Warrior Queens

WARRIOR QUEENS

The *Queen Mary* and *Queen Elizabeth*
in World War II

Daniel Allen Butler

STACKPOLE
BOOKS

Published by
STACKPOLE BOOKS
5067 Ritter Road
Mechanicsburg, PA 17055
www.stackpolebooks.com

Printed in the United States of America

All photos courtesy of The Mariner's Museum, Newport News, Virginia

10 9 8 7 6 5 4 3 2 1

FIRST EDITION

Library of Congress Cataloging-in-Publication Data

Butler, Daniel Allen.
    Warrior Queens : the Queen Mary and Queen Elizabeth in World War II / Daniel Allen Butler.— 1st ed.
      p. cm.
    Includes bibliographical references and index.
    ISBN 0-8117-1645-7
    1. Queen Mary (Steamship) 2. Queen Elizabeth (Ship) 3. World War,
1939–1945—Naval operations, British. 4. Great Britain. Army—Transport
service—History—20th century. I. Title.

D772.Q83 B88 2002
940.54'5941—dc21
                                       2001049745

To the three Butler brothers—
Harold, Robert, and Edwin—
who went off to war
and came home again

Built for the arts of peace
and to link the Old World with the New,
the Queens challenged the fury of Hitlerism
in the Battle of the Atlantic.
Without their aid the day of final victory
must unquestionably have been postponed.
—Sir Winston Churchill

CONTENTS

Author's Note xi

Prologue   *Queens at War* xiii
Chapter One   *A Tale of Two Queens* 1
Chapter Two   *A Dash to Freedom* 21
Chapter Three   *A Royal Escape* 33
Chapter Four   *The Queens Go to War* 45
Chapter Five   *The Enemy* 65
Chapter Six   *The Grey Ghosts* 79
Chapter Seven   *A Royal Tragedy* 99
Chapter Eight   *Life Aboard a Troopship* 123
Chapter Nine   *Triumph!* 141
Chapter Ten   *Peace* 157
Epilogue   *The Hand of Fate* 169

Appendix   Facts About the Queens 175
Acknowledgments 177
Index 185

AUTHOR'S NOTE

"Of arms and the man I sing . . ."

—Virgil

WHEN I SERVED IN THE U.S. ARMY, ONE OF THE FIRST BITS OF WISDOM imparted to young officers aspiring to higher rank was the need to learn and understand the importance of logistics, that branch of military science devoted to supplying, equipping, and moving troops. It certainly didn't sound glamorous, dashing, or exciting—in fact, it seemed to be a subject more suited to would-be accountants and shipping clerks than to a bunch of would-be Pattons and Rommels.

Good officers at any level soon disabuse themselves of this notion and realize that the most gifted commander in the world is impotent without sufficient numbers of properly equipped and supplied troops to lead. Even the wartime careers of Patton and Rommel (and MacArthur, and Zhukov, and von Manstein, and Yamashita, and Schwarzkopf, to name just a few others) are powerful testimony to how dramatically logistics can shape a battle or campaign, for weal or woe.

A sad aspect of much of military history written for the general reader is that this truth is often ignored or glossed over; the attraction is to write of gigantic tank battles and clashes of massive armies, of great navies striking hard, spectacular blows at each other, of aerial armadas raining destruction on the enemy. There is little, if any, room in such histories to tell the tale of how those armies, navies, and air forces gathered the strength necessary for such mighty efforts. It isn't exciting enough.

Or is it?

Warrior Queens isn't a discourse on Allied logistical management in the Second World War, nor did I ever intend it to be. From the outset I wanted to give the general reader an insight into how a pair of ships, never meant to see any kind of wartime service, were caught up by what must have seemed like an almost Gilbert and Sullivan–like idea. It was proposed to turn the two largest passenger liners in the world into troopships and sail them through seas filled with enemy submarines and warships to distant ports, moving whole divisions from continent to continent, transporting more troops than had ever been carried aboard a ship before. How those two ships, the *Queen Mary* and the *Queen Elizabeth,* succeeded in that improbable task, and in succeeding changed the course of a war, is the stuff of legend, and deserves a better memory than to be relegated to a backwater of history. *Warrior Queens* is meant to bring their story out of that backwater and demonstrate how their war was every bit as intriguing and exciting as the great battles their work made possible.

It's a rousing good story, and deserves to be told as such, without the tedium of academic language or posturing, or the endless recitation of statitics. *Warrior Queens* is a red-blooded tale of two great ships, set squarely in the middle of largest, bloodiest war in history, and that's how it tells their story. It's neither exposé nor revisionism; rather, it's an opportunity for anyone with even a passing interest in the history of those two great transatlantic liners to discover an amazing chapter in their careers. It's a chance for those who are intrigued by some of the lesser-known aspects of the Second World War to gain a better understanding of how those ships, and the crews who served on them, which never fired a shot in anger, made the Allied victory possible. To make the text "friendlier" to the general reader, I've dispensed with footnotes and endnotes, believing as I do that in a book like this one, which is nonargumentative in nature, they are a distraction and all too often are simply the trappings of a false academia. All the sources I consulted in preparing this book, both documentary and personal, have been listed in the Acknowledgments or the Sources sections at the end of the text, and I take full responsibility for the accuracy of the information presented. Out of respect for the Queens, and the priceless service they performed, for me to do anything less would be a disservice to them.

—Daniel Allen Butler

Queens at War

I send thee a shell from the ocean-beach;
But listen thou well, for my shell hath speech.
Hold to thine ear
And plain thou'lt hear
Tales of ships.
—Charles Henry (John Paul) Webb

WHEN THE ARMIES OF NAZI GERMANY STORMED INTO POLAND IN SEPTEMBER 1939, Great Britain was again thrust against her will into another world war. The tremendous sacrifices of the "war to end all wars" had been made only two decades earlier, and Prime Minister Neville Chamberlain had returned less than a year previously from a conference with Adolf Hitler in Munich, declaring "peace in our time"—surely the thought of another war to save Europe from German tyranny would be more than Britain could bear. But the German blitzkrieg destroyed Chamberlain's illusion that peace and Nazism could coexist, and so Great Britain was compelled to come to the aid of her Polish ally.

The decision to once more defend Europe created a critical need for Great Britain to bring home troops from all corners of her empire. Transporting them swiftly and safely would be a formidable task; fortunately, Britain's still-dominant position as the world's greatest maritime power ensured that the solution to the problem was at hand. The passenger liners of her merchant fleet could be transformed into troopships capable of carrying thousands of soldiers on every passage, bringing the far-flung garrisons of Britain's colonies and Commonwealth home to the defense of the British Isles. With their great speed and size, the crown jewels of this transport fleet would be the mighty Cunard Queens: the *Queen Mary*, less than four years old, and her as yet uncompleted sister, the *Queen Elizabeth*. Together they would carry many thousands of the troops needed to defend Britain and her allies. They would become the Warrior Queens.

The achievements of the *Queen Mary* and the *Queen Elizabeth* would become the stuff of legend. Together they logged over a million nautical miles and carried more than a million British, Canadian, and American soldiers and airmen. Conversions in America had made the two Queens capable of each ferrying as many as sixteen thousand troops during a single crossing—the equivalent of an entire army division. They would carry the ground crews and technicians who maintained the bombers and fighters of the mighty Eighth Air Force; the construction crews, ordnance personnel, and medical and supply staffs who constructed the staging areas for the invasion of Europe; and the infantry and armored divisions that would cross the English Channel and break into Hitler's "Fortress Europe" on D-Day.

The concept of requisitioning passenger liners during wartime in order to use them to transport troops wasn't new. The British first did it during the Crimean War in 1854, and most recently the tradition was carried on in 1982, when both the Cunard liner *Queen Elizabeth 2* and the P.&O. liner *Canberra* were pressed into service during the Falklands War. But the troopships' greatest achievements came during the Second World War, when the Allies had to bring their powerful but scattered resources to bear against the advancing forces of tyranny in both Europe and the Pacific. The war-torn years of 1939 to 1945, in which the darkness of imminent defeat turned into the brightness of triumphant victory, were their finest hours. And preeminent among them were the two great Cunard ships, the *Queen Mary* and the *Queen Elizabeth,* whose prodigious feats of transport Sir Winston Churchill would credit with shortening the war in Europe by as much as a year. Much like the tens of thousands of soldiers they carried, they were products of a peacetime world compelled by circumstances to become warriors. So they donned their uniforms of wartime gray, and sailed forth to confront enemies who were daring, skillful, and ruthless. They were well and truly Queens, were the *Mary* and the *Elizabeth,* but more than that, they were Warrior Queens.

This is their story.

CHAPTER ONE

A Tale of Two Queens

She moves a goddess, and she looks a queen.

—Homer

IT WAS THE WORST OF TIMES.

The iron grip of the Great Depression was slowly strangling the Clyde-side, that stretch of the River Clyde that reaches west of Glasgow toward Gourock and the Western Approaches. For almost a century the banks of the Clyde had been the home of the finest shipyards in the world, so much so that the phrase "a Clyde-built ship" had become an assurance that any vessel so described was sound, sturdy, and built to last. But as the world's economy descended into a stagnation that seemed to offer no hope of relief, trade and travel between nations steadily declined, and with them went the demand for ships to carry cargo or passengers across the world's oceans. One by one the shipwrights' hammers were being stilled in the Scottish shipyards along the river, as the orders for new ships dwindled, then vanished.

And now that stillness had come to the yard of John Brown and Co., Ltd. One of the greatest, proudest shipyards on all of the Clyde, indeed in all of Great Britain, John Brown and Co. had built dreadnoughts for the Royal Navy, freighters by the hundreds that sailed to all corners of the globe, and some of the greatest ocean liners the world had ever seen, including the magnificent *Lusitania*. But on December 11, 1931, when the whistle sounded "down tools," the silence in the John Brown works was deafening. Thirty-five hundred workers were suddenly unemployed, with little prospect of finding other work.

Towering over the yard, its brooding presence soon to become a constant reminder of all the glories there had been on the Clyde and might never be again, was the huge gray mass of an unfinished, unlaunched passenger liner known only as Hull 534. Begun in early 1930, the 534 was to be a fantastic new liner for the venerable Cunard Line, which had a long and prosperous relationship with John Brown and Co. that spanned three-quarters of a century. But the Depression caused the number of fare-paying passengers crossing the Atlantic to plummet, and Cunard had finally run out of money. When the hull of the 534 was almost 80 percent complete, all work was stopped on it. The 534 was supposed to have been as great a triumph of British shipbuilding as the *Lusitania* had been a quarter century before, but now it was nothing more than an empty shell, unpainted, unfinished, lacking engines, its deck open to the wind and rain, sitting desolate and empty. It would have been wrong to refer to the 534 as "she"—after all, it wasn't really a ship. It didn't even have a name.

The World War (the number would come later) had dramatically and permanently altered the passenger trade on the North Atlantic, and not necessarily for the better. Before the cataclysm that began in 1914, the North Atlantic run had been characterized by a fierce commercial struggle between Great Britain and Germany over two distinctly different yet closely related features: the quest for the Blue Ribband and the immigrant trade. The Blue Ribband, the mythical appellation that went to the liner that made the fastest Atlantic crossing, east- or west-bound, was by the end of the nineteenth century so coveted a prize that the competition became filled with nationalistic and jingoistic overtones, so much so that it almost ceased being a simple commercial rivalry between shipping firms.

When the Cunard Line's *Campania* captured the Blue Ribband with a speed of nearly twenty-one knots in 1896, the title had been in British hands for nearly two decades, usually being handed off between ships of the White Star Line and Cunard. After modest starts, however, two German shipping firms, Hamburg-Amerika and Norddeutscher-Lloyd, decided that there was no reason why their ships shouldn't compete with the British liners. The first challenge to result was the Norddeutscher-Lloyd's mean-looking, imposing, unmistakably German *Kaiser Wilhelm der Grosse,* which romped across the North Atlantic on her maiden voyage in early 1897 at nearly twenty-two knots. Not content in merely besting the British, the Germans embarrassed them by next introducing the *Deutschland,* which belonged to the Hamburg-

Amerika Line, crossing the "Big Pond" a year later at a speed of nearly twenty-three knots. Her preeminence was to last less than a year as, adding insult to injury, the new *Kronprinz Wilhelm* set a new record at twenty-three and a half knots; the year after that, the *Kaiser Wilhelm II* proved a shade faster still.

Just as significant as their speed was the magificence (some said extravagance) of the German ships' decor. In the words of John Malcolm Brinnin, they ushered in "a period of steamship history when the landscapes of Valhalla enscrolled on the walls and ceilings of grand saloons would all but collapse under their own weight, as well as a period when Teutonic efficiency united with matchless engine power would give Germany all the honors on the northern seas. And when the wits of the first decade of the [Twentieth] Century began to say something was 'hideously' or 'divinely' 'North German Lloyd' they meant, according to one American contemporary, 'two of everything but the kitchen range' then gilded."

This Teutonic monopoly on the Blue Ribband was more than Great Britain could stand; a head-to-head showdown was approaching between these upstart Germans and the established maritime power of the British. France and the United States, once serious contenders, were soon left in the wakes of these two great rivals as the race for the Blue Ribband became a vicious cycle of building ever bigger, faster, and more expensive ships.

Cunard played its ace in 1907 when it introduced the big, four-funneled *Lusitania* and *Mauretania,* a pair of turbine-powered behemoths that were each nearly eight hundred feet in length, weighed more than thirty-three thousand tons apiece, and were capable of speeds of over twenty-six knots—and appointed with the most luxurious and expensive accommodations yet seen aboard any ships. Just four years after that, the White Star Line trumped Cunard's aces when the *Olympic* went into service, with plans for her sister ship, the *Titanic,* to enter service eight months later, and a second sister, *Gigantic,* to follow soon after that. The White Star trio were ships nearly nine hundred feet long, weighing over forty-five thousand tons, and provided with a degree of luxury in their public rooms and first-class cabins that was never seen before or since on any ship. Their only shortcoming was their speed—capable of little more than twenty-five knots, that was their only concession to the two Cunard ships. Given that the difference in speed meant only that the White Star ships would arrive a few hours later than the Cunard vessels on any given crossing, the White Star Line was confident that the sheer opulence in their ships' appointments would more than make up for the difference. But tragedy fatally disrupted White Star's plans when the *Titanic* was lost on her maiden voyage, colliding with an iceberg and sinking two and a half hours later on April 15, 1912, taking 1,502 of her passengers and crew with her. Likewise, the *Gigantic* never fulfilled her promise for the White Star Line. Requisitioned as a hospital ship when war broke out in August 1914, just weeks before her maiden voyage was scheduled to take place, the *Gigantic,* which had quietly been given the less pretentious name *Britannic,* struck a mine and sank in the Aegean Sea in 1916.

Cunard had built a follow-up to the *Lusitania* and *Mauretania,* a ship called the *Aquitania,* which entered service in 1913. While almost as large as the *Olympic* and *Titanic,* the *Aquitania* wasn't quite as handsome in appearance as the two White Star ships, but so well thought out were her interiors that they were once described as "a silent sermon on good taste." The German steamship lines watched this succession of British ships take to the sea, and they carefully planned their responses. Norddeutscher-Lloyd took its time, but in 1913 Hamburg-Amerika produced the *Imperator.* She was to be the first of three nine hundred-foot, fifty-two-thousand-ton ships, with the *Vaterland* and the *Bismarck* to follow her in successive years.

The incredible growth in the size of the ships in the two decades before the Great War—the *Campania* of 1896 weighed a mere eighteen thousand tons; the *Imperator* of 1913 was three times her size—certainly was due in part with the later Victorians' and Edwardians' obsession with size, just as there was a very real game of one-upmanship being played between the British and the Germans, but more importantly, the growth of these ships was propelled by the burgeoning immigrant trade. Despite the glamour of Grand Staircases, veranda cafes, ornate and gilded Smoking Rooms and Dining Saloons, the immigrant trade was the bread and butter of the steamship lines; whatever additional income could be generated by transporting the rich and famous in overstuffed splendor was merely icing on the cake for the corporate stockholders. Consequently, the steamship lines worked very hard to make the immigrants' passage as safe, memorable, and—within limits—as comfortable as possible.

Aided by a spate of romanticized reporting, dramatic (and often staged) photographs, and evocative artwork more notable for its sensationalism than its accuracy, a great many myths have built up around the flood of immigrants that flowed to the shores of the New World at the end of the nineteenth century and the beginning of the twentieth. All too often these "steerage" or Third Class passengers ("Third Class" being the designated category for immigrant passengers) are portrayed as "tired, poor . . . huddled masses," as babushka- and shawl-beclad mothers gripping the hands of small, wide-eyed children, or as young men in ill-fitting clothes clutching their few belongings in loosely tied bundles, all hoping to find their fortunes in such exotic locales as New York, Pittsburgh, or Chicago.

As with so many subjects of the journalism of that day, the truth was a good deal more mundane. The majority of those leaving the Old World for the New were Teutons and Anglo-Saxons, although the numbers of immigrants from Southern and Eastern Europe increased steadily with each passing year. Many were Germans who were unable to cope with all the social dislocations the Fatherland was undergoing in its bewilderingly rapid transformation from an agrarian society to an industrial juggernaut. Many others were Britons, often skilled or semiskilled workers, sometimes craftsmen, occasionally members of the professions, forced to seek employment in America as Britain began her slow decline industrially and economically. Still more were Irish, part of a constant hemorrhage by which much of Ireland's best blood left her, forced by poverty and hunger to seek a better life in America. To these people, a ship was transportation, its sole purpose to take them from Southampton (or Cherbourg or Queenstown) to New York; their interests lay in clean quarters and decent food. It didn't take a stroke of genius to realize that if Seamus Mulvaney or Klaus Mueller arrived in New York warm, well fed, and dry, it wouldn't be long before he would be writing back to cousin Patrick in County Cork or brother Heinz in Dusseldorf about the fine time he had aboard the *Lusitania, Olympic,* or *Imperator* and that when the time came for Patrick or Heinz to make his own crossing, he should take the same ship.

Typically, Third Class berthing was concentrated in the forward and aft ends of the ship, with appropriate berthing arrangements for single men and women, married couples, and families. The cabins were spacious, spotless, and if a bit austere, were by all reports comfortable enough. The unmarried men or women shared a room with three to five other passengers of the same sex, while married couples and families had rooms to themselves. The accommodations included a large number of permanent cabins, as well as large sections of berths formed by movable wooden partitions, so that the numbers and sizes of the cabins could be adjusted to the number of passengers and the unused space given over to open common areas. The days of the cramped, dark hold, reeking of unwashed humanity and bilge, were long since a thing of the past. The Third Class galleys provided a fare that, though unspectacular, offered good food and plenty of it; in some cases, especially those from the more impoverished Irish counties, the steerage passengers ate better aboard ship than they ever had at home. All in all, given that a one-way ticket in Third Class on one of the larger liners cost as little as $36, most of the steerage passengers felt that they had gotten a good deal for what they paid for their passage.

Consequently, the economics of running a steamship were straightforward enough: The larger the ship, the more immigrants it could carry; and the faster it was, the more crossings it could make every year, more crossings meaning more fare-paying passengers. At the same time, the costs of operating the ship increased by only a fraction of fares paid. Certainly the number of immigrants justified the effort and expenditure—in each of the five years before the Great War, over seven hundred thousand men, women, and children left the Old World for the New.

All of this changed after the First World War. Simply put, the German merchant marine had ceased to exist; all of Germany's great prewar liners had been either hunted down and sunk by the Royal Navy or interned by the Americans, who promptly seized them when the United States declared war on Germany in April 1917. The three German leviathans, the *Imperator, Vaterland,* and *Bismarck,* were declared prizes of war and distributed as reparations. The United States was given the *Vaterland,* which was promptly rechristened the *Leviathan,* as a sort of reward for American participation in the war. The *Imperator* went to Cunard to become the *Berengaria,* given to the line as a replacement for the *Lusitania,* sunk by the *U-20* in May 1915. The *Bismarck,* which was unfinished when the war began and sat deserted on the ways for four years, was launched in 1922 and turned over to the White Star Line as compensation for the destruction of the *Britannic.* She entered service as the *Majestic.*

While the big German liners went a long way toward making good the lost passenger capacity of Cunard and White Star, and gave the United States a presence on the North Atlantic that had been lacking for decades, they were far from truly successful. The years of neglect while they sat rusting in American ports or German shipyards had taken a toll on them, and their crews had sabotaged every possible system aboard them before the ships were turned over to the Allies. Their electrical systems were faulty and prone to minor fires, and their interiors never quite lost their Teutonic flavor, making them less than popular with a large number of would-be passengers.

By the late 1920s it had become clear to Cunard and White Star that not only were their German prizes a disappointment, but many, if not all, of their prewar liners were nearing the end of their useful service lives. Replacing them on a one-for-one basis was out of the question, for the North Atlantic passenger trade had changed profoundly after the war, and declining numbers of passengers meant that the money to build whole new fleets of ships simply wasn't there. Another quantum leap in size would be necessary, for often a single hull would have to take the place of two or three smaller, older ships. Liners displacing eighty thousand tons or more, and over a thousand feet in length—ships that had been the stuff of fantasy before the war—would have to be built.

White Star was the first line to venture in those uncharted waters of steamship design. In 1928 the line placed an order with Harland and Wolff, the Belfast shipyard that had been building White Star ships for nearly sixty years, for a sleek, graceful ship that was to be called the *Oceanic.* Her keel was promptly laid and the framing of her hull had begun when the financial disaster of October 14, 1929, overtook her, Harland and Wolff, White Star, and the rest of the world. White Star's capital dried up, and work was suspended on the *Oceanic* for lack of money; soon the whole project was canceled completely. The White Star Line found itself struggling for survival.

Cunard had followed White Star's lead a year after work began on the *Oceanic,* laying the keel of Hull Number 534 at the John Brown works on December 1, 1930. It was a dark, murky, typically Scottish winter day, but it was bright with promise for the Clyde and for scores of communities for miles around. Cunard had decided in the later 1920s that two fast, powerful superliners, larger than any ever built, would be able to provide a regular, weekly transatlantic service—something that heretofore had required three ships. Each ship would be expected to make the crossing in five days; spend two days in "turnaround," where fuel, provisions, fresh linen, and all the other supplies required to the next crossing would be brought aboard; and set out on the return crossing with almost clocklike punctuality.

Alas, it was a vision that would quickly fade, and with it all hope of returned prosperity for the Clyde. What had promised to be four or five years of steady work building the two new ships (they were to be so large that they could only be built one at a time—John Brown's slipways weren't large enough to allow them to be built together) turned to ashes as Cunard, faced with continually shrinking passenger lists and growing deficits, slowly ran out of money to pay for the new ship. Within a year, Cunard was forced to suspend work on the 534, the line's finances by that time barely in better shape than White Star's, and the possibility of dissolution loomed on the horizon.

What had brought both of the British giants to such straits—indeed, what brought every passenger line on the North Atlantic to such straits—was a profound change that had overcome the passenger trade on the Big Pond. An act passed by the United States' Congress in 1921 forever altered the North Atlantic run, and in many ways brought about its doom. Called the Emergency Quota Act, it was popularly known as "The Three Percent Act," as it implemented a restrictive system of quotas on immigration that allowed only 3 percent of a nation's population, based on the 1903 census, to be admitted into the United States. Immigrant traffic naturally plummeted; by the mid-1920s the annual number of immigrants to the United States was less than a third of what it had been before the war.

This hit the steamship companies hard, as they had built their liners to accommodate that immigrant trade, some ships devoting as much as 75 percent of their cabin space to immigrants. What had been a reliable and rewarding source of income for the steamship lines vanished almost overnight, and there was nothing they could do about it. Ships were sailing with vast areas of their passengers' accommodations sitting empty and unused. Travel agents and shipping executives alike scrambled to find solutions.

The one that seemed to hold the most promise appears to have occurred more or less simultaneously to almost all the shipping lines. The answer was to upgrade what had been the Third Class areas of their ships, improve the amenities and appointments somewhat, and quietly drop the words "steerage" and "Third Class" from the corporate lexicons. Third Class became "Tourist" or "Cabin" class, and the advertising brochures were filled with colorful copy detailing how crossing on one of the great North Atlantic steamships was no longer just a means of travel, but was now an integral part of the experience of journeying abroad.

For a while it worked. The concept was the most popular among the American middle class, as thousands of families exploited the newfound affluence offered by the economic boom of the 1920s and, intrigued by the Europe described by the returning doughboys, for the first time created a demand for comfortable, economical passage in the eastbound direction that a few years before would have seemed impossible. It was more than the steamship companies had dared hope for, and as their revenues once again rose, they began to consider building larger and faster ships, and the fiscal caution had been their collective watchword in the early twenties went by the wayside. Briefly, the fortunes of the White Star Line were sufficiently bright to cause the line to begin construction of the *Oceanic;* Cunard similarly prospered and began the 534. The French Line (more correctly known as CGT, Compagnie Generale Transatlantique) decided to assert its presence on the

North Atlantic in a way it never had before and began work on what was to become the *Normandie*. The Germans even made an attempt to regain their lost pride of place by launching the *Bremen* and *Europa,* a pair of speedy, powerful-looking ships, roughly the same size as the ships of the *Imperator* class, though with far less pretentious interiors, that briefly recaptured the Blue Riband for Germany. Even the Italian Line got into the act, introducing the *Rex* and the *Conte di Savoia,* two smart, fast ships that proved the most popular vessels on the Mediterranean run.

But it didn't last. When the crash came, it wasn't just the great financiers and tycoons who saw their fortunes dwindle: Huge numbers of middle-class Americans had invested in the stock market and lost their life's savings. Suddenly, for many of them, there was no longer any question of being able to afford a trip to Europe—now the issue was survival. Almost overnight, as it were, not only did the steamship companies' capital reserves dry up, but their single largest source of income vanished as well.

White Star was the first to give up, canceling the *Oceanic,* and then slowly sinking into a sea of red ink. In 1931, Cunard's operating deficit approached $20 million, and work was suspended on the 534 less than a year after it had begun. Meanwhile, the French Line was able to keep its ships in service by virtue of hefty government subsidies, but the future of the *Normandie* was in doubt. Only the German companies continued to show a profit, but they were being propped up by Berlin, being underwritten by the Weimar Republic until 1933, by the National Socialists after that.

The French Line was the first to bite the bullet. Hardly had work stopped on the *Normandie* than officials from the company approached the French government with the idea of a massive loan to fund the completion of the new ship. Despite heated, sometimes rancorous debate within the National Assembly, where Socialist deputies demanded that the money be spent on social programs and welfare relief for unemployed Frenchmen, the loan was swiftly approved and work resumed on the *Normandie* with only the briefest of interruptions.

A similar arrangement seemed to be the only solution to Cunard's debacle. And there were powerful arguments in Cunard's favor—after all, it wasn't just national pride or the prosperity of the company at stake. Thousands of jobs were on the line: There were the workers in the yards and the factories that would build the ship and her equipment; chandlers who would supply the necessities for day-to-day operations; joiners and carpenters who would complete the interiors; and the stewards, stewardesses, waiters, cooks, galley

hands, stokers, engineers, and seamen who would make up the crew. With the
welfare rolls growing weekly, the idea of putting the many thousands of men
to work building and serving on the new ship had an undeniable appeal. Hat
figuratively in hand, Cunard's board of directors approached the one man
who had the means and authority to provide the solution to their dilemma—
Neville Chamberlain.

History hasn't been kind to Neville Chamberlain, and justifiably so—his
tenure as Prime Minister was unarguably the most disastrous in all of Great
Britain's existence. However, he *was* a businessman *par excellence,* and so was
admirably suited to the position he occupied in 1933, that of the Chancellor
of the Exchequer, the keeper of the British government's purse strings. He
welcomed Cunard's overture for government assistance, for with a shrewd
merchant's eye, he perceived the shared plight of Cunard and White Star as an
opportunity to bring an end to what he regarded as unnecessary competition
between the rival steamship companies. "My own aim," he recorded in his
diary, "has always been to use the 534 as a lever to bring about a merger
between the Cunard and White Star Lines, thus establishing a strong British
firm on the North Atlantic trade." He called the managing directors of both
steamship companies to a series of meetings in London in December 1933.
The terms of the government's offer as he outlined them were generous, but
Chamberlain's delivery was blunt. He made it perfectly clear that neither
White Star nor Cunard would be able to survive independently, while His
Majesty's Government was in no position to support both. The only way the
Government would loan the money to complete the 534 would be if the two
rival shipping lines merged.

Admittedly, it wasn't a difficult idea to sell—the management of both
companies also realized that the only way either would survive was to become
the Cunard White Star Line. The Government was offering the new company
a total of £9,500,000 ($47,000,000)—£3,000,000 to be used to complete the
534, £1,500,000 for working capital, and £5,000,000 to be set aside for the
construction of a future sister ship for the 534. The offer was accepted with
almost indecent haste, and by the end of January 1934, the loan was approved
by Parliament.

It took a couple months to work out the definitive terms and complete
the final arrangements for the merger, but in April 1934, while massed pipes
played and thousands of voices sang Scottish national songs, the workforce at
John Brown and Company, Ltd., returned to work on the 534 and the shipyard came to life again—and with it the towns and factories for miles around.

Although no one had worked on the hull for nearly two and a half years, the workers were astonished to find that all they needed to do was pick up where they had left off. Instead of a deteriorating hulk that would require months of refurbishing before new work could even begin, they found the 534's scantlings, frames, shell plating, decks, and machinery in first-class condition: The relative handful of workers who were retained at John Brown after work had been suspended had justified their employment by looking after the 534 with the same attentiveness a father pays to his smallest child. No rust was allowed to build up, no dirt to accumulate; each piece of machinery was carefully oiled and maintained.

Just how well those men had done their jobs was shown to the world when, just six months after work on the 534 resumed, she was ready for launching. It was even fitting to call the 534 "she" now, for the newly formed Cunard White Star Line had agreed on a name for her. In the past, Cunard had followed the tradition of giving its ships names ending in "-*ia*" while White Star had a similar tradition of names ending in "-*ic.*" In order to avoid any association with either of the parent lines and demonstrate a clean break with the past, the two component lines of the new company agreed to name the new ship the *Queen Mary.*

The story is often told that the new liner's name was originally to be the *Queen Victoria,* and a representative from Cunard White Star was dispatched to Windsor Castle to seek the Crown's approval for using the late monarch's name. When the somewhat flustered envoy broached the subject to King George V, he reportedly phrased it, "Your Majesty, we wish to name the new ship after Great Britain's greatest queen," thinking his meaning would be obvious. The King, whose wife was named Mary, promptly replied, "Splendid! I'm sure my wife will be very pleased!" Nonplussed, the company representative withdrew without further comment—after all, correcting the Crown is simply not done!—and the company, caught in a quandary, simply accepted that the new ship's name would be the *Queen Mary* and not the *Queen Victoria.* The story is so charming that one wishes it were true, but alas, it isn't.

There was one genuine problem with the name *Queen Mary* that Cunard White Star hadn't anticipated: There was already a ship on the registry of the British Board of Trade by that name. But the owners of a small Scottish coastal steamer allowed themselves to be persuaded by Cunard to rename their little ship the *Queen Mary 2,* and that obstacle was overcome.

The *Queen Mary* was launched on September 26, 1934. In what should have been Scotland's most beautiful month, the notoriously fickle Scottish weather brought a day full of wind and drenching rain, but nothing could dampen the spirits of nearly a quarter million cheering Scots who had gathered to watch as for the first time in history, the reigning king and queen presided over the launch of a merchant ship. Built alongside the ship's starboard bow was an enclosed platform, some thirty-five feet above the floor of the slipway, where King George V and Queen Mary would shelter from the rain. There was an elevator for their use, but they chose to mount the platform via an open walkway, sharing for a few minutes at least the sodden discomfort of their subjects who were waiting patiently for the ship to be launched.

The King addressed the assembled throng, and his speech was carried worldwide by the BBC. "Now, with the hope of better trade on both sides of the Atlantic, let us look forward to her playing a great part in the revival of international commerce. It has been the nation's will," he declared, "that she should be completed, and to-day we can send her forth . . . a ship . . . alive with beauty, energy and strength." It fell to him, he said, to perform "the happy task of sending on her way . . . the stateliest ship in the world." The Queen used a pair of golden scissors to cut the cord holding back a bottle of Australian champagne, which promptly broke against the bow of the ship, at the same time making the traditional announcement, "I name this ship *Queen Mary!* May God bless her and all who sail on her." Then, not realizing that the microphone was still live, she turned to her husband and in a stage whisper asked, "Shall I press the button now?"

Receiving an affirmative answer, the Queen pressed the button that triggered the hydraulic rams that would set the new liner in motion. For a fraction of a second, it seemed as if the ship wouldn't move, but then the white-painted hull began to tremble and, slowly gaining momentum, slide down the ways toward the waiting waters of the Clyde. There was a brief gout of flame under her keel as the weight of the hull scorched the stocks supporting it. Drag chains attached to the launching cradles rattled and roared, but the crowd remained strangely silent. An anxious minute passed as the hull continued to gain speed, causing some watchers to wonder if she would bury her stern in the opposite bank of the river, then suddenly there she was, what poet laureate John Masefield called "a rampart of a ship" floating high and proud on Scotland's most famous river.

Instantly the crowd broke into deafening cheers. No longer a forlorn hope, a painful reminder of what might have been, a stillborn giant that could have given testimony to the greatness of British shipbuilding, the *Queen Mary* was real and alive. At last the hull of the 534 tasted water, she had been christened by a queen, and she had a proper name—finally, she was a ship.

And what a ship! Advertising shills for the shipping lines had been pushing the limits of hyperbole for decades, seeking to impress and overawe prospective passengers with the size, speed, splendor, or some combination of the three of each successive generation of steamships. In the case of the *Queen Mary*, their artifices eventually reached the level of the inane, offering such absurdities as comparing the power of the *Mary*'s four turbine engines to the muscle power of seven million galley slaves, or announcing that her displacement was twenty-two thousand tons greater than that of the entire Spanish Armada. The First Class Lounge was to be so spacious, it was said, that nine double-decker buses could be placed inside, with three Royal Scot locomotives placed atop them, with room to spare. The ship was described as "long as a street and lofty as a tower, loftier and wider than many a country church."

In truth, her dimensions were staggering enough without such embellishments. From end to end she measured 1,019 feet, with a beam of 118 feet and an average draught of 39 feet. She displaced 80,677 tons. Compared to the largest warship in the world at the time, HMS *Hood*, the *Queen Mary* was 150 feet longer and 12 feet wider in the beam, with twice *Hood*'s displacement. In fact, the *Queen Mary* would dwarf any warship ever built until the American aircraft carrier USS *Enterprise* entered service in 1963. Over ten million rivets were used in constructing her hull, which contained over two thousand portholes. The distance from the keel to the top of her forward funnel was 181 feet, while her Boat Deck, or Sun Deck, was 75 feet above the waterline. She had twelve decks: four in the superstructure, the uppermost being the Sports Deck, running down through the Sun Deck and the Promenade Deck to the Main Deck; the seven below that lettered from A Deck down to G Deck; and the very bottom deck, the Orlop Deck, where the boiler rooms and engine rooms of the power plant were found.

That power plant was probably the finest such installation to ever be put inside a ship. Cunard was determined to recapture the Blue Ribband for Great Britain as swiftly and decisively as the *Lusitania* had done three decades earlier. The *Queen Mary* was driven by four screws, or propellers, powered by four sets of Parsons single reduction steam turbine engines. Each shaft had one forward and one reverse turbine, which were turned by the steam produced by a total of twenty-four water-tube boilers, divided among three boiler rooms. The boilers were oil-fired, each heating steam at seven hundred degrees Fahrenheit and at a pressure of four hundred pounds per square inch. All told, the *Queen Mary*'s engines produced 160,000 shaft horsepower. It was believed that she would be capable of speeds up to or even exceeding thirty-two knots.

She spent the months from September 1934 to March 1936 fitting out in the Clyde and conducting her sea trials. Her superstructure was completed along with the remainder of her machinery installation, and the funnels stepped; her galleys, laundries, and cold rooms installed; her public rooms and passenger cabins finished. The hull was painted satin black, her upper works gleaming white, and her three funnels the traditional Cunard red topped by a black soot band on the upper quarter of each. Most of the month of March 1936 was spent in extensive sea trials. There was an anxious moment when the *Mary* ran aground as she steamed out into the Clyde for the first time under her own power, but the soft river bottom did no damage to the hull, and the ship soon pulled free. Once out of the mouth of the Clyde and into the waters of the Western Approaches, she began three weeks of testing, running at varying speeds up and down the western coast of England and Scotland. There were prolonged high-speed runs, dashes along measured miles, and tests for maneuverability and stability. When all of these were completed, she was ready to head for Southampton, there to begin taking aboard all the provisions, supplies, and necessities required for her to fulfill her role as a passenger liner.

As the *Queen Mary* steamed into Southampton for the first time in May 1936, the sight of her was breathtaking. Towering over the Ocean Dock where she was moored, there was no question that she was the epitome of traditional British shipbuilding. Her gracefully raked stem and gently flared bow gave way to the rounded bridge and superstructure front that had been a hallmark of Cunard ships for nearly half a century. Fully enclosed, the superstructure ran unbroken for nearly three-quarters of the ship's length, eliminating the fussy, cluttered look that had characterized the *Mauretania* and *Aquitania*. The three red-and-black funnels, gently decreasing in height from fore to aft, were carefully proportioned to bring a sense of balance to the ship's appearance, giving her a purposeful, thrusting look without creating an illusion of top-heaviness.

At the same time, Cunard avoided the worst of the aesthetic pretensions of the ship that would be the *Queen Mary*'s closest rival, the *Normandie*. The *Normandie* inside and out embodied the ideal of pure Art Deco, her French decorators applying their knowing skill in the manner that initially created the Art Deco style. Unfortunately, this style didn't always work: The *Normandie*'s sharply raked clipper bow contrasted bizarrely with her conventional counter stern, and her three funnels looked outsized in proportion to her hull, giving the *Normandie* a squat, almost bloated look. Cunard was far more traditional in its approach to the Art Deco style, and in the *Mary*'s decor utilized over fifty different exotic and rare woods, collected from all over the British Empire, in places where the *Normandie* was given over to crystal, chrome, and glass. The result was a distinctly British atmosphere, a combination of the traditional and the modern that was considered too sedate by some critics of the 1930s.

Aboard the *Queen Mary*, passengers were never left unaware that they were on a ship, whereas the *Normandie*'s designers tried to disguise her interiors as a Paris hotel. Cunard openly rejoiced in the fact that the *Mary* was a ship. Round portholes were proudly exposed rather than hidden behind false window sashes, and nautical touches, ranging from mementos of other Cunard ships to signal flags to simple informational signs that unashamedly used words like "port," "starboard," "fore," and "aft," were found in every part of the vessel. One observer best quantified the disparity between the two: "The French built a remarkable hotel and put a ship around it. The British built a beautiful ship and put a hotel inside it."

Nowhere was that difference more readily apparent than in the *Queen Mary*'s First Class Lounge. Though its two-deck height and huge pillars might have made it too imposing a space for most people to feel comfortable in, the half dozen working fireplaces with little clusters of leather wing chairs and tables about them, along with the numerous corners and nooks the columns created, ultimately gave the lounge a cosiness that the *Normandie*'s lounge, too reminiscent of a hotel foyer, could ever match.

Certainly the centerpiece of the *Queen Mary*'s interior was the First Class Dining Saloon. The White Star Line's *Olympic* and *Titanic* had been the first to introduce small tables for four or eight dinner guests, eliminating the long tables that had been found on all ocean liners previously. The *Queen Mary* copied that excellent idea, allowing the guests to seat themselves in whatever numbers and combinations they wished at tables covered in snow white linen, set with spotless crystal and sterling tableware, surrounded by gleaming oak and mahogany paneling and polished brass fixtures. On one wall was a giant map of the North Atlantic, with an indicator showing the exact position of the *Queen Mary* during each transatlantic voyage. (When the *Queen Elizabeth* entered service, a similar map was installed in her First Class Dining Saloon, with indicators showing the positions of both ships so that passengers could see when they would meet.) One of the most popular features was the small and exclusive Verandah Grill, found at the aft end of the superstructure, just below the main mast. The *Queen Mary*'s design allowed her to carry 776 passengers in first (or "Cabin") class, 784 in second ("Tourist") class, and 579 in third ("Tourist Third") Class, a total of 2,119, with a crew of 1,035.

When the *Normandie* set out on her record-setting maiden voyage on May 29, 1935, the French had been extremely secretive about whether she would attempt to take the Blue Ribband away from the Italian liner *Rex*. By contrast, when it was announced in May 1936 that the *Queen Mary*'s maiden voyage would take place in July, it was no secret that Cunard intended for her to snatch the Blue Ribband away from the *Normandie*. On May 27, 1936, the *Queen Mary* left Southampton on what would be a crossing marked by remarkably fair weather and very high speed. As the *Mary* approached the American shore, it became clear to her passengers and crew alike that the Blue Ribband was in her reach. Almost at the last moment, though, the *Queen Mary* found herself surrounded by fog barely a day out of New York. Her captain, Cmdre. Sir Edgar Britten, cut her speed back to barely more than steerage way, rightly being more concerned with the ship's safety than with the record. Once the fog lifted, he pushed the *Queen Mary* as hard as he dared, averaging just over thirty-two knots for the rest of the voyage, arriving in New York in four days, twelve hours, and twenty minutes after she left Southampton. The time lost in the fog had been crucial, for *Normandie*'s record-setting crossing had been just thirty-eight minutes faster. The *Queen Mary*'s performance had left no doubt, though, that the Blue Ribband was hers for the taking.

That it hadn't been a record crossing made little difference to the Americans, as New York seemed almost delirious with the celebration of the *Queen Mary*'s arrival. A flotilla of fireships, spraying water hundreds of feet in the air, surrounded her, as hundreds of pleasure craft followed in the great liner's wake as she steamed up the Hudson River. Tens of thousands of people lined the waterfront, while untold thousands more watched from windows in the skyscrapers overlooking New York Harbor. They had never seen such a ship. The *Normandie* had been impressive, but from the very first, there was a sense of majesty, a "presence," about the *Queen Mary* that inspired a sense of near awe in those who saw her. It would be a presence that the *Queen Elizabeth* would share with her, but it would never again be duplicated.

Though the *Mary*'s performance made it clear that the Blue Ribband was within her grasp, before any record-setting crossing could take place, there was the usual assortment of teething problems found in any new ship that needed to be corrected. At high speed the *Queen Mary*'s stern shook violently, and in heavy seas she developed a pronounced corkscrew motion. She also had a marked tendency to roll in almost any kind of seaway (this was not cured until gyroscopic stabilizers were installed in 1956). As far as the passengers were concerned, the most annoying problem was that smoke from the funnels would drop soot and oil on the after promenade decks. The interior structure of the stern was stiffened to better resist the vibration and corkscrewing, and a switch from three-bladed to four-bladed screws eliminated the worst of the vibration. The problem of soot dropping on the passengers was solved by the installation of special ventilators in the funnels.

The worst of these problems remedied, the *Queen Mary* had another go at the Blue Ribband on August 31, 1936. Arriving in New York on September 3, she had made the crossing in three days, twenty-three hours and fifty-seven minutes—the first time the crossing over the Atlantic had been made in under four days, her average speed being an amazing 30.63 knots. Though the *Normandie* took the Ribband back the next year, on March 1937, the *Queen Mary* would finally prove the faster in August 1938, with an eastbound crossing time of three days, twenty hours, and forty minutes—an average speed of 31.69 knots. The Blue Ribband had returned to Great Britain. Surely, it was the best of times.

It wasn't in speed alone that the *Queen Mary* established her supremacy over the *Normandie:* Passengers heavily favored the British ship. The *Normandie* rarely sailed with a full booking of passengers, whereas the *Mary* frequently had a waiting list. In 1937, her first full year of service, the *Queen Mary* carried 56,895 passengers, almost twice the number carried by the *Normandie* that year. While it was probably inevitable that the British aristocracy would prefer the *Mary* over the *Normandie,* it did take the French by surprise when ordinary businessmen and American tourists passed on their fashionable, trendy ship with its cold, pretentious interior to book passage on the *Queen Mary* instead. Despite what the critics thought, the unique combination of traditional decor with touches of Art Deco produced a far more welcoming and comfortable atmosphere for everyone aboard.

That there *were* passengers aboard was due to a remarkable rise in the number of people who were crossing the Atlantic in all classes. After having declined steadily—and occasionally plummeting—for five years, in 1935 the number of passengers the steamship lines carried to and from the New World and the Old increased. The economies of Europe and the United States had begun to recover from the worst depredations of the Great Depression, though by no means had they returned to their pre-Crash prosperity. Nonetheless, their numbers had grown sufficiently to allow the Cunard White Star Line to begin to retire its oldest ships, as well as those that were perpetually losing money. Within little more than a year, the *Olympic, Mauretania, Berengaria,* and *Majestic,* along with several smaller vessels, were withdrawn from service and sent to the breakers.

To make up for the loss in carrying capacity those retired ships represented, the line decided that the time was right to avail itself of that £5,000,000 that Parliament had earmarked for the construction of a sister ship for the *Queen Mary.* The announcement was made that the new ship would be built in the same yard as the *Mary,* John Brown and Co. Ltd. Her name was to be the *Queen Elizabeth.*

Actually, it is probably more correct to refer to the *Elizabeth* as the *Mary's* running mate rather than a true sister ship, as they were not built from the same original design, though it was clear that the earlier ship had provided the inspiration for her. While the public had made it clear that it preferred the *Queen Mary's* more conservative atmosphere over the artistic pretensions of the *Normandie,* Cunard hadn't ignored the French ship and decided to work many of its better features into the *Queen Elizabeth* without surrendering the best aspects of traditional British shipbuilding. The *Elizabeth* was an engineering marvel. Over seven thousand experiments using scale models in a test tank were conducted before the final shape of her hull was determined. These models traveled over one thousand miles from one end of the tank to the other, as engineers studied each configuration to find the optimum combination of resistance, flow, and wake form.

In her construction, over ten million rivets were used. Her power plant was similar to the *Queen Mary's,* consisting of four sets of single reduction geared turbines capable of developing 160,000 horsepower. Each one of the 257,000 individual blades on each turbine (there were a total of eight, one forward and one reverse on each shaft) was tested and fitted by hand. The ships' four manganese-bronze propellers were each machined from a single casting and weighed thirty-two tons apiece.

Immediately noticeable was her more sharply raked bow, which flared into a long, unbroken, flush main deck, eliminating the small well deck forward of the *Mary's* superstructure. Her upper works were less crowded with ventilator cowls, of which there were very few, or deck houses, instead offering long expanses of open deck space for the passengers. The huge air intakes for the boilers and engine room vents were carefully worked into the superstructure, a styling cue that had been adopted from the *Normandie*. But the *Elizabeth*'s designers went the *Normandie* one better, reducing the number of funnels from three to two. Overall, her cleaner lines and thrusting bow gave the Elizabeth the appearance of a fast ship, which she was, although ultimately the *Mary* would prove to be the faster.

The *Queen Elizabeth* was also slightly larger than the *Queen Mary*. She was 1,031 feet in length, while her beam (118 feet) and deep draught (39 feet) were the same as those of the earlier ship. Her displacement of 83,673 gross tons made her the world's largest passenger ship, a distinction she would hold for sixty years. Her powerplant was almost identical to that of the *Queen Mary*, though it never quite matched the older ship in total power output, and like the *Mary*, she had four sets of Parsons turbines driving four screws. Her designed service speed was 28.5 knots, which she would easily surpass—in practice she would prove to be almost, but not quite, as fast as the *Queen Mary*. She was designed to carry 2,283 people with a crew complement of 1,100.

The *Queen Elizabeth*'s keel was laid on October 6, 1936, and work on her had absolute priority at the John Brown yard. She was given the hull number 535, but unlike the *Mary* was never known by it. So important was this new project considered that work on her hull went on around the clock, something almost unheard of among British shipbuilders in peacetime. But as the *Queen Elizabeth* grew, so did a sense of unease that slowly covered all of Great Britain. Although most Britons thought of Adolf Hitler as hardly more than an ill-educated, ill-mannered little man with a ridiculous mustache and an overinflated sense of his own importance, events were unfolding across Europe that suggested that this coarse little person, loud mouth, bad cowlick and all, was actually a rather dangerous fellow. He might be readily lampooned, but dismissing him was not so easily done.

Hitler's announcement that Germany would repudiate the terms of the Treaty of Versailles in 1935, followed a year later by the reoccupation of the Rhineland, had alarmed some Britons, while many others regarded these as acts of redress against a far too punitive peace forced on the Allies by the vengeful French. There was a certain amount of truth to that idea, but what gradually became more and more disturbing to the British people was that righting old wrongs did not seem to satisfy the German Führer. His requests evolved into demands and were presented with a temerity—even insolence—that would have made the most arrogant of the old Imperial German diplomats blush. Though the British Government, personified in the Prime Minister, Neville Chamberlain, tried its best to placate and satisfy Hitler

(Chamberlain's name for this policy was "appeasement"), it began to dawn on the British people, though the Prime Minister was never to share in this enlightenment, that the real "Mr. Hitler," as Chamberlain referred to him, was a far cry from the figure of caricature and mockery seen in the music halls. Instead, he was a very frightening individual: Here was a man who wanted, indeed craved, a war. More frightening still, he possessed the means of waging one, whether his neighbors were willing or not. Less than two decades had passed since the end of "the War to End All Wars," and the man who was the absolute dictator of a rapidly rearming Germany, whose mental and emotional stability were questionable, who in another time and place would have been dismissed as simply a sore loser with delusions of grandeur, was preparing to fight the whole thing over again. It was a terrifying thought.

But it was not a thought that the new Queen chose to dwell on. King George VI came to the throne following the death of George V in 1936 and the brief interregnum of Edward VIII. When the *Queen Elizabeth* was ready to be launched on September 27, 1938, Cunard White Star requested the presence of the royal couple, and George VI adopted the same protocol as his father: His wife, Elizabeth, would actually launch the ship. With the graciousness that would mark her whole life, Queen Elizabeth chose to speak of peace instead of war. As she prepared to break the bottle of champagne against the ship's bow, sending her on down the ways, she declared to a listening world, "We proclaim our belief, that by the grace of God, and by Man's patience and good will, order may yet be brought out of confusion, and peace out of turmoil. With that hopeful cry in our heart, we send forth upon her mission this noble ship." Barely more than a minute later, the *Queen Elizabeth* was floating high and proud in the River Clyde, and was quickly towed to the fitting out basin. But the threat of war loomed over the shipyard, for despite Neville Chamberlain's triumphant return from Munich three days after the *Queen Elizabeth*'s launch, declaring "Peace in our time!", the triumph soon soured and Britain began to look to her defenses. The needs of the Royal Navy took precedence in every shipyard in the country, and work on the *Queen Elizabeth* was slowed as manpower and materials were allotted to the warships awaiting refits and modernization that began to queue up along the banks of the Clyde.

Then, on September 1, 1939, the war came. Hitler's panzers had rolled into Poland, and two days later Great Britain declared war on Germany. Now, more than ever, it was the worst of times.

CHAPTER TWO

A Dash to Freedom

"Peace is the dream of the wise;
war is the history of man"
—M. Le compte de Segur

AS THE 1930S WANED AND A MEASURE OF PROSPERITY RETURNED TO THE middle and leisured classes on both sides of the Atlantic, bookings increased for all the big shipping companies. While every line had its partisans and every ship its admirers, unquestionably the most popular vessel on the North Atlantic run was the *Queen Mary;* the appearance of the *Queen Elizabeth* was eagerly anticipated.

Part of the *Queen Mary's* charm, which she never lost in any of her guises, was the way she seemed to bridge the gap between the old and new generations of transatlantic liners. The Germans, French, and Italians all seemed absolutely determined to make a complete break with the traditional decors— and appearances—of ocean liners for half a century. When the *Bremen* and *Europa* were introduced, they brought the stark simplicity of Germany's new Bauhaus school of design with them; in the *Ile de France* and *Normandie,* the French line overwhelmed its passengers with the pretense and self-conscious chic of Art Deco; the Italians were probably the most successful, giving their new liners handsome, rakish lines without affectation, and bringing a distinctly Mediterranean flavor to their interiors. The German twins and the French *Normandie* were praised among the self-proclaimed "smart set" of the day, and appealed to the sort of frantic, self-promoting minority that always fears not being seen to be part of the cutting edge of a new trend. However, it was telling of the tastes and preferences of the overwhelming majority of the traveling public that after the *Queen Mary*, the most popular ships of the day were the *Rex* and the *Conte di Savoia*.

In the *Queen Mary*, Cunard possessed something well and truly unique: a ship that combined tradition and innovation in a way that brought out the best of both. Tradition has had a stronger influence, both positive and negative, on British society than on possibly any other in the world. Nowhere was that influence more strongly felt than on British ships: several classes of British battleships in the late nineteenth and early twentieth centuries, for example, had the officers' quarters stationed at the extreme stern of the ship, probably the single most uncomfortable spot on the whole vessel, simply because that was where officers' quarters in sailing vessels had traditionally been placed.

In the last half of the 1930s, the *Queen Mary*'s primary running mate was the old *Aquitania*, the last of the four-funneled liners and the last British liner to actually enter service before the Great War began. With her straight up-and-down stem, counter stern, fussy superstructure, busy—almost cluttered—upper decks, and quartet of tall stovepipe funnels, each with its octet of round, cowl-shaped ventilators clustered at its base, she was the epitome of the traditional British ocean liner. The *Queen Elizabeth*, when she eventually entered service, would sport a raked stem and cruiser stern, an astonishingly clean superstructure, clear, open upper decks, and a pair of massive oval funnels, with their intakes built into their bases, eliminating the need for ventilators at all. The *Aquitania*'s interiors were dim, heavy with dark wood paneling, overstuffed leather chairs and settees, leaded glass, and elaborate carvings. The *Elizabeth*'s would be open and airy, bright with polished metals, etched glass, and lightly tinted veneers. The two ships were a generation and a world apart.

The *Queen Mary* somehow bridged this gap, and in doing so became probably the best-loved ship ever to sail the North Atlantic. She had her problems, of course: She rolled, and rolled heavily, in anything more than a moderate seaway, breaking several fortunes worth of crockery in her lifetime. But there was something in her lines that harked back to the tradition of the *Aquitania* while also looking forward to the future of the *Queen Elizabeth*. Her interiors embraced the Art Deco style without becoming enslaved to it; her funnels echoed but didn't copy the profile of the *Aquitania*, and served as the models for those of the *Elizabeth*; the lines of her superstructure foreshadowed the clean sweep of the *Elizabeth,* while her upper works still hinted at the fussiness and clutter of the *Aquitania.* She was unique in that she spanned, unlike any other ship afloat, the lost era of elegance and the new era of modernism.

Probably nothing sums up this apparent contradiction, nor demonstrates how well it worked in practice, than something as mundane as the flooring used on the decks of the *Queen Mary*'s public arcades, lounges, and passageways. A novel linoleumlike material called Korkoid was laid down, each room given a distinctive, stylish pattern. Daily these floors were buffed to a mirrorlike shine, but rather than make a great show of this new material and draw the passengers' attention to it, as would have been done on one of the French or German liners, parts of the decking were then covered with large woven oriental rugs or area carpets, similar to the treatments given to hardwood floors ashore. This sort of homeliness, while lacking any appeal to the critics, was attractive to passengers, who felt comfortable with such familiar touches.

It was this atmosphere, at once relaxing and exciting, that made the *Queen Mary* the toast of the North Atlantic, and assured a waiting list for almost every crossing she made. So successful was she that Cunard was actually able to pay installments in advance on the loan the government had made for the construction of the two *Queens.* Though the nature of the passenger trade on the North Atlantic had changed beyond all recognition from what it had been before the Great War, it had become as profitable as ever. Utter confusion, though, was about to overtake it.

While the threat of war overhung the *Queen Elizabeth* from the day of her launching (Neville Chamberlain was on his way to Munich to betray the Czechoslovakian republic to Hitler that morning), so that it eventually imperiled her completion and even her existence, that same threat took much longer to overshadow the *Queen Mary.* None of the succession of crises that passed across Europe between 1936 and 1939 ever caused Cunard to hesitate to continue her service across the Atlantic. The German Navy was small, its battleships puny and outnumbered by the Home Fleet of the Royal Navy, its renascent U-boat arm, once feared, now hardly more than a collection of coastal defense boats. Prime Minister Chamberlain, looking past Nazi Germany at the Communist monster to the east he feared far more—Russia—focused his energies on pacifying or "appeasing" Adolf Hitler, so that the German Führer would be a willing shield for Europe against what many French and British politicians feared was soon to become a militant Bolshevism.

Besides that, as Chamberlain was quick to point out to those who criticized his defense policies, particularly Winston Churchill, as the effects of the Great Depression ebbed, the reviving economic might of the Empire would make it sheer folly for any nation to seek war with Great Britain. The consequences would be ruinous for all involved, but especially for the aggressor, clearly something no sane man would want to bring about. But Europe had learned in 1914 that war can overwhelm a continent despite—and sometimes because of—the best efforts of supposedly sane men. More disturbing, it was becoming increasingly clear that the odd little man in Berchtesgaden with the funny little mustache was not particularly sane.

When Chamberlain returned from Munich announcing "peace with honor" and "peace in our time," he felt that he had finally gotten the measure of Hitler. Hitler, in turn, felt quite the same way about Chamberlain. Chamberlain believed that Hitler simply needed to be shown that there was a civilized way of settling disputes between major powers that didn't require bluster and threats—that face-to-face diplomacy and dialogue could be an effective substitute for saber rattling. He was, to Chamberlain's mind, a neophyte in the ways of international politics who simply had to be shown the ropes. Hitler, on the other hand, believed that Chamberlain, who had always *seemed* to be spineless, really *was* spineless, and that he would always back down to any demand made under a threat of war, provided it was delivered with a carefully calculated measure of theatrics and hysteria.

Both men were utterly, fatally wrong. When the German Army occupied the rump of Czechoslovakia in February 1939, in flagrant violation of the Munich agreement of six months earlier, Chamberlain was furious. He took it as a personal insult—after all it had been *his* signature on that agreement with Hitler; it was an affront to his personal honor. Never mind that he had sold a large measure of Britain's national honor down the river at Munich, this sort of personal offense wouldn't be tolerated again! So when Hitler began making acquisitive noises about the "Polish Corridor," that strip of land that the Treaty of Versailles had given to the newly reformed nation of Poland, which allowed her access to the Baltic Sea but cut off East Prussia from the rest of Germany, Chamberlain assured the Polish government that Britain would guarantee the integrity of Poland's borders.

It was a hapless, hopeless mistake, and a challenge that Hitler couldn't resist taking up. Poland's borders were as vulnerable as Czechoslovakia's had been near-impregnable a year earlier. And whereas the Czechs had possessed a large, modern, well-trained and well-equipped army, the Polish armed forces, though even more numerous, were poorly organized and badly equipped. The Polish soldiers were well trained and brave to the point of foolhardiness, but they were trained to refight the First World War, something Hitler had every intention of avoiding.

All this time, the German Navy was feverishly building ships and submarines. Originally Hitler had planned on beginning his war against France and Great Britain in 1944 or 1945, and all of the design and building programs of the three armed services, army, air force, and navy, were geared toward that date. In the navy, the expansion of the fleet had been given particularly close attention, with a carefully thought-out plan of construction (Plan "Z") drawn up to create a balanced fleet that could challenge the Royal Navy on something approaching an equal footing. Though the Germans realized, just as they had three decades before, that they could never match the building capacity of Britain's shipyards on a hull-for-hull basis, they were determined to build ships that ton-for-ton were superior to anything the British Navy possessed. Unfortunately for the Germans, their new ships were based on obsolete World War I–vintage designs, and the twenty-year hiatus imposed on their naval architects by the Treaty of Versailles meant that they had no experience with the latest developments in guns, armor, or propulsion. As a consequence, the full scale of Plan "Z" was never realized, and the ships that *were* built, though they looked impressive on paper, were poorly balanced, often overweight and undergunned, with poor sea-keeping qualities.

Not so the U-boat arm. Adm. Karl Doenitz, a modestly successful submarine officer in the First World War and a profound thinker in developing U-boat strategies and tactics, wanted a fleet of three hundred submarines to be able to complete his portion of Plan "Z." Though German warship designers had been unable to find work in the years between the wars, German submarine engineers and architects had been able to work for several dummy companies set up in neutral countries, most notably Holland. There they had the opportunity to keep abreast of the latest technological developments in submarine warfare, as well as scrutinize foreign boats and design submarines of their own. Recalled to Germany in the mid-1930s, these engineers were able to put their accumulated experience and knowledge to use. The U-boats they designed for the resurgent German Navy were built around the world's finest diesel engines and the accrued experience of wartime action and peacetime innovation. They were solid, workmanlike boats that, though not world-beaters in any given category, were well balanced and reliable. When the war began in 1939, Admiral Doenitz had only a third of the number of boats he had wanted, but they were operated by crews trained to a high standard, following a thoroughly thought-out tactical doctrine that would multiply their effectiveness out of all proportion to their numbers.

The *Queen Mary* put to sea from Southampton bound for New York on August 30, 1939, carrying a record number of 2,332 passengers, including Mr. and Mrs. Bob Hope, and a cargo of $44 million in gold bullion. Most of the passengers were Americans, as U.S. citizens were leaving the Continent in droves that August. It was clear that more than just a crisis was looming, and no one wanted to be caught on the wrong side of the Atlantic if the shooting started, as seemed more and more likely every day.

The crisis on the Continent that the *Queen Mary* was leaving behind was unlike those that had passed by in the previous three years: This one offered little, if any, chance of being resolved peacefully. Adolf Hitler had focused all of his malicious attentions on Poland, and he was determined that there would not be a diplomatic solution to the crisis as there was at Munich in 1938. He was bent on humiliating Neville Chamberlain and making a mockery of the Prime Minister's guarantees to Poland. Privately, Hitler expressed his belief that once Germany attacked Poland, Chamberlain would repudiate his assurances to the Poles, leaving them in the lurch. But even if he stood by his word, that would not prevent the Führer from attacking, for Hitler wanted to have a war, and nothing would stop him from having it.

On the morning of September 1, 1939, lunging columns of dark gray panzers, supported by vast columns of field gray infantry, roared into Poland and began systematically decimating the Polish defenses. On September 2, the British government issued an ultimatum to Germany, demanding that the Wehrmacht withdraw its divisions from Polish soil within twenty-four hours. Failing that, a state of war would exist between the Third Reich and the British Empire. Hitler responded to the ultimatum with all the courtesy he felt appropriate—he ignored it—and at 11:00 A.M. on September 3, 1939, Great Britain once again found herself at war with Germany.

The declaration of war promptly threw the docks at Southampton, as well as London and Liverpool, into utter confusion. Some sailings were canceled outright as ships were requisitioned by the British government; others were delayed when word reached the ports that the liner *Athenia* had been torpedoed off the north coast of Ireland on her way to Liverpool. In Southampton, as the *Aquitania* prepared to depart for New York that afternoon, notices were quickly printed announcing that she would set sail as planned. In their haste to prepare the notices, government officials overlooked the eerie echoes of a warning issued in 1915 before the *Lusitania* left New York on her last voyage when they announced: "American citizens are hereby advised that they are taking passage on a belligerent ship and are subject to sinking without notice."

Nor was the chaos limited to British and French ships. On August 29, just before the *Queen Mary* set out from Southampton, one of her erstwhile German rivals, the Norddeutscher-Lloyd's *Bremen,* was putting into New York for the very last time. The increase of international tensions and the likelihood of war between Germany and Great Britain had alarmed the American authorities, so before she was allowed to dock, the *Bremen* was searched from keel to masthead for possible stowaways, as well as any equipment or material that might be used for illegal purposes within the United States. The American Attorney General, Frank Murphy, defended the search, declaring, somewhat self-righteously, "There will be no repetition of the situation in 1917, when a democracy was unprepared to meet the espionage problem."

Once the *Bremen* was allowed to disgorge the travelers she was carrying, her captain, who clearly was privy to information that no one else in New York possessed, refused to take on any passengers for the trip back to Germany. Instead, a minimal amount of provisions were brought aboard and the *Bremen*'s fuel bunkers were quickly topped off. Barely more than twenty-four hours after she had arrived, the *Bremen* set out to return to Germany, empty save for her crew, on what would be her last crossing of the Atlantic ever.

As the *Queen Mary* made her way across the Atlantic, her captain, acting on instructions from the Admiralty, was following a course nearly a hundred miles south of the track she normally followed, a precaution taken to avoid any U-boats that might have been lying in waiting for the huge liner. Shortly before midnight on September 2, a few hours after the British ultimatum was delivered to Germany, a signal was sent to the *Queen Mary* ordering her to go to full alert, instructing the captain to take "all necessary precautions . . . paying particular attention to the threat of submarine attack" in order to bring the ship safely into New York Harbor. Immediately the crew was set to work painting over all the portholes and rigging blackout curtains at all the doorways that led out onto the ship's upper decks. Additional lookouts were posted, and a zigzag course was laid out for the ship to follow.

At the same time that these precautions were being taken, the following notice was being posted throughout the ship:

R.M.S. *"Queen Mary"*

As a purely precautionary measure, all passengers are forbidden to smoke, strike matches, or show any kind of light on
any of the outside decks between sunset and sunrise. Passengers are also requested to use the outer decks as little as possible during darkness, and are forbidden to use the Sun
Deck during the aforementioned hours. The Commodore
requests that all passengers will co-operate with the forego-
ing instructions.

It is worth noting that rather than arousing an outcry among the passengers at what might have been regarded as an infringement on their preroga-
tives, the notices served to underline the seriousness of the situation, and the
passengers, for the most part, were readily cooperative.

In the lounges and dining rooms throughout the *Queen Mary*, passengers
huddled around radios to catch the latest news. The atmosphere throughout
the ship became increasingly anxious when Prime Minister Chamberlain
announced that war had been declared. Thoughts of the fate that had befallen
the *Lusitania* weren't far from anyone's mind, as a similar fate could easily
overtake them. As the most visible symbol of Great Britain's maritime power,
the ship would offer a target that no U-boat commander could resist.

Fortunately, the *Queen Mary* encountered no lurking German submarines,
and on the morning of September 5, she steamed into New York Harbor. That
same day Admiralty instructions directed all British merchant ships to remain
in whatever friendly or neutral ports they were docked. On September 6
Cunard canceled all sailings of the *Queen Mary* "for the foreseeable future" and
made arrangements for the crewmen who were part of the Royal Naval Reserve
to return to Britain, where their skills were urgently needed. Within days of her
arrival, only a handful of her officers and crew remained, keeping themselves
busy with maintenance tasks. Before the month was out, however, British and
American intelligence officers, as well as American law enforcement officials,
including the FBI and the New York Police Department, began organizing a
protective cordon around Pier 90, as German saboteurs who were determined
to cripple the *Queen* were rumored to be operating in New York.

Whether there ever actually were Axis sabotage experts in New York at
the time has never been proven one way or the other, but if there had been,
the *Queen Mary* wouldn't have been their only target as, in a curious twist of

fate, she was moored alongside her great French rival, the *Normandie*. Like the British, the French were taking no chances with the pride of their fleet and had ordered the *Normandie* to remain in New York when the war broke out. Unlike the British, who quickly ordered their ships painted in wartime "light sea grey" as a protective measure to be ready when they were needed again, the French couldn't seem to make up their minds about what to do with the *Normandie,* and so she remained in her black, white, and red prewar livery, while her British counterparts donned a more sober mien. With only a small crew of caretakers aboard, she sat motionless, all but forgotten.

While the *Queen Mary* sat idle in New York, and her sister, the unfinished *Queen Elizabeth,* sat equally idle in the Clyde in Scotland, a furious debate was raging through the British Admiralty in Whitehall, as well as in the House of Commons, about what to do with these two monstrous ships. Critics were quick to call them "white elephants," and while acknowledging that their vast size meant that they could carry larger numbers of troops than any ships ever had before, they tried to argue that the *Queens'* sheer size would also mean that the Royal Navy would have to assign valuable cruisers and destroyers to escort them wherever they went, cruisers and destroyers that the Royal Navy simply could not spare. Also, the thousand tons of fuel oil that each liner would burn every day could be better used, they claimed, by ships of the Royal Navy, and their holds were too small for them to be useful as cargo ships.

The *Queens* were not without their defenders, however, and their arguments were ultimately compelling. The sheer size of the two ships, which the critics claimed was their greatest liability, was in fact their greatest asset. By being able to bring unparalleled numbers of troops from anywhere in the world to the places where they were needed most, the *Queens* would allow the British to deploy their limited forces more effectively and decisively. Not only would the size of the ships allow them to move as many troops as several smaller ships, but their speed would allow them to outrun any German warship afloat, eliminating the need for escorts except in confined waters.

Eventually the views of those people in the Admiralty and the Government who wanted to utilize the *Queens* as transports prevailed, and on March 6, a memo from the Admiralty was forwarded to Cunard's board of directors, informing the company that the services of the *Queen Mary* were required by King and Country, further stating that "His Majesty's Government relies on the goodwill of yourselves, your staffs and agents in carrying out these instructions and preparing the ship for the King's service, especially as regards clearing cargo, fueling, storing and manning."

It was a crucial decision, made in the nick of time, since it would take several weeks for the *Queen Mary* to be readied for trooping duties. Britain's strategic situation, while not perilous, was precarious: There were only a handful of divisions in the British Isles at the time. Many more were stationed overseas and could be recalled, and Britain could also draw on the forces of the Commonwealth, the armies of South Africa, India, and Australia, for even more reinforcements. But those units would take weeks, sometimes months, to reach Europe, so any means of moving troops in larger numbers at greater speeds were embraced. Consequently, the value of the *Queen Mary* and *Queen Elizabeth* became evident, assuring their survival.

What would happen next was, to a large extent, up to the Germans. The *Queen Mary* was now safe in New York, though the *Queen Elizabeth,* still sitting in the Clyde, was quite vulnerable to German bombs. From the end of September 1939, when Poland was finally overrun, until the spring of 1940, the German and Allied armies glared at each other across the Franco-German border, but neither side seemed to be interested in doing much more than making fierce faces at one another, the conflict degenerating into what became known as the "Phony War" or the "Bore War." The Allies had lost a tremendous opportunity that autumn, for Hitler had practically denuded his western defenses in order to assure an overwhelming superiority of numbers against the Poles. Had the French struck while the Wehrmacht was preoccupied in Poland, they could have driven deep into Germany, occupied most of the German centers of heavy industry, crippling the German Army, and almost certainly toppled Hitler from power.

Instead, France displayed the same infuriating lack of good judgment that would characterize French foreign policy for the rest of the century, remaining haplessly immobile when bold action could have ended the war in a single stroke. Chamberlain did little to encourage the French to action, the resolve that had driven him to stand by Poland suddenly vanishing as quickly as it had come. In truth, Britain could have done little more than offer moral support, even had Chamberlain summoned the courage to try; there were only two British divisions in France, hardly enough to launch or sustain an offensive. Hitler had counted on French timidity when he was planning his Polish strategy, and his intuition was rewarded. It would be further rewarded when he and his generals were drawing up their plans for the invasion of the West.

That such an invasion had to come sooner or later was obvious to the more perceptive minds in Whitehall, and when it did, Britain would require every man and weapon she could muster. Getting them to Britain would be up to the *Queen Mary* and the *Queen Elizabeth,* but before they could begin, both of them would have to undergo major conversions into proper troop-ships. Before that could happen, the *Queen Elizabeth* had to be taken out of harm's way.

CHAPTER THREE

A Royal Escape

It was England's greatest crisis. . . .
This time Britain stood alone.

—William Manchester

THOUGH THE WARCLOUDS WERE CLEARLY GATHERING OVER EUROPE IN THE months following her launch, the *Queen Elizabeth's* completion was given absolute priority at the John Brown yard, and workers continued to labor on her around the clock. There was always a chance that war could be averted, and Cunard still had hopes of making a reality of its plan for a two-ship transatlantic service, so the line and the shipyard were putting their best efforts in her. By being the first ship to exceed a thousand feet in length and eighty thousand tons displacement, the *Queen Mary* had been called "the inevitable ship," and the *Queen Elizabeth,* being longer and larger than her consort, as well as the French Line's *Normandie,* was soon dubbed "the ultimate ship."

Even though the three ships were almost exactly the same size, each one's individual appearance made a quite different impression. The *Queen Mary* was the most traditional, big and powerful, four-square looking, imposing from any angle; the *Normandie,* with the elliptical lines of her superstructure, strangely short foredeck, and oddly outdated counter stern could, in turn, appear yachtlike from one angle, squat and dumpy from another. The *Queen Elizabeth* was perhaps the most beautiful of the three: The long foredeck, unusually clean superstructure, and sweeping lines of her hull and upper works created a sense of grace and power that no other liner ever matched, before or since.

Her interiors were somewhat different from the *Queen Mary*'s as well, again reflecting a certain amount of influence by the *Normandie*. While never abandoning the "English country home" atmosphere that had been the hallmark of British passenger liners for more than a half century, the *Queen Elizabeth* designers did shy away from the walnuts and mahoganies of the *Mary* in favor of lighter woods. The main lounge was paneled with a veneer of Canadian maple burl, which had a warm beige-pink tone, highlighted by being mixed with panels of light blue, pale gray, and beige leather. The captain's cabin received special treatment, with unique paneling made from wood taken from rock elm piling that had been driven in the Thames River for the original Waterloo Bridge in 1911 and removed in 1936 when the bridge was replaced. The waters of the river had worked a chemical reaction on the wood, creating a subtle, handsome shade of light gray unmatched by anything else in the world. Art Deco motifs were found throughout the ship, though not with the stridency with which they sometimes confronted the *Normandie*'s passengers. One particularly graceful theme carried throughout the ship echoed the way the *Queen Mary*'s designers had acknowledged rather than concealed the fact that she was a ship: Motifs and panels in staircases, over fireplaces and along the *Elizabeth*'s passageways, were variously made from steel, copper, bronze, white metal, aluminium, lead, and glass—all materials used in the construction of the ship. It was an aesthetic tour-de-force that would never be equaled.

At least, that was the vision that the designers had for the *Elizabeth,* and thankfully it would one day be realized, but the likelihood that it would be accomplished in the near future began to fade almost as soon as she was launched. Despite the joy and celebration that marked the launch of the *Queen Elizabeth* on September 27, 1938, and the enthusiasm that the workers were putting into her completion, a growing air of foreboding was spreading over Great Britain. The Munich Crisis had passed, war having been narrowly averted when British Prime Minister Neville Chamberlain and French President Edouard Daladier sold Czechoslovakia down the river to a gleeful Adolf Hitler, but an awareness was growing among the British people that all was not right in Europe, and that the price paid by their Prime Minister was probably too steep. They were right: Though Chamberlain had declared that the Munich Agreement had brought Europe "peace in our time," within six months of its signing Hitler had trampled all over the accord. Belatedly, Britain began to look to her defenses, and refitting and modernizing the ships of the Royal Navy became a growing priority in every British shipyard.

Consequently, the focus of the work at the John Brown yard began to shift away from the *Queen Elizabeth* as work gangs were reassigned to military jobs. Starved of funding for new ships by the skinflint (parsimonious is too kind a word) Governments of Stanley Baldwin and Neville Chamberlain, the Royal Navy was forced to increase its numbers of active warships by drawing out of reserve a large number of worn and aging—and in some cases antiquated—ships, mostly of First World War vintage, modernizing them as best it could, and sending them out to the fleet. Sometimes this meant simply upgrading or modifying a ship's armament and equipment, which was fairly easily accomplished. Other times it meant extensive reconstruction of a ship's hull or superstructure, always a long and often difficult process. Usually the task was somewhere in between the two. In any case, it became clearer with each passing month that the *Queen Elizabeth* was most likely going to become an expensive luxury, and though the work on her never stopped, the number of work gangs dwindled weekly as the Royal Navy demanded more and more of John Brown's resources.

One of the reasons for this was the newly launched battleship *Duke of York*. A thirty-five thousand-ton behemoth armed with ten 14-inch guns and a battery of sixteen 5.25-inch antiaircraft guns, she was one of the most modern battleships in the world, and was being readied to take her place with the Royal Navy's Home Fleet at Scapa Flow. A decision would have to be made, and made quickly, as to which of the two—*Queen* or *Duke*—would be finished first.

But then, on September 1, 1939, Hitler's Wehrmacht smashed into Poland. Neville Chamberlain suddenly discovered a backbone no one suspected he had (though he was to soon lose it again) and honored Great Britain's alliance with the Poles, issuing an ultimatum to Germany to withdraw from Polish soil within forty-eight hours or face war with the British. Hitler ignored the ultimatum, feeling that he had the measure of Chamberlain and the British people—he was right about the first but fatally, for him, wrong about the second. For the second time in two decades, war swept across the Continent.

For those were expecting a reprise of the high drama of the autumn of 1914, where the French and British, fighting shoulder-to-shoulder to stop and then turn back the German invader, the first eight months of the Second World War were a disappointment. Chamberlain, continuing in his delusion that eventually Hitler would be reasonable and negotiate a fair and lasting settlement, was unwilling to countenance any aggressive operations against

Germany, while France, falling into a timorousness—long on brave words and short on action—that would come to be her trademark for the rest of the century, refused to undertake any offensive against the Germans for fear of German reprisals. After the first flurry of bold words and meaningless activity, the conflict between Germany and Great Britain settled down to a rather dull routine that was soon dubbed the "Phony War."

Admittedly, Winston Churchill was doing his best to change that. Churchill had returned to the Admiralty—site of some of his greatest accomplishments before and during the Great War—as First Lord on the same day that Britain declared war on Germany. He had been foisted on Chamberlain, who wanted no part of him, by a House of Commons that had belatedly come to understand the clarity and veracity of the warnings Churchill had been sounding about the Nazi menace for years. The House had made it clear to Chamberlain that unless he brought Churchill into the Government—and in post suitable to his unique talents, not merely as a figurehead—then they were quite prepared to turn Chamberlain out of office. Chamberlain, who cordially detested Churchill, a sentiment Churchill never felt inclined to return, was the consummate political animal, and so he acquiesced and gave Churchill the Admiralty. After all, Chamberlain was a businessman, and a good manager is always willing to use talented subordinates, no matter what his personal feelings.

Churchill was a busy man at the Admiralty. While finding that in 1939 the Royal Navy was far from the "somnolent service" he had discovered it to be in 1911, it was being stretched to near the breaking point by its responsibilities. The morale of the officers and ratings was good, their competence unquestioned, their dedication unchallenged. He had confidence in the men he was to lead, and they had confidence in him: When word of his appointment as First Lord was announced, the signal was flashed throughout the fleet, "WINSTON IS BACK!" The respect and admiration implicit in the signal was unmistakable: It was fully reciprocated.

The problem faced by the Royal Navy was not with its human elements, but rather with its ships. While the supremacy of the Home Fleet's capital ships would never be seriously challenged during the whole course of the war, in 1939 the gravest danger lay in the lack of lighter units, particularly light cruisers and destroyers, the ships that would be required to escort and protect the convoys on which Britain's survival would depend. Even as it was drawing heavily on the Reserve Fleet, the Royal Navy was hard-pressed to provide adequate protection for all of its charges.

Within days of war being declared, the "pocket battleship" *Deutschland* was prowling the Western Approaches, the waters to the north and west of Scotland's Western Isles, while her sister ship, *Graf Spee,* was patrolling the South Atlantic, threatening the sea lanes that tied Great Britain to South Africa, India, and South America. In the great German naval base at Kiel, *Scharnhorst* and *Gneisenau,* a pair of battleships masquerading as battle cruisers, were preparing to put to sea. And even though Adm. Karl Doenitz, the commander of Germany's U-boat fleet, possessed only a fraction of the U-boats he felt would be required to wage a successful submarine war against Great Britain, he had every submarine he could muster infesting the waters surrounding the British Isles, and they were soon taking a heavy toll on British shipping. Just as dangerous were the swift raids of the squadrons of torpedo craft—*Schnellbooten,* or S-boats (the Allies knew them as E-boats)— that would strike hard at the British shipping that had to steam down the North Sea or up the English Channel to reach the Thames Estuary and the Port of London.

Every destroyer, every light cruiser that was seaworthy or could be made seaworthy was pressed into action. The shipyards of the River Clyde were desperately needed to refurbish the older ships drawn out of reserve, build new ships for the Royal Navy, and allow bomb- and torpedo-damaged merchantmen and warships to be repaired, so work on the *Queen Elizabeth* stopped entirely, and she sat idle at her fitting-out basin—a large dry dock—at the John Brown yard.

The rather thorny issue of what was to be done with the *Queen Elizabeth* now confronted the Admiralty. Clearly there was now no need for a new passenger liner, and completing any more work on her would mean diverting time, materials, and workers from badly needed warships. Though scrapping her might be a painful, even wrenching, task for the Scottish shipwrights who built her, the strategic value of the thousands of tons of steel in her hull was undeniable. On the other hand, it seemed that *something* could be done with her—the *Elizabeth's* boilers and engines were complete, and most of her superstructure was finished, including her two funnels, though she was still a long way from being ready for sea.

The fate of the *Queen Elizabeth* was left in the hands of the Admiralty— Cunard couldn't do anything with her at this point. Much of Cunard White Star's fleet had already been requisitioned for service with the Royal Navy, and most of the line's officers—who were Royal Naval Reserve—were already in service with the navy, while almost all of the company's administrative staff was busy coordinating the movements of its ships to meet the needs of the Royal Navy. Heated debates took place at the highest levels of the British Government over how the liner could best serve the needs of the Empire. The Germans wouldn't ignore her forever, no matter how phony the Phony War seemed to be. Some serious thought was given to the idea that the *Queen Elizabeth* be sold to the United States in her unfinished state in exchange for war supplies. There was also some talk of cutting away her superstructure and converting her into an aircraft carrier, but although a few design studies were begun to test the feasibility of the idea, no actual work on such a conversion was ever begun.

Therein, though, lies one of history's great "what ifs?" With her immense size, the *Queen Elizabeth* would have dwarfed any other aircraft carrier in the world, and would easily have been capable of handling as many as 120 aircraft, or roughly twice the capacity of any other carrier in the world at the time. In point of fact, her dimensions would have rivaled those of the American *Kitty Hawk* class of supercarriers built in the early 1960s. While such bulk probably would have been a liability in the cut-and-thrust of operations in the Mediterranean, it would have made the *Elizabeth* perfectly suited to the vast expanses of the Pacific. Had the conversion begun in late 1939 or early 1940, it almost certainly would have been completed by the fall of 1941, which would have allowed the *Queen Elizabeth* (which would have needed to be renamed, as there was already a battleship *Queen Elizabeth* in service with the Royal Navy) to sail with Force Z, the task force composed of the battleship *Prince of Wales,* the battle cruiser *Repulse,* and the carrier *Victorious,* dispatched by Prime Minister Churchill to the Far East in an attempt to thwart a threatened Japanese advance into Malaya.

As events unfolded, Force Z, under the command of Rear Adm. Tom Phillips, sortied from Singapore the same day that the Japanese attacked the American naval base at Pearl Harbor, but *Victorious* had to turn back because of problems with her turbines. The two capital ships sailed on, now devoid of air cover, and were overwhelmed and sunk by Japanese dive bombers and torpedo planes in a matter of hours on December 10, 1941. Events may well have turned out quite differently, and the Japanese strategy for their advance into Malaya been thrown into turmoil, had the modified *Queen Elizabeth* accompanied *Prince of Wales* and *Repulse* on their last sortie, her fearsome air wing a deterrent to Japanese air attacks.

Instead, she sat in the bleak, gray waters of the Clyde, some work continuing in a rather desultory fashion, as her essential systems were completed, but all work on her interiors was understandably halted, leaving them mostly vast, empty shells. Workers gave her hull and upperworks a coat of wartime gray paint and added a degaussing coil, but nothing more was done to prepare the *Elizabeth* for any sort of wartime role. Finally, Winston Churchill decided that the *Queen Elizabeth* would be best employed as a troopship, and intervened to save her. At his direction, on November 2, 1939, the Ministry of Shipping issued urgent orders to complete the work necessary to make the liner ready for sea. She was going to America to join the *Queen Mary.*

The urgency was due to the fact that there were only two occasions in the next twelve months when the tides in the Clyde would be high enough to allow the *Queen Elizabeth* to steam down the river and into the open sea—the first was February 26, the next six months later, so February 26 it had to be. In the space of twelve hours, the *Elizabeth* was to be eased out of the fitting-out basin, with the battleship *Duke of York* to take her place.

Workers once again swarmed over the liner, finishing what was determined to be the essential work. It is interesting to note that in what was defined as essential and what wasn't, the *Elizabeth* would sail with part of her launching cradle still attached to her bow. All of the navigational systems were installed but were untried: All of the working up, testing, and corrections that normally would have been part of the *Queen Elizabeth*'s sea trials would have to be done during one mad dash to the safety of New York. In a sort of silent acknowledgment of what might happen, all of the lifesaving equipment—including a full complement of lifeboats—was installed, and most importantly, the power plant was completed in all respects. Inside, she might be little more than a "big empty," but she would go to sea as a proper ship.

There was no way that the preparations for the *Elizabeth*'s movement could be concealed—German reconnaissance aircraft were flying over Glasgow daily, and German spies made regular reports to Berlin on the liner's progress. But if the British couldn't hide the fact that the *Queen Elizabeth* was getting ready to put to sea, they could mislead the Germans about her destination. An elaborately detailed cover story was worked out to keep the Germans and their agents looking in the wrong direction.

Discreetly, so as not to arouse German suspicions that the story was a ruse, the word was leaked out that the *Queen Elizabeth* would be taken to Southampton to finish her fitting out. Stacks of packing cases, some empty and just for show, but most filled with the carpets, china, silverware, paneling, wallpaper, tables, chairs, beds, and bureaus that would have completed the ship's interior, began piling up in warehouses along the Ocean Dock of

Southampton's waterfront. The King George V dry dock was scheduled for an inspection of the *Queen Elizabeth*'s screws and rudder upon her arrival, and various hotels in the city near the docks were flooded with reservations for the shipwrights and artificers who would be completing the specialized work on the liner. The cover story was sufficiently convincing to cause the harbor officials at Southampton to ask Cunard for a docking plan for the ship, a serendipitous detail that merely added to the story's credibility.

That the Germans swallowed the tale hook, line, and sinker was proven by the swarms of Luftwaffe bombers that appeared over Southampton on the afternoon of March 3, the earliest that the *Queen Elizabeth* could have arrived, and every day for the next three days—until the Germans realized they had been had. That didn't mean there were no anxious moments up in Scotland—there was more than enough drama to last several lifetimes in the struggle to get the *Elizabeth* out to sea.

February 26 dawned gray and bleak, with a threat of rain, typical weather for a Scottish winter, and perfect for moving the *Queen Elizabeth* unobserved by German reconnaissance planes. Just before noon, a half dozen tugboats began edging the liner out of the basin, into the middle of the Clyde, hoping to catch the high tide at 4:00 that afternoon as she passed Rashilee Light, some twelve miles downstream, the spot where the *Queen Mary* had run aground four years before. In order to lighten the *Elizabeth* and allow her to ride as high as possible, all of her lifeboats had been lowered and towed downstream earlier, but it would still be touch and go.

It was a dismal departure compared to the sendoff the *Queen Mary* had been given four years before. Then, a crowd estimated at a quarter of a million people lined both banks of the Clyde as she departed for Southampton. Now, only a few hundred dockyard workers were watching as the *Queen Elizabeth* set out to sea for the first time. Edging her along at just over three miles per hour, the half dozen tugs attending her were careful to make certain she stayed in midchannel, where the deepest water was.

Things got tense as the *Elizabeth* reached the Rashilee Light, the most dangerous and difficult part of the passage down the Clyde. The riverbed rises slightly at this point and the river flows faster—but so does the incoming tide, the same tide that the *Queen Elizabeth* was depending on to allow her to clear the river bottom. The danger was real and immediate, for if the liner ran aground hard and fast here, the Luftwaffe might be able to deliver Britain a crippling blow: Sinking the *Queen Elizabeth* in the Clyde would not only deny the British the use of the port of Glasgow, it would also mean that the

Clydeside shipyards—and any ships in them—would be cut off as well, possibly for months.

Caught by the sudden surge of the incoming tide over the shallows, the bows of the *Queen Elizabeth* threatened to swing toward the shore and ground the ship, and for over an hour the tugs struggled with their huge, ungainly charge. The rush of the incoming tidal flow was so strong that despite the fact that all six tugs were straining to the utmost, the *Queen Elizabeth* was actually standing still. The coordination between the crews of the tugs and the liner was remarkable, their seamanship superb, for they held the liner steady until finally the flow subsided somewhat, and at 5:15 the *Elizabeth* finally steamed past Rashilee and dropped anchor off the Tail of the Bank at the mouth of the Clyde. There she picked up her lifeboats, and the crew began the final checks and last-minute maintenance to ready her for the open seas, a task that would consume the next three days.

Capt. Jack Townley was on the bridge of the *Queen Elizabeth,* in command of a skeleton complement of four hundred officers and men. On February 28 he conducted a series of engine and compass trials in the mouth of the Clyde Firth, then settled down to wait for further orders. It wasn't a comfortable wait, as the *Elizabeth* was far from out of danger: She was still within range of the Luftwaffe's bombers, and despite the precautions being taken by Royal Navy destroyers, there was still a chance that a U-boat could slip past them and put a torpedo or two into the new liner before anyone could do anything about it.

Apparently Captain Townley had a good idea of where the liner was bound—after all, no port in Europe was safe for the *Elizabeth,* and she wasn't prepared for a run as far as Cape Town, let alone Singapore or Sydney. She had been designed for only one port in North America—New York. There was no other realistic choice, but official confirmation hadn't yet arrived. What information was given to Townley and his crew was that the *Elizabeth* was not bound for Southampton, and that the ship's articles that the crew had signed would have to be modified to conform to oceanic rather than coastal regulations. Some thirty crewmen objected, reasonably as it were, that they hadn't signed on for a transatlantic trip (the crew could see the obvious as well) and asked to be taken off the ship. A tender took the men to Gareloch, where for security reasons they were detained for the next five days until the *Elizabeth* had safely arrived in New York. As events turned out, they may have regretted not making the crossing, as the crewmen who did were paid an extra £30 "inconvenience money" in addition to their regular wages.

Dawn comes late in the Scotland winter, so it was still dark on the morning of March 2, 1940, when a tender pulled alongside the *Queen Elizabeth,* and a King's Messenger stepped aboard. Escorted to the bridge, he presented Captain Townley with a set of sealed sailing orders to be opened only after the ship was on the high seas. Within minutes, the *Elizabeth* was under way, accompanied by an escort of four destroyers and an umbrella of aircraft. It wasn't until ten hours later and night had fallen, when the flotilla was two hundred miles past the Western Isles, that, in a flurry of lamp signals wishing the *Queen Elizabeth* "Good Luck!" the destroyers and aircraft departed, leaving the liner on her own. It was time for Captain Townley to open his orders.

As he expected, the *Queen Elizabeth* was ordered to make her best possible speed for New York, zigzagging the entire distance to confuse any U-boats that might stumble across the liner on the way. Once there, she was to remain in New York until further instructions from His Majesty's Government were received. Within minutes, the liner was working up to 24.5 knots, the fastest she could go without straining her new and untried engines. Captain Townley laid out a zigzag course to follow—he had to improvise one—and all over the ship, crewmen were double-checking portholes and decklamps, making sure the ship's blackout was absolute.

Inside, the nearly four hundred crewmen rattled about in the vast, empty passageways and unfinished decks. Each man had his own First Class cabin, although the accommodations and furnishings were sparse, with few amenities. The food was good, and a daily menu was produced on the ship's own printing press, but it was an uncomfortable five days nonetheless. One engineer remembered it this way: "We had no carpets, just bare floors [the steel decks], no heating, and the light fixtures were just hanging wires." All of the fixtures and furnishings were left sitting in dockside warehouses in Southampton, part of the scheme to deceive the Germans.

It was a tense crossing: The only protection the *Queen Elizabeth* had was her speed and maneuverability—two qualities that were very much unknowns on the untested ship—and the secrecy surrounding her departure. The weather helped; always bad in midwinter on the North Atlantic, it was windy, with squalls and heavy seas, and visibility was poor, which drastically reduced the chances of any German warship spotting the liner. Captain Townley was ordered to maintain strict radio silence, while the British worked hard to maintain the deception that she was actually bound for Southampton. Even the Cunard officials in New York were unaware that she was coming until the day before she was due to arrive, kept in the dark by the Admiralty.

On the morning of May 7, a Transworld Airlines DC-3 was flying into New York when, forty miles east of Fire Island, it radioed a report of seeing a huge gray ship zigzagging furiously toward New York Harbor. The ship appeared strangely deserted—two men on her stern were the only people visible on her decks—and she seemed to be in a fair state of disrepair: Part of her launch cradle was still attached to her bow, sections of the superstructure were unpainted, and huge patches of red primer showed in her hull where the hastily applied coat of gray paint had been worn away by the wind and waves. It was the *Queen Elizabeth,* and her dramatic, unannounced appearance created a sensation in New York. In many ways, it was reminiscent of the *Queen Mary's* arrival four years earlier. The first ship to meet the *Elizabeth* was the dredger *Coney Island.* When she sounded her whistle in salute, it was the signal for every ship in the harbor to join in a cacophony of greeting. The *New York Post* captured the moment vividly:

> As she slowly made her way up the river, she was accorded the tumultuous welcome befitting the most distinguished representative of maritime royalty ever to reach America's shores. Thousands of spectators thronged the windows and tops of West Side buildings. More than a dozen planes circled overhead and dipped time and time again in salute, while scores of tugboats churned the water on all sides of the great grey Majesty with whistles and sirens wide open. The waterfront personnel took to the piers en masse to watch her pass.

A small fleet of tugs guided the *Queen Elizabeth* into her slip at Cunard's Pier 90, alongside the *Queen Mary.* The *New York Times* called the *Queen Elizabeth* the "Empress Incognito," remarking that "many sagas of the sea have begun and ended in our harbor, but can the old-timers remember anything to compare with the unheralded arrival of the biggest and fastest liner in the world, after the most daring of all maiden voyages?" It was John Maxtone-Graham who best put in the event into context: "If she was scarcely dressed for the occasion, the brilliance of her escape from the Germans gave the moment a particular drama all its own. That vast, sombre ship, nudged delicately into the slip just north of her sister, gave symbolic presence to the war that America was yet to enter."

With the arrival of the *Queen Elizabeth*, one of the most amazing array of liners ever assembled in New York Harbor was complete. Alongside the

Elizabeth was the *Queen Mary;* other Cunard ships moored there were the *Mauretania,* which carried on the name of the great Blue Ribband holder, and the *Aquitania,* the last of the great four-funneled liners, and the only liner to serve in both World Wars. Along with them were the French Line's *Normandie* and *Ile de France* and the Italian Line's sleek but forlorn *Rex.* Armed guards patrolled their decks, as well as the piers where the ships were tied up; at night, powerful searchlights kept them illuminated, as American intelligence officers had learned that German agents were hoping to put bombs aboard the British and French ships to prevent them from being used by the Allies. The future for the French and Italian ships was really quite uncertain, but that of the Cunard ships had already been decided—on March 1, 1940, His Majesty's Government had informed Cunard that its fleet was being requisitioned for the duration of the war for service with His Majesty's Armed Forces. The *Queens* were going to war.

CHAPTER FOUR

The Queens Go to War

Wake, soldier, wake, thy war-horse waits
To bear thee to the battle. . . .

—Thomas Kibble Hervey

IN *THE INFLUENCE OF SEA POWER UPON HISTORY*, ONE OF THE MOST INFLUENtial books written in the last two hundred years, Capt. Alfred Thayer Mahan described "sea power" as a nation's capacity to use the world's oceans to transport the flow of raw materials and finished goods necessary to sustain a nation's economy in peacetime, as well as transport troops and supplies in wartime, while simultaneously denying that capability to the enemy. No nation has so thoroughly understood or expertly executed that concept as Great Britain.

That the two *Queens* could be used to exercise sea power in ways that Britain's enemies could never effectively counter was an idea that the Admiralty was not long in appreciating. What the *Queens* offered the Allies was the means of combining Mahan's theory with Gen. Nathan Bedford Forrest's homely dictum for victory, "Gettin' there the firstest with the mostest."

In the First World War, some of the more enlightened members of the British government and military leadership had come to appreciate that while the Central Powers of Germany and Austria-Hungary enjoyed the advantage of interior lines of communication, the superior mobility that the Royal Navy offered the Allies held out the promise of negating that advantage by allowing the Allies to strike at several points around the Central Powers' perimeter, diluting their overall strength and draining their reserves of manpower. For a variety of political and military reasons, some valid, some not, the British were never able to effectively exploit that advantage, but the lesson was not lost. In 1940, though Britain's land and air forces were small compared to the huge numbers that Germany had mobilized, the resources of the Empire were still vast, and the manpower that the British could call upon from India, Australia, and Canada could prove decisive. The challenge for the British was to get that manpower to the places where it could be brought to bear against the enemy.

That was what made the *Queen Mary* and the *Queen Elizabeth* so valuable—their sheer size meant that each of them could transport more than twice as many troops as any other ship in the British fleet, allowing more ships to be given over to carrying materiel, supplies, and equipment, making for a more rapid buildup of combat units in critical areas. More to the point, perhaps, their capabilities were critical: Age and the Great Depression had sadly depleted the numbers of Britain's great liners. Of the huge ships built before the First World War, only the *Aquitania* remained; the *Olympic, Majestic, Berengaria,* and *Mauretania* had all gone to the breakers years before. Without the *Queens,* Britain's ability to draw on the resources of the Empire would be sharply diminished.

For that to happen, though, the *Queens* had to be transformed into ships suitable for carrying troops. Despite the fact that the *Queen Mary* had been sitting at the pier for nearly seven months, very little work had been done on her in preparation for trooping, aside from covering the black, white, and red paint of her hull, upper works, and funnels with a coat of paint in a shade the Royal Navy was pleased to call "light sea grey." Admiralty lethargy wasn't to blame for the delay, however. Painting the ship to make it less visible to prowling U-boats was a permissible step for Cunard to take, even if it was at Admiralty direction. More obvious changes and modifications, though, stood a good chance of running afoul of American neutrality legislation and the isolationist segment of the American population that was ever anxious to enforce it.

More than a half century after the end of the Second World War and the Nazi horrors that were revealed, it may seem incredible that a large portion of the American population in 1939 and 1940 had no desire whatsoever to get involved in another European war. Feeling what was perceived as ingratitude on the part of the very people whom the Americans believed, with some justification, that they had saved from German domination in 1918, and appalled at the punitive peace of Versailles (not realizing that their own President Wilson had, through his political maneuverings, squandered any chance of the United States having a positive influence on the peace treaty), the isolationists were dedicated to the idea of allowing Europe to stew in its own juices, so to speak. The problems that led to the outbreak of the war were of Europe's creation—they should be of Europe's solution as well. It wasn't up to the United States to rescue France and Great Britain every time they got themselves into trouble. The isolationists were not a collection of crackpots, Fascist and Nazi sympathizers, and opportunists looking to further their own self-aggrandizing schemes, although they have at times been depicted as such. That there were Nazi sympathizers—and agents—who exploited the isolationist movement for the benefit of their German masters is undeniable, as is the fact that there was an appreciable representation from the lunatic fringe within the movement. Their presence was meaningless, for there were just as many extremists and oddballs among the more vocal ranks of the interventionists. The overwhelming majority of isolationist Americans were ordinary, level-headed people who simply believed that America's first duty and responsibility was to America.

What made the isolationist position seem so plausible at the time was that any "threat" the totalitarian powers in Europe, Nazi Germany in particular, posed to the United States was still very hypothetical indeed. Those Americans who were urging the United States to take up arms against Hitler could only muster arguments premised with "If . . ." as they tried to persuade their fellow citizens of the danger they saw inherent in the Nazi government and its Führer. In Great Britain, the dire warnings sounded so long by Winston Churchill eventually fell on receptive ears as the Third Reich loomed more sinister and menacing with each new acquisition of territory, each new humiliation of the Western democracies—but Germany was only a hundred or so miles from Great Britain as the bomber flies, and she shared a common border with France. That proximity made the German threat one that the French and British had to honor. The three-thousand-mile wide moat of the Atlantic Ocean caused that threat to appear to dwindle, if not into insignificance, then at least into one of very minor proportions.

Consequently, the isolationist movement—which, while it was never a real majority of the population, was far too large to be labeled a mere "faction"—had used its considerable influence to get legislation passed by Congress that had the expressed intent of keeping the United States out of war, avoiding the "mistakes" that had drawn America into the First World War. Three pieces of legislation, collectively known as the Neutrality Act, were enacted in successive years from 1935 to 1937. The first of them prohibited the sale of any weapons of American design or manufacture to any belligerent power, without making any distinction between aggressors and nations defending themselves from those aggressors. The second forbade American financial institutions from making loans for any purpose to any warring nation, or businesses of those nations—again without making any distinction between aggressors and victims. The most significant part of the third was a provision that banned travel by U.S. citizens on ships owned by any belligerent nations. The origin of these laws was easy to perceive, as they were specifically drawn up to prevent a repetition of the circumstances that had embroiled the United States in the First World War, which the isolationists believed to have been a major blunder on America's part. The third act was written to prevent another incident like the sinking of the *Lusitania,* the British passenger ship that was torpedoed and sunk by a German U-boat in May 1915, with the loss of 1,198 lives, 128 of them Americans. This act did allow the president to draw up a list of nonmilitary goods, such as grain, that the United States could sell to belligerent nations, but strictly on a "cash and carry" basis. Belligerent nations would have to pay up front and transport the goods on their own ships.

Specific details of these collective acts also strictly limited what business belligerent powers could conduct within the United States, as well as proscribing what types of and to what extent repairs and modifications could be carried out on their ships when they put into American ports. More to the point, protective measures meant to safeguard and protect passenger ships and merchantmen from submarine attack were permitted, but work on a ship preparing for a combatant role—which included troopships—was forbidden under penalty of seizure and internment of the violating vessel. So in order for the *Queen Mary* to be converted for trooping duties, she had to return to a British port. All that could be done in New York, in addition to the coat of gray paint, was to remove most of the luxury furnishings aboard her. So in mid-March 1940, some 220 cases of china, silver, and crystal from the dining rooms were packed away, along with six miles of carpet, 500 chairs and settees, 400 tables of various description, and roughly 450 deck chairs. Some extra protection was added to the bridge, mostly in the form of sandbags, and a half dozen 20-millimeter Oerlikon guns, along with the same number of machine guns, were mounted for antiaircraft defense.

The morning of March 21, 1940, saw the *Queen Mary* leave New York, with Capt. William Irving on the bridge. She was bound for Sydney, Australia, where the work to fit her out as a troopship would be done. It was actually going to be a rather roundabout trip, as she was first to carry a small number of passengers to the Caribbean, then put into South African ports before heading "Down Under." Her first stop was the small island of Trinidad, where she arrived on March 24 and dropped off a few hundred passengers. She set out for Cape Town the next day. On this leg of the voyage, she was carrying more than fifty-three hundred people, some fifteen hundred of them crewmen (or at least Cunard personnel) and the rest troops sent to bolster the garrison at the Cape. It was an uncomfortable eight days, as the *Mary* was not air-conditioned—she had been designed for the North Atlantic, after all—and she was badly overcrowded. In fact, poor ventilation would plague both of the Queens for the next two years as they moved British and Commonwealth troops back and forth between the Far East and Great Britain.

Back in New York, speculation was rife about the whereabouts of the *Queen Mary*—British security measures had been so effective that hardly anyone knew she was leaving until after she had gone. In order to throw the Germans off her scent, carefully cultivated rumors were spread over the next few days, some of them finding their way into the press, where they were given the cachet of authority. One story that appeared in the *New York Sun* on March 23 was typical. It reported that the *Queen Mary* and the *Mauretania,* which had left New York the day before the *Mary,*

> will become vital links in Canada's huge air training pro-
> gramme, carrying men and supplies between Australia and
> western Canada. . . . There will doubtless be a need for ship-
> ping training planes and supplies back to Australia from
> Canada, so it will not be an entirely one-way job for the big
> liners. It would be relatively safe to use the luxury ships for
> such work. Their chance of being waylaid by submarine or
> pocket battleships on the run between Sydney and Vancou-
> ver would be extremely remote.

There was a certain amount of truth to the story, which is probably why it was so effective, in that the *Mauretania* did go to the Pacific to transport equipment and personnel between Canada and Australia, but the *Queen*

Mary was taking an entirely different route to Sydney, and for an entirely different purpose.

The *Queen Mary* arrived in Sydney on April 13—she had stopped off at Freemantle for two days first—and as soon as the troops disembarked, she was moored at the Cockatoo Docks and Engineering Company. Working round the clock, swarms of Australian shipwrights began to transform her into a seagoing barracks, taking off any remaining interior furnishings that could be removed, including some two thousand stateroom doors. The wooden doors were flammable, and splinters from doors shattered by bomb blast or gunfire could be as lethal as metal fragments from bursting shells. They installed triple-tiered wooden bunks in all the cabins and put up racks for slinging hammocks in her public rooms.

The Main Hall, a broad passageway that in peacetime had been lined with shops where passengers could purchase anything from jewelry to perfumes to a complete suit of clothes, was converted into offices, while the galleys were enlarged and additional lavatories and showers were installed throughout the ship. Hinged metal shutters were welded into place to protect the windows of the bridge, and hundreds of additional sandbags were brought aboard and piled around vulnerable sections of the superstructure. In just over two weeks, the *Queen Mary* was modified to carry fifty-five hundred troops, as well as a crew of over nine hundred. The work didn't stop there: Another two dozen twenty-millimeter guns were added, as well as twelve rocket launchers, a score of machine guns, rangefinders, and a central antiaircraft director.

On May 5, 1940, the *Queen Mary* began her trooping duties in earnest, as she set sail from Sydney, bound for Gourock, Scotland, with five thousand Australian soldiers aboard. She sailed in convoy with two Cunard stablemates, the *Aquitania* and *Mauretania;* three Canadian Pacific liners, the *Empress of Britain, Empress of Canada,* and *Empress of Japan;* and the steamer *Andes,* of the Royal Mail Line. The cruisers HMAS *Australia* and *Canberra* escorted the lot of them. Britain was calling on the strength of the Commonwealth; Australia was responding by sending the 6th Australian Division, vanguard of the Second Australian Imperial Force, successor to and heir of the fearsome fighting reputation of the AIF of World War I, the famous "Diggers." Along with the Australian infantry, the convoy was carrying a contingent of New Zealand infantry, respected fighting men in their own right, as well as artillery and support units, some fourteen thousand men all told.

The *Mary* would not be able to show off her vaunted speed on this passage, since the convoy was limited by the top speed of the slowest vessel, the

Andes—a shade over twenty-one knots—though there would be plenty of opportunity for that later. And while she was carrying only a third of the number of troops that she would eventually be called on to transport at one time, the *Queen Mary* was already beginning to fulfill the promise that her vast size offered. The seven ships of the convoy that left Sydney that May 4 were the physical embodiment of "sea power"—and Britain was soon to be in need of all the succor that her Empire could provide.

In mid-April 1940 the British had sent an expeditionary force to Norway to thwart an invasion attempted by the Germans. Though considerable damage had been inflicted on the German Navy, the British were unable to prevent the Luftwaffe from airlifting additional troops into Norway, and before long the British forces, hampered by a lack of coherent strategy and lackluster leadership, were bottled up in a handful of coastal towns, awaiting evacuation. As if that were not bad enough, when the convoy put into Table Bay off Cape Town on May 27, instead of being allowed to disembark the troops a few days ashore, the officers of the convoy were informed that their visit was being cut short and they should make for the Clyde "with all possible speed."

While the ships were at sea, Great Britain's strategic situation had badly deteriorated. On May 10 the Germans launched their invasion of the West, marching their infantry into Holland and Belgium, and then launching their panzer divisions in a lightning-swift strike through the Ardennes Forest, *behind* the Anglo-French armies that had advanced into Belgium to meet what they thought was the weight of the Nazi onslaught. Division after division of the French Army dissolved in chaos, then melted away in panic. Unsupported by their suddenly impotent allies, the handful of British divisions sent to France conducted a stubborn fighting withdrawal to the sea, but they were trapped around the French port of Dunkerque and seemed to be at the mercy of the approaching German armored divisions. About the only good news was that on May 10, Winston Churchill replaced Neville Chamberlain as Prime Minister. At least the Australians and New Zealanders aboard the troopships could count on Britain continuing the fight.

As the convoy left Cape Town on May 28 and shaped a course toward Gourock, Scotland, the news only got worse. Beginning on May 27 and carrying on through June 3, most of the British troops trapped at Dunkerque were successfully evacuated, along with roughly a hundred thousand French soldiers, but almost all their heavy equipment—trucks, artillery, antiaircraft and antitank guns—had to be left behind. On June 8 the last British forces were withdrawn from Norway. What was left of the French Army was offering pathetically little resistance to the Germans, and on June 14 Paris fell to the German Army. Four days earlier, after maintaining a careful neutrality until it became obvious which side was going to win, and hoping to acquire a share of the spoils, Fascist Italy had declared war on France. Helpless, the French asked for surrender terms on June 17. Britain was now facing Nazi Germany alone.

The worsening strategic situation didn't stop the Australian troops from finding ways of displaying their customary high spirits. One of the most memorable was a daily newspaper published by one of the supply sections called the *Ammo Daily.* An engaging collection of news, gossip, parody, and the occasional needling of the British by the Aussies, it was a good way for the troops to stay up-to-date on news from around the world, and it provided a diversion from the tedium of the long voyage. It wasn't until June 16, six weeks after leaving Sydney, that the *Queen Mary* finally reached Scotland.

When she docked at Gourock, she was greeted by cheering crowds who wanted to welcome her back home. This was the first time the *Mary* had returned to the Clyde in five years, and to the men who built her, as well as their families, she would always remain "their" ship. The reception was somewhat muted, as the news had just broken of the French request for an armistice with Germany, but it was no less heartfelt for all that. In some sense, there was an element of relief in the welcome, since the Australian and New Zealand troops were tangible proof that Britain wasn't quite as alone as she sometimes seemed to be.

In any case, for several reasons, the *Mary's* stay at Gourock wasn't destined to be a long one. With Southampton denied to the *Queens,* the only port in Great Britain that could accommodate their huge size was Gourock, and despite the vigilance of the Royal Air Force, some German reconnaissance planes were bound to get through and spot one of them as they sat tied to the dock. At the same time, there was always the chance that a German agent unknown to or unaccounted for by British Intelligence could be operating in western Scotland, and the *Queens* were impossible to miss. The longer the *Queen Mary* stayed in port, the more vulnerable she was.

The British had prepared well, though, both for her security and for making a quick turnaround. Local newspapers were informed that severe penalties, including suspension, would be exacted for any published reports of the *Queen Mary's* movements, while local photographers were liable to have their cameras and film confiscated—and spend a day or two behind bars while their backgrounds were checked—for taking photos of the liner. Overly talkative sailors would find themselves swiftly transferred to shore duties, and maintenance parties onboard were escorted to and from the places they were working and were constantly watched by military police.

The turnaround was accomplished in twelve days—quick work, all things considered, although quite slow by later standards. Captain Irving took the *Queen Mary* down the Clyde, and the next morning, once she was well clear of the Western Approaches, he opened a set of sealed orders that directed him to take the liner to Singapore for further modifications, stopping at Cape Town on the way. The trip to Singapore was uneventful, if long, and on August 5, 1940, the *Queen Mary* put into the huge Admiralty dry dock for a much-needed overhaul.

One of the first priorities was scraping the marine growth off the ship's bottom. It had been more than two years since the *Mary* had been drydocked, and the accumulation of barnacles and seaweed was considerable. The whole process of scraping, inspecting, and repainting the lower hull took five weeks. While that was being done, a de-gaussing coil was added for protection from German magnetic mines. Consisting of five miles of copper wire wound lengthwise around the *Queen Mary*'s hull, when charged with an electric current, this coil effectively neutralized the ship's magnetic field, rendering the magnetic mines sown by German minelayers, submarines, and aircraft in coastal waters around Great Britain harmless. This was an important protective feature, as in the first year of the war, magnetic mines, which reacted to the magnetic field of a ship's steel hull and would explode only when a ship was directly overhead, exacted a severe toll of British ships sunk or damaged. An idea of how powerful these mines were can be gauged by the fact that repairs to HMS *Belfast,* a Royal Navy cruiser that ran afoul of a magnetic mine, took three years to complete.

At the same time that all this work was being done, the *Mary*'s steering gear was refurbished, and vital machinery in her engine rooms was overhauled. The same could be said of the crew, as they were finally given some hard-earned and well-deserved shore leave. The numbers and resources of the Singapore police department were sorely taxed as the sailors cut a wide swath across Singapore's waterfront, but before things could get too far out of hand, work on the *Queen Mary* was finished and she was ready to get back into the war. It wasn't a moment too soon.

While the *Queen Mary* was being fitted out and beginning her service as a troopship, the *Queen Elizabeth,* left behind in New York Harbor, was far from idle. Six weeks after the *Queen Mary* departed for Sydney, the *Elizabeth* was moved across the Hudson River to the Todd Shipyard in Hoboken, New Jersey. There, swarms of electricians and plumbers were brought aboard to finish installing the liner's light fixtures and connect her toilets, sinks, and showers. They expanded the galleys and completed storerooms, refrigerators, and freezers for provisions. Workers scraped off the river growth that had built up on her hull during the months she had sat idle, first in the Clyde, then in the Hudson. They removed the remains of her launching cradle, still attached to her bow, then inspected her bottom and pronounced it seaworthy. Like the *Queen Mary,* she was given a handful of antiaircraft guns, along with a three-inch popgun on her after deck for protection, and her bridge was heavily sandbagged. On November 19, 1940, she set sail for Sydney, where her conversion into a proper troopship would be completed.

She would be urgently needed. While the *Queen Mary* was refitting in Singapore and the *Queen Elizabeth* was still sitting in the Hudson River, the war took an unexpected turn, and the focus of Great Britain's war effort shifted to the Middle East and North Africa. Motivated by the same opportunism that had led him to declare war on France after she was all but beaten by the Germans, Italy's Fascist dictator, Benito Mussolini, launched an offensive into the lightly held British colony of Somaliland on August 6, overrunning the entire country in less than two weeks. Three weeks after that, on September 16, 1940, his ponderous Libyan army staged a massive invasion of Egypt, which was a British protectorate.

Although in some ways the Italian attack was a genuine threat to the Empire, in others it was almost a Gilbert and Sullivan type farce of a military operation. The danger was that the Italians might overrun Egypt and seize the Suez Canal, effectively cutting the Empire in half. The British forces defending Egypt numbered barely thirty thousand troops, while the Italian Army in Libya mustered nearly eight times that number. Nevertheless, after being prodded rather forcefully by Mussolini, who had first ordered the attack in June, Gen. Rodolfo Graziani, the Italian commander, advanced his forces a mere sixty miles in the first week of the attack, then halted to rest and refit his allegedly exhausted units.

As the German general Erwin Rommel was later to learn, the Italian soldier, when properly led, can be a fine fighting man, but the officers leading the Italian "invasion" of Egypt were incompetent nincompoops. After halting his army's advance, Graziani sat motionless for three months, claiming he was awaiting promised reinforcements and supplies. In the meantime, his opposite numbers in the British Army, Gen. Archibald Wavell and Gen. Richard O'Connor, were planning a daring counterattack that would drive deep behind the Italian positions, cut them off from their supply routes, and bag the lot of them as prisoners, effectively ending any Italian threat to Egypt and the Suez Canal.

Attacking in the second week of December, Wavell and O'Connor's offensive went off even better than they had planned, and the bulk of the Italian forces were "bagged" within a matter of days. The British commanders immediately set about exploiting their success, and the British Western Desert Force drove west across Libya, capturing Alam Halfaya, Tobruk, Sollum, Bardia, and Benghazi—all places that were to become known around the world in the months to come—in rapid succession, pushing the Italians back into Tripolitania and threatening to drive them from North Africa entirely.

The need to reinforce the Western Desert Force became paramount, and immediately the *Queen Mary* was put to the task; the *Queen Elizabeth* would follow as soon as her refit was complete. On September 25 the *Queen Mary* left Singapore, once more bound for Sydney, where additional bunks were installed, increasing her capacity to eight thousand troops. On October 20 she set out for Suez, this time with most of the Australian 9th Division aboard. Before she could reach Suez, though, she was diverted into Bombay, where the Australians were transferred to other, smaller ships, the Admiralty having decided that the confined waters of the Red Sea were too dangerous for the *Mary*. If she was lost, nearly 20 percent of Britain's troop-carrying capacity would be lost with her.

From October 1940 to February 1941 the *Queen Mary* shuttled back and forth between Australia and India. She put back into Singapore in March for another, briefer, refit, then in April 1941 the *Queen Mary* and *Queen Elizabeth* sailed together for the first time, carrying ten thousand Australians and New Zealanders, this time going all the way to Suez.

These Sydney-to-Suez-and-back passages were hardly the type of service that the *Queens* had been designed for, and the heat, rather than the Axis navies, proved to be the greatest threat to them. Built for the North Atlantic, where even the best days could be chill, their ventilation systems simply weren't up to the task of keeping a dozen decks cool in the tropics, particularly when the ships were loaded with twice as many human beings as they had originally been designed to carry. As the liners made their way across the Arabian Sea and up the Red Sea, the heat defeated the ventilators entirely, turning the spaces below decks into something akin to vast ovens. Even for healthy, fit young men like the Australians and New Zealanders, the heat could be deadly, and nearly every such passage was marked by a handful of deaths among the troops, attributable to heatstroke or heat exhaustion. The crews of the two *Queens* did what they could, rigging saltwater showers above decks, jury-rigging extra fans, spreading awnings where possible, but the heat remained an oppressive enemy.

When the *Queens* were returning to Sydney, things would be even worse: On those passages their purpose had shifted from carrying Imperial and Commonwealth troops to carrying prisoners of war, most of them the tens of thousands of Italians captured by the Western Desert Force. There were considerable numbers of wounded among the POWs, many of them serious. The heat would often prove too much for men already weakened from wounds, and on the return from Suez, burial services were sometimes held as often as every four hours as the heat exacted its toll. Inevitably something had to give, and it did.

It happened on board the *Queen Elizabeth,* as she was steaming toward Suez in July 1941. On the fifth day of the voyage, tempers, which had been rising, suddenly flared, and soon the officers of the *Elizabeth* had something approaching a mutiny on their hands. A fight broke out on one of the mess decks among the Australian infantry—no one ever found out what started it—and within minutes, the brawl evolved into wholesale fisticuffs and thrown crockery. Australian infantry had a rightfully earned reputation for fighting, whether with the enemy or among themselves, and the scrap might have soon sorted itself out had not some of the crew decided to get involved.

The crew, even more than the troops, had legitimate grievances; many had not been off the *Elizabeth* for nearly a year, their quarters were located in some of the hottest areas of the ship, and their diet—food is always a priority with sailors—had become bland and monotonous to the point of insult. The Australian brawl seemed to serve as a catalyst for all the pent-up resentments among some of the *Elizabeth*'s crew, and they began a small riot of their own. Where the Diggers had limited themselves to breaking knuckles and dishware on various parts of their collective anatomies, the crewmen quickly escalated to hurling kitchen utensils and pans and pots of boiling water at one another, and at one point, a cook who was clearly in the wrong place at the wrong time was forced into his own—heated—oven. The senseless brutality of the act suddenly seemed to take the heart out of the rioters, and when a company of Royal Marines was hastily brought on board the *Elizabeth* from the cruiser HMS *Cornwall,* they were quickly rounded up, arrested, and placed in detention. The unfortunate cook survived, although he was severely burned, and his assault was the basis for the charges brought against the crewmen. The ringleaders of this violent episode were eventually taken to England for trial and given long prison sentences.

But the episode cast a harshly revealing light on the conditions the essentially civilian crews of the *Queens* had to endure for months on end. That such an incident should occur is understandable in hindsight; that there were no recurrences speaks volumes about the level of professionalism and dedication to duty those men possessed. Together, Cunard and the Admiralty took steps to alleviate as many of the causes of the crewmen's discontent as they could, although there was little they could do about the heat.

It was in April 1941, the same month that the *Queens* sailed together for the first time, that the war in North Africa took another dramatic turn, one that made their services even more vital than before. Determined not to allow his Italian ally to be further humiliated by the British, Adolf Hitler directed a small German contingent to go to Africa to bolster the Italian defense of Tripolitania. With that force went a short, stocky panzer general who had his own ideas about how the war in North Africa should be fought, and who wasted no time putting those ideas into practice. Gen. Erwin Rommel, soon to become know around the world as the "Desert Fox," was aggressive, imaginative, opinionated, arrogant, and born with a gift for improvising strategies and tactics. Above all, he was charismatic, inspiring not only his German troops, but those of his Italian allies as well. Though the Italian soldiers never fought with as much enthusiasm as their German counterparts, they were far more willing to fight for Rommel, in whom they had confidence, than they were for their own generals, in whom they had none.

Rommel struck almost immediately at the forward British positions, driving them back across Libya to the gates of Tobruk and beyond. Rommel timed his attack shrewdly, since the Western Desert Force had been stripped of the equivalent of three divisions, some of its best troops having been sent to the aid of the Greeks, who had been attacked by Italy in November 1940, but who drove their attackers back in a series of humiliating defeats.

There is an almost comic-opera air that surrounds Italy's war effort—at least, it would be comical if it hadn't meant death or mutilation for so many people. While Mussolini, like Hitler, had proven his personal bravery in the

First World War, there all valid comparisons stopped. Hitler was an evil genius, but a genius nevertheless; his strategies, which would become more and more rigid and unimaginative in the war's later years, had flashes of true brilliance in the first. He never attacked without sound plans, or without sound political or economic reasons behind them. Mussolini was essentially an egotistical buffoon who continually tried to engage Hitler in a game of military one-upmanship, a game that he lacked the manpower, equipment, resources, and intelligence to win. The invasion of Greece was as ill advised as the invasion of Egypt had been, and it produced the same results—an embarrassing defeat for the Italians, who then had to be rescued by their German allies.

It had one unexpected consequence, though, in addition to bringing General Rommel into the fray: For the first time in the war, the attention of the Germans, as well as the Italians, was focused on the Mediterranean Sea. Almost overnight, the threat to the Suez Canal and the lifeline of the Empire loomed larger than ever. From being something of a sideshow, "the Med" was transformed into a major theater of war, and a new urgency was imparted to the duties of the *Queens*. From April to November 1941 they brought more than eighty thousand Australians and New Zealanders to North Africa. Other transports were bringing Commonwealth divisions from India and South Africa, as the advantages of sea power gathered momentum and Britain began concentrating the strength of her Empire in anticipation of making a decisive effort against the Axis powers in the Med in 1942.

The *Queens* didn't return to Australia empty: In the seesaw battles of the Western Desert, where the front line could move hundreds of miles in a matter of a few days, there were always prisoners taken by either side. Those captured by the British were taken back to Alexandria, Egypt, processed, then eventually put aboard one of the waiting *Queens*, bound for a prisoner-of-war camp somewhere in the Australian outback. The majority of these prisoners were Italians, who always seemed more ready to surrender, and in greater numbers, than the German troops. Good soldiers though the Italian troops could often be, they lacked the motivation of their German counterparts. Rommel may have been a charismatic leader, but he couldn't overcome the lingering doubts among these latter-day Roman legions that they were fighting for the glory of Mussolini, not Italy.

Events on the other side of the world that December caused Britain's plans to dissolve in utter confusion. The Japanese attack on the U.S. naval base at Pearl Harbor, Hawaii, on December 7, 1941, fundamentally changed the strategic balance of the war, bringing the full weight of American manpower, industry, and economic might into the conflict on the side of the Allies. A more immediate cause for concern to the British, though, were the Japanese offensives launched down the Malay Peninsula and into Indonesia the same day as the attack on Pearl Harbor. The British were hard-pressed to hold the Japanese back, as many of the Royal Navy ships that had been stationed in the Far East had been recalled to the Atlantic, while the best squadrons of the RAF's Far East Air Force had been redeployed to Egypt or the British Isles. Many of the British and Indian divisions that had been posted in Burma and Malaysia had been transferred to North Africa, as well as most of the Australian Army. The Land Down Under was almost defenseless.

This was a situation the Australian Prime Minister, John Curtin, would not tolerate. As soon as the magnitude of the Japanese threat became apparent, Curtin demanded that the Australian divisions fighting in North Africa be brought home. Prime Minister Churchill and the British High Command at first refused, but Curtin didn't allow himself to be intimidated by Churchill and asserted his rights as the Prime Minister of a Dominion power, fully Churchill's equal. After some heated exchanges between the two men, Churchill relented. The Australian divisions were ordered home.

The ships that would take them home wouldn't be the same ships that carried them to North Africa, though. The *Queens* were diverted from the Sydney-to-Suez run and ordered to Cape Town to take them out of range of the advancing Japanese. In mid-December Churchill and his military staff traveled to Washington, D.C., for a conference with their American counterparts. It was at this conference that the Americans and British decided on a "Germany first" strategy, rightly perceiving that Nazi Germany posed not only a greater, but also a more immediate, threat to the Allies. For the time being, they would have to simply hold the line in the Pacific.

But "holding the line" meant that the Japanese would have to be stopped first, and stopping them meant holding Australia. It would take time for the Australian units in North Africa to be withdrawn and sent home, and in the meantime the U.S. Army would have to defend the continent. In that December conference, it was decided that the Americans would be responsible for the operations of both *Queens*—the crews would remain Cunard employees, but the costs of operating the two ships would be paid by the U.S. government. This arrangement also meant that the *Queens* were subject to American naval regulations—something Winston Churchill would run afoul of in the near future. Each liner underwent a two-month-long refit, the *Mary* in New York, the *Elizabeth* in San Francisco, which increased the transport capacity of each to fifteen thousand troops. By March 1942 both were carrying American reinforcements to Australia, mainly artillery units and engineers, along with a large number of Army Air Corps personnel, the vanguard of some twenty thousand GIs that they would carry to Australia in the next four months.

The *Queen Mary*'s first voyage carrying GIs was one of the most dangerous passages she would make during the entire war. Leaving New York on February 18, 1942, she was bound for Sydney via Trinidad, Rio de Janeiro, Cape Town, and Freemantle. U-boats were taking a heavy toll on American shipping in the Caribbean, and the *Mary* was forced to put into Key West, Florida. It was there that Capt. James Bisset took over command, replacing Captain Irving, who had reached mandatory retirement age.

Bisset was a legend among Cunard captains and merchant skippers on the North Atlantic. Having spent thirty-five years with Cunard, he was now the senior skipper of the line. Thirty years before taking command of the *Queen Mary*, he had been the second officer on a small Cunard steamer called the *Carpathia* in the early morning hours of April 15, 1912. The *Carpathia* was commanded by Capt. Arthur Rostron, one of the bravest and most conscientious men to command a ship on the North Atlantic, a fact that he demonstrated that morning as he guided the *Carpathia* through iceberg-infested waters to come to the rescue of the survivors of the *Titanic*. The rescue, brilliantly carried out, made Rostron's career, and it made a lasting impression on Bisset, who followed in Rostron's footsteps by becoming one of the best captains in the British Merchant Marine.

As the tender took Bisset out to the *Queen Mary* for the first time on the morning of February 24, the sight of the ship in the morning mist made a lasting impression on him:

> [She had] the appearance of a great rock set in the middle of the sea. Two U.S. destroyers were patrolling around the anchored ship, on the lookout for U-boats. As we drew nearer, I could make out two tankers, one moored on each side of her, amidships, feeding her with oil-fuel and fresh water. Though the tankers were vessels of 6,000 tons, they were dwarfed by her tremendous bulk. Gazing up at her I felt overawed at the responsibility soon to be mine.

Once the ship was provisioned, Bisset took her on a westward swing around Cuba, then out of the Caribbean through the Anageda Passage and into the Atlantic. Unknown to anyone, the *U-161* and *U-129* were following almost the same course. Just moments after the *Mary* cleared the passage, a tanker was torpedoed ten miles away. Operating under strict orders not to stop or respond to distress signals, Bisset ordered the *Queen Mary* to make all possible speed and quickly cleared the area, then set course for Rio de Janeiro.

The *Mary* dropped anchor off Rio on March 6, with Captain Bisset determined to make the stop as brief as possible. It was good that he did, for German and Italian diplomats in Rio were working with their intelligence services, frantically trying to get word to one of their submarines that the liner was in port. Bisset had been tipped off by Allied intelligence officers, who had intercepted the signals, and once the ship was refueled and reprovisioned, the *Queen Mary* put to sea again, several hours ahead of her scheduled departure time. It was a shrewd decision, for unknown to the Allies, there was at least one German submarine that reached Rio about the time that the *Mary* was originally scheduled to sail. The U-boat missed the liner's departure but was able to sink a tanker just outside of Rio. (This didn't stop the Germans from announcing that they had sunk the *Queen Mary*—the first but not the last time they would claim one of the *Queens* had fallen victim to their submarines.)

The rest of the voyage was uneventful, and the *Mary* docked in Sydney on March 28. She would be in harbor for nine days while she refueled, restocked her storerooms, and recovered from the effects of carrying American troops for the first time. Overall, the GIs had behaved themselves, but one habit they brought aboard provoked an instant and imperious reaction from Captain Bisset. Chewing gum is one of the less notable American contributions to Western civilization, and after the voyage was over, the *Queen Mary's* crew had to use scrapers and caustic soda to remove the layers of discarded gum that the GIs had dropped on her decks. Bisset banned its use aboard the *Mary*, and the ban remained in force until the war was over.

When the *Mary's* turnaround was finished and she set out for New York on April 6, she passed the *Queen Elizabeth*, just entering Sydney Harbor after her voyage from San Francisco. Unlike the *Mary's* passage, the *Elizabeth's* crossing of the Pacific had been uneventful, the most exciting part of the voyage being a minor security scare aboard during the last few days of the crossing. Fifty thousand bottles of Coca-Cola had been loaded aboard for the crew and GIS to drink on the three-week voyage, and all of the empty bottles had to be accounted for at the end of it. They were—or, rather, 49,999 of them were. The sole exception had been kept by a GI who had painted it red, white, and blue, then wrote a message giving the name of the ship, the date, and a few particulars about the voyage. Shipboard MPs caught him before he could throw the bottle overboard. The GI was disciplined, and the bottle—along with the rest—was returned to Coca-Cola.

The *Queen Mary's* adventures continued on the voyage back to New York—for some reason, she always seemed to be more prone to this sort of thing than the *Queen Elizabeth*. Just after dawn on May 6, while she was still some six hundred miles southwest of New York, lookouts on the bridge sighted a group of six lifeboats, all of them under sail and apparently on course for Bermuda. Captain Bisset knew better than to stop, for a clever U-boat captain could have been shadowing the lifeboats in the hope that some ship would be foolish enough to do just that, presenting the submarine with a sitting duck for a target. Bisset did, however, signal to the little flotilla by Aldis lamp that he would notify the U.S. Navy of their position. He did so, and American destroyers picked up the lifeboats the next day. They were from the Canadian transport *Lady Drake*, which had left Halifax bound for Bermuda three days earlier. Among the survivors was the son of the *Queen Mary's* purser, who sent his family word of his safe arrival with the cheerfully cheeky cable: "Dad useless as usual, passed us by. But we made it."

The *Queen Mary* returned to Pier 90 on May 7, having spent seventy-eight days at sea on the round-trip, covering some thirty-five thousand miles. But the welcome was somewhat muted, for it was a melancholy docking: At the next pier lay the remains of the *Normandie*, the magnificent French liner that had been the *Mary's* great transatlantic rival before the war. An unexplained fire had broken out aboard her on February 9, and although it had been brought under control, the thousands of tons of water used to fight the blaze had caused her to roll over onto her port side, a total loss. Though she was eventually righted two years later, she never sailed again, but instead was broken up for scrap.

The loss of the *Normandie* underscored the grave toll the war would take among the transatlantic liners. Already the Canadian Pacific's *Empress of Britain, Laconia,* and *Athenia* were gone. In the months to come, the *Ceramic, Gloucester Castle,* and *Empress of Canada* would all be lost. In the Mediterranean, Italy was to lose the *Rex, Conte Rosso, Neptunia,* and *Oceania*. Germany's *Bremen* was already a blackened wreck lying in the harbor of her namesake city, and in the last few months of the war, the *Wilhelm Gustloff* would become the setting for the greatest loss of life at sea in history. Over five thousand Allied merchant ships would be lost to German torpedoes, bombs, or shellfire in the North Atlantic during the Second World War. The *Queens* were about to sail into the heart of the longest, most bitter campaign ever fought, the Battle of the Atlantic. If they survived, they would change the course of history.

CHAPTER FIVE

The Enemy

We've fought with many men acrost the seas,
An' some of 'em was brave an' some was not. . . .
—Rudyard Kipling

THOUGH NEITHER THE JAPANESE NAVY OR AIR FORCE EVER REALLY POSED much of a threat to either the *Queen Elizabeth* or the *Queen Mary,* when the two ships were transferred to trooping duties in the North Atlantic, they found themselves sailing into the middle of the longest, costliest, and most hard-fought campaign of the Second World War: the Battle of the Atlantic. The North Atlantic was simultaneously the lifeline by which Britain survived and the Allies brought their mounting offensive power to bear against the Axis, and the hunting ground of two of the Allies' always tenacious, often brilliant, and sometimes ruthless foes: the German Luftwaffe and the German Kriegsmarine. To defeat them, the Allies had to be as tenacious, brilliant, and ruthless, sometimes more so. In the air, on the sea, and under the sea, no other campaign in World War II would be fought with the ferocity of the Battle of the Atlantic. The reason was quite simple: Whichever side lost the Battle of the Atlantic lost the war.

The war fought in the Atlantic was a war of attrition, nothing more, nothing less. For the Germans, the goal was to sink ships at a greater rate than the Allies could replace them, while building new U-boats faster than the Allies could inflict losses. For the Allies, the goal was exactly the opposite: sink U-boats faster than Germany could build replacements, and keep their own shipping losses to a minimum. For both sides, the prize was Great Britain.

Though it is often overshadowed by the sheer volume of postwar German apologia and Soviet propaganda, the strategic key to the Second World War in Europe was the island kingdom of Great Britain. As long as she continued to resist Germany, Britain would serve as the base for the increasingly destructive Combined Bomber Offensive, allowing the Royal Air Force and the American Army Air Corps to attack key German industries, sap the strength of the Luftwaffe, and cause valuable resources to be diverted from new construction to rebuilding bomb-damaged factories and towns. Equally important was the continued British presence on the periphery of the Nazi empire, a constant threat that drew men, tanks, trucks, and supplies away from the fighting fronts to defend vulnerable points along a perimeter that stretched from Narvik, above the Arctic Circle, down to the Mediterranean coast of North Africa. Most crucial of all, as long as Britain stood, she could serve as the staging ground for the Allied invasion of Western Europe, the Second Front, which would spell certain doom for Nazi Germany.

While it is true that most of Germany's manpower and the majority of her tanks and artillery were posted to the Russian Front, which in terms of sheer numbers was the largest war ever fought, Great Britain's continued defiance of Hitler meant that Germany never had the luxury of turning all of its resources against the Soviet Union. The men, vehicles, fuel, materiel, aircraft, artillery pieces, and resources that the Germans were forced to deploy in Norway, the Low Countries, France, Italy, and even within Germany itself were denied the overstretched and exhausted Wehrmacht units on the Eastern Front. They were needed either to defend against an invasion that might come at any time, in any place, or to protect the Reich from the Allied bombers that everyone knew would come nearly every day and every night; Great Britain's belligerence made possible the huge Soviet victories at Stalingrad and Kursk, and the Red Army's crushing rout of the Wehrmacht in the summer of 1944.

Nor was it difficult for the strategists of the German high command to realize the potential threat that Great Britain represented to the Third Reich's hopes of victory, especially after December 1941. While the British Empire posed a threat to Nazi Germany, the manpower and industrial strength of the United States combined with Britain's strategic advantages could well prove fatal to those hopes. So it was that the German armed forces threw themselves into the Battle of the Atlantic with a fury rarely seen elsewhere in the war.

The Luftwaffe, the German Air Force, had never been organized or equipped as a strategic striking force, nor had much thought ever been given to any possible maritime role for the German bomber force. There were no aircraft designed for long-range reconnaissance or attack, and few of the aircrews had any training or experience in flying extended missions over open water. But the officers and men of the bomber squadrons of Luftflotte (Air Fleet) X and XII, stationed in France and Norway, quickly adapted their aircraft and tactics to meet the challenge. Even before the Battle of Britain began in late summer 1940, the Luftwaffe was attacking British shipping in the English Channel, the North Sea, and the approaches to the Irish Sea. It was after the Battle of Britain, when it became clear to the German high command that there would be no invasion of Britain and no negotiated peace, that the assault on British shipping and the effort by the Luftwaffe to sink as much tonnage as possible began.

There were three main types of aircraft that British ships had to face in the waters around Great Britain, and for some distance out into the Atlantic. The first was the Junkers Ju-87, a single-engine, gull-winged dive-bomber best known by its nickname "Stuka," a contraction of *Sturz Kampfflugzeug,* or "diving battle aircraft." Slow, underarmed, and vulnerable to enemy fighters, the Stuka was nevertheless a terrifying menace to any ship. Each aircraft was capable of carrying an eleven hundred-pound bomb slung under the fuselage, along with two one hundred-pound bombs under each wing. As the aircraft dived down from altitudes of twelve thousand to fifteen thousand feet, the sound created by its engine racing at maximum speed combined with the shriek of the slipstream across the wings was enough to unnerve men on the aircraft's target below. Some Ju-87 pilots had a siren mounted on one of the landing gear struts, its howl adding to the frightening cacophony of the dive. Just as demoralizing as the sound the Stuka produced was the knowledge shared by the men below that the Stuka pilots, most of them veterans of two, three, sometimes four campaigns, were capable of delivering their bombs with near-pinpoint accuracy. Only the most gifted ship handling could save a vessel from devastation by a Stuka attack pressed home with determination.

But the Stuka had its drawbacks. It was slow, with a top speed of barely two hundred miles per hour, which meant it could be "bounced" by Royal Air Force fighters at will, with no chance of running away. And it was poorly armed for self-defense—all the firepower a Ju-87 could muster for its two-man crew of pilot and gunner were a single forward-firing 7.92-millimeter machine gun in each wing and a single flexible rearward-firing machine gun in the cockpit. The RAF's Hawker Hurricane mounted four .303 machine guns in each wing, while the Spitfire Mk V boasted an armament of four machine guns plus two twenty-millimeter cannons. Any Stuka caught by British fighters was as good as lost.

More important than the shortcomings of the Stuka's defensive armament was the relatively short range of the type. With a combat radius of less than 250 miles, the Stuka lacked the ability to strike at ships and convoys approaching Great Britain from the west, where the somewhat short-legged Hurricanes and Spitfires could not reach it. While that was no doubt good news to the men aboard ships bound for Liverpool or Glasgow, in practice it meant that the Germans were able to concentrate their Ju-87 squadrons against Britain's Channel ports, and the vital Channel convoys steaming for the Thames estuary. Since the dive-bomber was able to operate there while under friendly fighter escort, the pesky Spitfires and Hurricanes could be kept at bay, and the Stukas were used with terrible effect on Channel traffic. Southampton was one of the ports within range of the Ju-87, which meant that it wasn't available to either of the *Queens,* leaving Gourock as the sole port in Great Britain where the two ships could dock.

The Heinkel He-111 was a twin-engine, elliptical-winged aircraft, originally employed as a medium bomber for the Luftwaffe, that became a workhorse of sorts as the war progressed. Originally designed as an airliner in 1935, the He-111 was first used by the Luftwaffe in 1937, when it made a name for itself as a weapon of terror in the Spanish Civil War, being used indiscriminately against civilians and troops alike, dropping heavy bomb loads and proving too fast for Republican fighters to catch easily. It was the Battle of Britain that exposed the weaknesses of the type, when its defensive armament of five single machine guns scattered throughout the aircraft was shown to be pitifully inadequate against the RAF's fighters, and its once-brilliant speed was no match for the Hurricane or Spitfire, though in the Blitz these bombers devastated many of Britain's cities, most memorably Coventry on November 14, 1940.

The bomber variant of the He-111 that the Luftwaffe used against Atlantic shipping was armed with one 20-millimeter cannon, one heavy 13-millimeter machine gun, and five 7.92-millimeter machine guns, while its bomb load was an impressive 7,150 pounds, heavier than any other German bomber. Never known for the accuracy of its bombing patterns, when the He-111s could be brought to bear against Allied convoys in squadron strength or greater, the sheer volume and weight of bombs dropped ensured that there would be crippling damage and ships sunk.

A modified version of the He-111 was soon produced for a maritime combat role, fitted with shackles under the wings that allowed it to carry two torpedoes. Usually deployed in flights of three or four at a time, these torpedo bombers inflicted damage all out of proportion to their numbers. This same airplane was also used as the launching aircraft for the Hs-293 glider bomb.

This unusual weapon was the predecessor of today's "smart bombs." Used against ships or ground targets, it was a glider airframe built around a 650-pound warhead. Carried under the wings or in the bomb bay of its parent aircraft, it was boosted by a rocket motor that ignited for ten seconds as soon as it was launched. What made the Hs-293 so destructive—and hence so feared by seamen—was that rather than leaving its point of impact to chance and ballistics, it was guided by the bombardier, who used a joystick in the aircraft to send radio commands to the glider and fly it into its target. First used in mid-1943, Hs-293s sank or severely damaged a number of Allied ships in both the Mediterranean and the Atlantic.

Strangely enough, the aircraft that was the most dangerous to the Allied convoys was not designed to be a warplane. The Focke-Wulf Fw-200 Kondor was a huge, four-engine aircraft that bore more than a passing resemblance to the Douglas DC-4. Like the DC-4, the Kondor had begun life as an airliner, first entering service in 1936 with Lufthansa, the German national airline. In 1937 it made headlines around the world by flying nonstop to several distant cities, including New York and Tokyo. These flights brought the aircraft to the attention of the Luftwaffe, and though there were initially no plans for the aircraft to be put to any military use, when the Germans suddenly realized in 1940 that it had no long-range reconnaissance aircraft capable of ranging out over the Atlantic, the obvious answer was the Fw-200C. A modification of the basic Kondor design that allowed it to carry a bomb load as well as cannon and machine guns for attacking shipping, the Fw-200C was a modest performer compared with British and American four-engine heavy bombers—hardly surprising, since it was essentially only a lash-up and not a purpose-built aircraft. Only 278 were built in all.

One major flaw in the aircraft was that it had a nasty tendency to come apart, either the fuselage buckling just forward of the tail assembly or one of the wings falling off, sometimes in the air, more often on landing. Nevertheless, it remained a thorn in the Allies' side until near the end of the war, and in the critical years of 1941 to 1943 its influence on the strategy and tactics used by the Allied convoys on the North Atlantic was completely out of proportion to the numbers of Kondors deployed.

The Fw-200 had a crew of seven, sometimes eight, and could carry a thirty-five hundred-pound bomb load in a long gondola under the fuselage and an additional one thousand pounds of bombs on external wing racks. As the war progressed and new weapons were introduced, a modified version with lengthened outboard engine nacelles carried the same Hs-293 glider bomb as the He-111. Defensive armament often comprised a twenty-millimeter or thirty-millimeter cannon at the front of the gondola, a fifteen-millimeter or twenty-millimeter gun in the forward dorsal turret, and as many as five other machine guns mounted at various points in the fuselage. On low-level strafing attacks, the heavy guns in the front of the aircraft could be brought to bear on the target ships. Despite this heavy (for a German aircraft) armament, the Kondors were very vulnerable to Allied fighters, and when small escort carriers began accompanying Allied convoys in late 1942, the Kondor squadrons were used almost exclusively for reconnaissance.

In that role the Kondor excelled. Able to range far out into the Atlantic and loiter there for hours, searching for and keeping track of Allied ships, the Kondor quickly became something of a fixture to the convoys. Communications between patrolling Kondors and the convoys they shadowed were not unknown, on more than one occasion the crew of a Kondor circling above a convoy bluntly asking it for its position. The reply invariably consisted of a very precise set of longitude and latitude figures that placed the convoy firmly on the other side of the world. There were several variations of the story in which a convoy signaled to the aircraft overhead, "Please circle the other way round, you are making us dizzy!"

In the simplest possible terms, the surface fleet of Hitler's Kriegsmarine, the German Navy, was an unmitigated failure. When the war began, nearly six years before the target for the completion of the German Navy's commander in chief Adm. Erich Raeder's Plan "Z," the numerical strength of the Royal Navy over the Kriegsmarine was nearly overwhelming. In 1939 the German Navy possessed only a handful of modern capital ships: three "pocket battleships," *Deutschland, Admiral Scheer,* and *Graf Spee;* and two big battle cruisers, *Scharnhorst* and *Gneisenau.* Two battleships were still being built—*Bismarck* and *Tirpitz*—that when finished would be bigger, faster, and better armed and armored than any ship in the British fleet, but neither would be completed before 1941. While it was arguable that ton for ton the German warships were superior to their British counterparts, the German Naval High Command seemed to have no real idea of what to do with them.

The first surface battle of the war came in December 1939, off the coast of Uruguay in the South Atlantic, where three British cruisers damaged *Graf Spee* and forced her to retreat into Montevideo Harbor, where she was scuttled by her captain, Hans Langsdorf. An even more dramatic battle occurred in May 1941 when the newly commissioned *Bismarck* sank the battle cruiser *Hood* and damaged the battleship *Prince of Wales* in the Denmark Strait, but she was hunted down and sunk a few days later by the battleships *King George V* and *Rodney* without ever even having sighted a single merchant ship. This was the last time a German capital ship ventured into the North Atlantic, partly because Hitler was afraid of losing the pride of his navy, but mostly due to the fact that the Naval High Command had no idea what to do with these ships. *Scharnhorst* was sunk in December 1942 by the British battleship *Duke of York* during a pointless sortie against the Murmansk convoys in the Barents Sea, and *Tirpitz* ended her days skulking from fjord to fjord in Norway.

The only real effect Germany's surface fleet had in the Atlantic was to force the Royal Navy to beef up the convoy escorts with additional cruisers and destroyers and, when possible, one of its older, slower battleships. Despite some small early successes by the battle cruisers and pocket battleships, not one Atlantic convoy was crippled or turned back by the surface fleet of the Kriegsmarine. More damage was done by small surface raiders disguised as merchantmen, which remained a hazard to Allied shipping through 1943.

Probably no single episode better illustrates the ineptitude of the German surface fleet—or demonstrates how the Luftwaffe and the U-boats could savage Allied shipping—than the ordeal of the convoy known as PQ-17. In July 1942 a large, fast convoy of British, American, and Panamanian ships, PQ-17, set out from Iceland for Murmansk, with a half dozen Royal Navy destroyers and perhaps a dozen corvettes and destroyer escorts, also Royal Navy, assigned as a close escort. An Anglo-American squadron of cruisers and destroyers was assigned to support the convoy if needed, while a shadowing force of one aircraft carrier, two battleships, three heavy cruisers, and a destroyer flotilla waited to the north of the convoy's projected course, ready to swoop down on any German capital ships that ventured out into the Atlantic to attack the convoy.

The convoy was to be the bait of the trap; the jaws of the trap, the shadowing force, was meant to close on *Tirpitz,* the huge fifty-three thousand-ton battleship that was moored in Alta Fjord in Norway. What incompetent nincompoop chose this particular time of year to attempt this operation, and why, has never been explained, for it was the worst possible time for such an attempt. In the summer months at those high latitudes, the darkest it ever gets is a bright twilight around midnight, so the Germans were able to keep the convoy under near-constant observation, making note of its position, speed, and course almost at will. The Germans knew that the Allies had set a trap (this was at a time in the Battle of the Atlantic when the Allies and the Germans were reading each other's ciphers with almost equal ease) and were well aware of the dispositions and movements of the surface units arrayed against them.

The battle began on July 4, with attacks by both the Luftwaffe and U-boats. *Tirpitz* set out from Alta Fjord but turned back, for reasons that have never been adequately explained, before it got anywhere near the convoy. Allied reconnaissance learned of *Tirpitz's* sortie almost immediately, and as soon as word reached the convoy, the escorts and the support group withdrew at high speed to the west, leaving the convoy totally unprotected. Had *Tirpitz* continued with her sortie, she would have been among the convoy within a matter of hours, and wreaked havoc on the merchant ships long before the shadowing force reached a point where they could have engaged her. What might have been *Tirpitz's* moment of glory—and there would never be another such opportunity—ended in humiliating idleness.

For the convoy, though, there was no respite. Over the next five days, twenty-three merchant ships were bombed, machine-gunned, or torpedoed to the bottom of the sea, and most of the survivors that staggered into Murmansk were damaged. For years the British merchant marine harbored a bitter resentment against the Royal Navy, believing—with some justification—that they had been betrayed and sacrificed for no purpose.

By contrast to the dismal performance of the surface fleet, the U-boat flotillas of the German Kriegsmarine were devastatingly successful. If Admiral Raeder had no idea of how to use his battleships and cruisers against the British, Adm. Karl Doenitz knew exactly how to strike hard at the Royal Navy and the lifelines of the British Empire.

The U-boat had nearly brought Great Britain to her knees in World War I. Admiral Doenitz, Commander-in-Chief (U-boats), drew up a building program in the late 1930s, structured like Raeder's Plan "Z," to be completed by 1945, based on his belief that improved classes of submarines could accomplish even more spectacular successes in the event of another war. Doenitz envisaged building a fleet of U-boats, over three hundred of them, that could deploy attack squadrons of fifteen to twenty submarines each—a concept that eventually evolved into the tactics of the "wolf packs"—that would decimate British convoys.

Doenitz's plans went awry when the war came in September 1939: Germany had just fifty-seven submarines, of which only twenty-two were fit for service in the Atlantic. Gradually the number of operational U-boats increased, but it wasn't until early 1942 that their numbers exceeded one hundred. Individual U-boats, however, operating with courage, skill, and daring—and sometimes ruthlessness—made their mark from the first days of the war. On the evening of September 17 the *U-29*, a small coast-defense submarine never designed to be taken out on the high seas, under the command of Cmdr. Otto Schuart, operating off the coast of Norway, fired three torpedoes at HMS *Courageous*, a British aircraft carrier. *Courageous* sank within fifteen minutes, along with her captain and 518 men. On October 13, 1939, Lt. Gunter Prien took his *U-47* into the British Fleet anchorage at Scapa Flow undetected. As luck would have it, most of the British Home Fleet was at sea, but Prien did find the battleship *Royal Oak*. He first fired four torpedoes at her; only one hit, and most of the damage it caused was above *Royal Oak*'s waterline. Prien then fired three more torpedoes, one of which caused a catastrophic explosion. *Royal Oak* sank in fifteen minutes, with the loss of 833 men.

But it was an incident that occurred on the third day of the war, September 3, 1939, that essentially set the tone for the submarine war, when the *U-30*, commanded by Lt. Fritz Julius Lemp, torpedoed the British passenger liner *Athenia*. The liner sank the next day, and though most of the passengers and crew were saved, 112 people lost their lives, including 28 Americans. Lemp torpedoed the *Athenia* despite explicit orders from Hitler himself not to fire on passenger ships. Propaganda Minister Joseph Goebbels tried to shift the blame for the *Athenia*'s loss onto the British, claiming that she had actually been sunk by a time bomb placed in her cargo hold by the Royal Navy, part of a scheme masterminded by then First Lord of the Admiralty Winston Churchill to create a confrontation between the United States and Germany, akin to the *Lusitania* incident of World War I. While Goebbels's fantasy may have fooled some of the German people, the rest of the world wasn't taken in by it.

The incident was hugely significant, though, because it established almost immediately for the Allies an image of the U-boat crews as heartless, fanatical Nazis with little regard for human life. Whether that image was correct, there was no denying that they were very good at what they did: In the first four months of the war, 221 ships, totaling more than 750,000 tons, were sunk by the U-boats.

The period between July and October 1940 became known as the "Happy Time" for German submarines. It was during this time that the U-boats first began to employ "wolf pack" tactics. An incredible toll of 217 ships sunk, more than a million tons of shipping, was exacted from the Allied merchant fleets—in exchange for the loss of only six U-boats. And though the Allies didn't know it, that was only the beginning of the U-boat onslaught.

The wolf pack, known to the Germans as *Rudeltaktik,* was the best known—and most effective—tactic used by the U-boats. In the First World War, the convoy had been the key to the Allied triumph over the U-boats, as the attacks by the German subs were never coordinated, and the convoy's escort would usually overwhelm a single marauding submarine. Doenitz thought long and hard about how to counter the convoys' advantages and finally concluded that the U-boats in their turn should overwhelm the convoy's defenses. When he finally had enough U-boats and facilities to try his idea, after the fall of France in 1940, he wasted no time in putting his theories into practice. The idea was elegantly simple: A flotilla of U-boats, ranging from as few as five to as many as twenty, would set up a patrol line to scout for convoys. Whichever boat first spotted a convoy acted as a shadower and would follow the convoy, giving regular reports on the convoy's course, speed, and bearing. The other boats would converge on the shadower and take up positions around the convoy, coordinating their attack, usually striking on the surface at night.

When the U-boats were manned by determined commanders, this meant that the convoy's escorts would be overwhelmed, with more boats attacking than they could defend. The success of these tactics can be shown by a handful of stark statistics: In 1940 the U-boats were sinking an average of 200,000 tons of Allied shipping a month; in 1941 the average rose to 211,000 tons a month; and in 1942 it was still more than 187,000 tons a month. It was a loss rate that the Allies could not make good, and in 1942 the outcome of the Battle of the Atlantic—and of the war—hung in the balance.

In 1941 the tide had briefly turned against the U-boats, as additional escorts and air cover—and more tellingly, American escorts for the convoys halfway across the Atlantic, which allowed the badly overstretched British forces some relief—caused the rate of sinkings by the U-boats to drop dramatically. In the months that followed the United States' entry into the war, however, the rate of sinkings skyrocketed again, as hundreds of vessels sailed unescorted along America's east coast, often conveniently illuminated or silhouetted at night by seaside towns and resorts that hadn't learned the need for effective blackouts.

The Allies managed to hang on—barely—and by early 1943 the tide was turning against the U-boats. The numbers of Allied escort ships steadily increased, and the introduction of escort carriers allowed the convoys to have air cover all the way across the Atlantic, finally trumping the ace of the Luftwaffe Kondors. Without their reconnaissance reports, it became harder for the U-boats to locate the convoys, and with the Allies being able to consistently crack the U-boats' Enigma ciphers, it became easier for the escorts to track down the German submarines—the hunters were becoming the hunted. By mid-1944 one U-boat was being lost for every Allied ship sunk, a rate of exchange Germany could ill afford.

The threat of the U-boats wasn't ended, however, though they no longer had the ability to influence the outcome of the war. The German submarines still had teeth that could bite hard. In late 1944 they were still sinking more than one hundred thousand tons a month, and the Allies continued to take no chances with the *Queen Mary* or the *Queen Elizabeth*. The secret routings, the heavy escorts off New York and in the Western Approaches, the nonstop high-speed crossings all would continue to be standard operating procedure for the Queens until the end of the war.

The question remains to be answered, though, about the U-boats and the men who served in them: Were they cold-blooded murderers, steely eyed, fanatical Nazis who preyed on helpless merchant ships, striking unseen and undetected, killing without mercy or compunction? Certainly, the First World War had seen more than its share of ruthless U-boat commanders—was this next generation heir to that mantle? In a narrow sense, yes, they were. It is a matter of record that when Lt. Fritz Julius Lemp, commanding the *U-30*, torpedoed the *Athenia*, there was no doubt in his mind that he was sinking an unarmed passenger liner, and even if it was done in contravention of the Führer's orders, there is no record of Lemp ever being disciplined or reprimanded for his action. Yet there were U-boat skippers who were as humane as Lemp was barbaric.

On September 12, 1942, at 2207 hours, the *U-156*, under the command of Capt.-Lt. Werner Hartenstein, torpedoed a large target in the South Atlantic. The ship was the British liner *Laconia*, carrying a crew of 136, with 348 civilians and military personnel, a small cargo of military supplies, and some 1,800 Italian prisoners of war, guarded by 160 Polish soldiers. The ship sank quickly, and Hartenstein surfaced to confirm his kill and try to learn the identity of his victim.

He was astonished to hear Italian voices coming from the lifeboats and among the people struggling in the water. Realizing what they had done, Hartenstein and his crew immediately began pulling people from the water. He signaled for assistance from nearby U-boats and also sent out a clear, uncoded signal to any vessel nearby, asking for help and promising not to fire on any ship assisting in the rescue.

The *U-156* took some two hundred survivors aboard, most of then crowding the U-boat's narrow deck, while a string of lifeboats with another two hundred survivors was towed behind. The *U-506,* under Capt.-Lt. Erich Woerdemann, arrived and began picking up other survivors; a few hours later the *U-507,* under Lt. Harro Schacht, and the Italian submarine *Cappellini* also appeared. The four submarines headed for the African coast, towing lifeboats behind them, and with hundreds of survivors standing on their decks. Though they were attacked by an American B-24, they were able to successfully deliver more than fifteen hundred survivors to the care of the Vichy French, who had sent their warships out to intercept Hartenstein's little convoy.

Clearly Hartenstein came from a far different mold than Lemp, but the aftermath said much about the U-boat service and the men who served in it. The incident prompted one of the most notorious orders Admiral Doenitz ever issued: In what became known as "the *Laconia* order," Doenitz made it absolutely clear that under no circumstances were U-boats to take part in any kind of rescue operations of the crews of the ships they sank—the men were to be left in the water.

> 1) Any attempt to save survivors of sunken ships, including pulling swimming men from the water and putting them on board lifeboats, the righting of overturned lifeboats, and giving food and water to survivors will be discontinued. Such actions interfere with the primary demands of warfare esp. the destruction of enemy ships and their crews.
>
> 2) The orders concerning the rescue of captains and chief engineers of merchant ships sunk remain in effect.
>
> 3) Survivors are only to be rescued if their knowledge could be of importance to the U-boat fleet.
>
> 4) Stay hard. Remember, the enemy has no regard for woman and children when bombing German towns.

Doenitz's orders, while harsh, reflected the realities of the U-boat war from the perspective of the submariners themselves. If abandoning survivors from a sinking ship in the middle of a freezing ocean seems cruel, it was no worse a fate than they faced when the destroyers and corvettes escorting the convoys hunted them down. The German sailors had little chance of rescue when their U-boats were sunk, their usual fate being a slow death by asphyxiation in a crippled submarine lying on a shallow bottom, or being smashed into a pulp when the hull of their sinking boat finally passed its crush depth and collapsed. It was a hard, cruel war they were fighting, with no quarter asked or given—the stakes were far too high for such niceties. So the German U-boat crews became efficient, hard, and sometimes cruel themselves. A measure of their determination can be gleaned from a few simple facts: Between September 3, 1939, and May 7, 1945, German submarines sank nearly twenty-five hundred merchant ships, totaling almost thirteen million tons—more than half of all the merchant ships lost by all the Allied and Axis nations *combined* during the war. How many people died in those ships will never be known for certain; just Britain's losses, her merchant marine and the Royal Navy together, totaled 104,890 men.

If the U-boat crews were determined, they were also incredibly brave. Of the more than forty thousand young men who served aboard the German U-boats during World War II, fully three-quarters of them lie forever on the bottom of the Atlantic Ocean.

CHAPTER SIX

The Grey Ghosts

And sweep through the deep,
While the stormy winds do blow,—
While the battle rages loud and long,
And the stormy winds do blow.
                                        —Thomas Campbell

WHEN THE *QUEEN MARY* AND *QUEEN ELIZABETH* WERE TRANSFERRED TO the Atlantic, not only were they entering a new war, confronting a new foe, but they also were facing a whole new set of priorities. In the last week of December 1941 Prime Minister Churchill and his military staff came to Washington, D.C., for the first of what would be several joint strategic planning sessions between American and British military leaders, this one being known as the Arcadia Conference. Sometime during the conference, the U.S. Army Chief of Staff, Gen. George C. Marshall, met with the Prime Minister to discuss the possibility of further modifying the *Queen Mary* and *Queen Elizabeth* with an eye to drastically increase their capacity to carry troops. Marshall wanted to look into the possibility of having each ship carry as many as ten thousand soldiers—the equivalent of an entire division—at one time. If it could be done, it would give the Allies the capability to decisively alter the course of the war in Europe.

What motivated Marshall's inquiry was a coalescing grand strategy that the Americans were developing. Within days of America's entry into the war, President Roosevelt, along with Adm. Ernest King, the Navy Chief of Staff, and General Marshall, had decided that the defeat of Nazi Germany should be the Allies' first priority, a decision that the British didn't hesitate to endorse. Even at that early date, it was obvious that in order to make that objective a reality, the Allies would have to invade continental Europe. It was equally obvious that such an invasion would be the most complex and difficult military operation ever attempted, and that the first requirement for the assault would be to gather sufficient troops.

On the question of where the invasion should take place, the British and Americans disagreed sharply. The British believed that the most vulnerable spot for such an assault would be somewhere along Europe's Mediterranean coastline, what Churchill referred to as the "soft underbelly of Europe." The Americans, with typical bluntness, wanted to stage the invasion directly across the English Channel, into occupied France. The two strategies were mutually exclusive, since it would mean a division of resources that the Allies weren't certain they could support. Both sides had valid military and political reasons to support their strategic concepts, and it shortly became clear that the debate over where the invasion of Europe would take place would not be easily settled.

Regardless of where the invasion would be staged, though, the most fundamental requirement was to build up the forces needed for invading Europe. And this had to be accomplished in a reasonable period of time, for the longer the Germans were allowed to retain their grip on Europe, the more formidable their defenses would become. The entire process had to be methodical and systematic, and would be limited by the transport capacity of the Allies, principally the Royal and U.S. Navies and their associated merchant marines. That the American and British staffs were able to base their planning on sound estimates and evaluations of each nation's capabilities was due in no small part to the foresight of American and British staff officers, along with President Franklin Roosevelt and Prime Minister Churchill.

A year and a half before the United States was drawn into the war, in the summer of 1940, the Navy Department sent a permanent "observer" to London with the mission of laying the groundwork for cooperation between the Royal Navy and its American counterpart should the United States come into the war. Army observers were also sent to London during 1940, but only on special missions; it was not until the spring of 1941 that the War Department set up a permanent liaison. Among them was Maj. Gen. James E. Chaney, who went as a Special Army Observer, reporting directly to General Marshall. The British, in turn, set up the Joint Staff Mission in Washington, D.C., representing the British chiefs of staff. In both cases, the observers were to act as channels for exchanging information between the two countries' armed forces.

This coordination was made easier as a result of two formal Anglo-American military conferences held in the spring and summer of 1941. One of the most important subjects discussed at both conferences was defining a combined strategy for Europe along with formulating policies that would govern joint conduct of the war should the United States become involved. The results of these conferences, known as ABC-1, were used by the American War and Navy Departments as a basis for American planning in the increasingly likely event that the United States was drawn into the war. Although decisions reached at ABC-1 were not binding on either Great Britain or the United States—President Roosevelt was legally barred from officially recognizing them at the time—they were to prove invaluable after the Japanese attack on Pearl Harbor obliterated America's neutrality.

It was as a result of the efforts by the various observers, military missions, and joint conferences that General Marshall was able to ask Churchill such informed questions about the troop-carrying potential of the *Queen Mary* and *Queen Elizabeth*. Despite the fact that the United States had been in the war for less than a month, Marshall's mind was already preoccupied with laying the groundwork for an operation code-named Bolero.

Operation Bolero would eventually transform England into what Supreme Allied Commander Dwight D. Eisenhower would call "the greatest operating military base of all time." It officially began in May 1942, when the first twenty-five thousand American troops were sent to England. This was the beginning of a buildup that would gradually increase until by the spring of 1944 as many as 220,000 troops were being ferried across the Atlantic every month.

General Marshall, who had what amounted to a genius for logistics, did some quick calculations and determined that given the current Allied shipping capacity, by the end of August 1942 sufficient American reinforcements would have reached the Pacific to halt any further advances by the Japanese, and that in the Atlantic, enough U.S. troops would be available to garrison Iceland and Northern Ireland. Once that was accomplished, the United States could concentrate on sending troops and equipment to Great Britain to begin the buildup for the invasion. Marshall believed that at least two infantry divisions, one armored division, and nine hundred American aircraft could be in the United Kingdom by September 15, 1942. It was an ambitious plan, but as events turned out, it was a successful one. One of the most important consequences of this rapid deployment of American troops was that it allowed the British to withdraw three trained, seasoned divisions from Northern Ireland. They were promptly sent to North Africa, where they helped tip the scales in favor of the Allies in the decisive battles around El Alamein in the autumn of 1942.

Operation Bolero came into being in April 1942, more than two years before the D-Day invasion on June 6, 1944. Its purpose was the transfer of fighting men and equipment from the United States and Canada to England to support an envisioned cross-channel invasion in 1943. Before Allied forces in the West were strong enough to gain and maintain a lodgment on the European continent, a massive buildup of supplies would be required to support such an endeavor. The U.S. Army Services of Supply (SOS) was given the job of handling the most colossal logistical effort in history. Not only was it necessary to get the soldiers and equipment to the British Isles, but once they were there, they had to be fed, clothed, and housed. Finding places to store the tens of thousands of tanks, trucks, armored vehicles, and artillery pieces necessary to wage war on the continent—not to mention the thousands of bombers, fighters, and other aircraft—meant that every open field in Great Britain was a potential parking lot.

At its height, the demands of Operation Bolero choked British ports with shipping of every description. Eventually more than sixty-nine hundred vessels were involved in bringing more than five million tons of supplies to Great Britain, along with over one and a half million men. When the invasion was finally launched, the support forces included six battleships, twenty-two cruisers, hundreds of destroyers, landing craft, and support ships, as well as more than ten thousand aircraft of all description. But the centerpiece of this effort would be the *Queens.*

It was at the Arcadia conference that the decision was made to place the *Queens* under the control of the U.S. Navy, although they would continue to be manned by Cunard personnel—who also paid their wages. This was sort of "lend-lease" in reverse, with Great Britain for once able to supply the United States with the "tools to finish the job." It also made sense from a logistical standpoint: The majority of the troops to be carried were American, and the United States would be providing the supplies and provisions for each crossing. Placing the *Queens* under American control would greatly simplify that procedure.

At one point in the discussion with Churchill, Marshall registered his concern over the terrible number of casualties that could result if one of the ships were to be torpedoed and sunk. It seemed to be an unusual observation, given the context of the discussion. Each ship's complement of lifeboats could hold more than three thousand people, and it would be easy enough to bringing additional rafts and floats aboard to raise the lifesaving capacity to eight thousand. Marshall, though not a seaman, was astute enough to realize that

The *Queen Mary* off Gourock, Scotland, March 5, 1936. She is about to put to sea for the very first time, to undergo her sea trials. Note how high the ship is riding out of the water and the absence of most of her lifeboats.

The bow of the *Queen Mary* as she anchors off Rashilee Light at the mouth of the Clyde. She has just finished her sea trials. Six years later, a little more than one hundred miles from this spot, this bow would cut the cruiser HMS *Curacoa* in two.

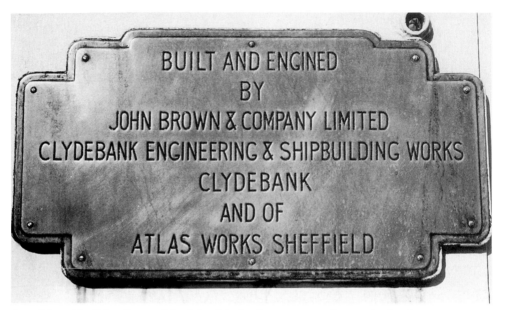

Scottish pride. The *Queen Mary*'s builder's plate, mounted near the bridge.

The *Queen Mary* arrives in New York on her maiden voyage, June 1, 1936. Fog just a few hours out of New York had kept her from capturing the Blue Ribband by 38 minutes. Two months later it would be hers.

The dignity, grace, and power of the *Queen Mary*'s lines show why she was called "the stateliest ship afloat." New York Harbor, June 1, 1936.

Four years later, war has overtaken the *Queen Mary*, and she sits idle at Cunard Pier 90, wearing a fresh coat of "Light Sea Grey" paint, facing an uncertain future. The doomed French liner *Normandie* casts a shadow on the *Mary*'s starboard side.

Making good a daring escape from the besieged British Isles, the unfinished *Queen Elizabeth* thunders toward the United States at more than 30 knots. Note the missing lifeboats and near-deserted decks.

At last safe in American territorial waters, the *Queen Elizabeth* has slackened her speed as she approaches New York. The unexpected arrival of the giant new liner in early March 1940 caused a sensation in the United States.

The three largest ships in the world, from left to right, the *Queen Elizabeth*, the *Queen Mary*, and the *Normandie*. The two British ships are already painted wartime gray, but the *Normandie* still wears her peacetime colors.

The *Queen Mary* goes off to war, March 21, 1940. On her way to Australia to be fitted out as a troopship, she is being eased from the Cunard pier for the first time in seven months.

Above: The *Queen Mary* steaming out of New York harbor on her way to Australia. Almost two years would pass before she returned.

Left: The *Queen Elizabeth* leaving New York, bound for Gourock, Scotland. Thousands of GIs crowd her upper decks to catch a last glimpse of the United States. This photo gives an excellent impression of the huge numbers of troops both Queens were able to carry on each crossing.

Wearing her peacetime colors for the first time, the *Queen Elizabeth* sets out from Southampton on her true maiden voyage, October 16, 1946.

Restored to her prewar glory, the *Queen Mary* resumes her interrupted passenger service on July 31, 1947.

Last salute to a Warrior Queen: The crew of HMS *Hermes* cheer the *Queen Mary* as she leaves Southampton for the last time, October 31, 1967.

A good look at how crowded the berthing was aboard the Queens during their days as the "Grey Ghosts." The official caption of this photo claimed that these American airman were studying technical manuals, although from the grins on their faces, it seems more likely a crap game was in progress.

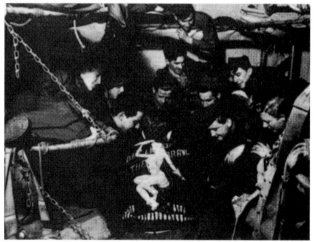

The British light cruiser HMS *Curacoa* as she appeared in the summer of 1941. A little over a year later, she would be cut in two off the northern coast of Ireland.

these figures were only at best a theoretical ideal, and that the chaos aboard a sinking ship would result in thousands of lives being lost. The question that Marshall had to answer for himself—and for the Allied planners—was whether the strategic opportunities offered by the *Queens* were worth specific risks.

What Marshall had in mind was exploiting the carrying capacity of the *Queens* to the maximum. Given that the space available for boats, rafts, and floats limited their capacity to roughly eight thousand persons, that meant that figure was the maximum number of troops each of the *Queens* should carry. If that limitation was ignored, then the liners could be fitted out to carry nearly double that number of troops, allowing entire divisions to be moved in one voyage by one ship, a feat never before attempted or accomplished. Marshall, never one to mince words, bluntly questioned Churchill whether they should take the risk. Churchill, with equal bluntness, replied, "I can only tell you what *we* should do. You must judge for yourselves the risk you will run. If it were a direct part of an actual operation we should put all on board that they could carry. If it were only a question of moving troops in a reasonable time, we should not go beyond the limits of lifeboats, rafts, etc. It is for you to decide."

Marshall didn't immediately respond, but a few days later he visited the *Queen Mary* when she was in New York and was taken around the ship by Harry Grattidge, the liner's Staff Captain. When Marshall sounded him out about the idea of converting the *Queens* to carry as many as fifteen thousand men, Grattidge thought of only one objection. The two ships' normal draughts were identical—twenty-nine feet, six inches. Grattidge did some calculations and determined that with fifteen thousand troops aboard, this figure would increase to something like forty-four feet. This was so deep that it would barely clear the Holland Tunnel in New York Harbor. If the soldiers on board were to crowd to one side of the ship to get a last glimpse of New York as they departed for Europe—as it seemed likely they would do—their combined weight would cause the ship to list considerably. Even a five-degree list would cause either of the *Queens* to foul the tunnel, with dangerous consequences for the ship and disastrous consequences for the tunnel and those inside it. The only way it could be done, Grattidge explained, would be "for the troops to remain wherever they are and stay perfectly still until we're over the . . . tunnel. When they could move again without fear of the ship listing . . . we could give them a green light. But from my experience of trooping that's a pretty tall order for 15,000 troops."

That was good enough for Marshall, who obviously had more confidence in the discipline of American troops than Grattidge, and the orders went out within a matter of days for the conversion to begin on both of the *Queens*. Work on the *Queen Elizabeth* would be done in San Francisco at the same time the *Queen Mary* was taken in hand in New York. While not quite identical conversions, they were very similar in most respects.

The work done in Australia to convert the *Queens* to troopers had increased their capacity to fifty-five hundred people, but this program was far more ambitious, as it planned to triple that figure. The Australian shipwrights had installed rows of fixed wooden triple-tiered bunks in the liners' cabins and used some of the public rooms for slinging hammocks; the Americans had an entirely different concept in mind. The American plan hinged—quite literally—on a device called a standee bunk. This was a rectangular frame of tubular steel, mounted on hinges and bolted to a bulkhead. Its arc of travel was limited by snubbing chains at both ends of the frame so that it could lie horizontally. Within the frame, laced tautly to it, was a fitted length of heavy canvas. The standee bunk's occupant slept on this. It was an ingenious design, easily cleaned, reasonably comfortable (for six or seven nights, at least), and since it could be folded up and out of the way when not in use, it allowed for more room to move about than did the fixed bunks used by the Australians.

Another difference between the Australian and American approaches was the sheer ruthlessness of the American conversion. No place on either ship, aside from the crews' quarters and the engineering spaces, was considered sacrosanct. On the *Queen Mary*, the First Class Smoking Lounge was converted to a hospital; the tourist-class cocktail bar became a pharmacy; the cabin-class restaurant was filled with mess tables and benches; the Observation Lounge and Midshipman's Bar were unceremoniously filled with bunks; and the tailor shop became a detention center and the headquarters of the military police detachment permanently stationed aboard. And standee bunks went *everywhere*—a stateroom originally designed for four people could be converted into sleeping space for as many as twenty-one GIs. Not even the swimming pool was spared; bunks were mounted in there seven high.

While the *Queens'* first missions after being taken over by the United States were to carry American troops to Australia to bolster the defenses there, it was clear from the nature of the refits and modifications made to both of them that they were ultimately destined for service in the Atlantic. It was decided then that each ship should carry a defensive armament equal to that of a light cruiser, so the number of twenty-millimeter antiaircraft guns was increased to twenty-four, while ten forty-millimeter guns in five twin mounts were added. Additionally, six three-inch guns in high-angle/low-angle mounts were emplaced, similarly disposed on both liners, with two guns in front of the bridge and the other four mounted on the after decks. Finally, the four-inch popguns originally mounted on the stern of each ship for defense against submarines were replaced with far more imposing—and more effective—six-inch weapons. Though certainly not meant to allow either of the *Queens* to slug it out with a conventional warship larger than a destroyer, it was an armament heavy enough to discourage any raider or surfaced U-boat that might mistakenly want to pick a fight with the liners.

That some measure of self-defense was required was due to the fact that the *Queen Mary* and *Queen Elizabeth* almost always sailed alone. Their best defense—in fact, their only defense—against submerged U-boats lying in ambush was their speed. Making a steady twenty-eight to thirty knots, while following carefully designed zigzag patterns, they could easily outpace any submarine the Germans had. Even if a U-boat skipper was lucky enough to draw a bead on one of the *Queens,* the target would not be in range long enough for him to make any corrections to his initial approach or line up for a second shot—he would have one chance and one chance only to get his torpedoes off, and if his calculations were not perfect, he would never get another. That same speed, though, also meant that the *Queens* were much faster than any other merchant vessel afloat, and faster than many escorts.

There was always the chance of a carefully set ambush, with U-boats lying in wait for the approach of an unsuspecting *Queen.* To avoid this, the liners followed a zigzag course as they crossed the Atlantic. The zigzag was a seemingly random series of course changes that would prevent the ship from staying on any one bearing long enough for a submarine to target it and fire its torpedoes. In reality, there was nothing random about it, since it was necessary for the ship to make steady and constant progress toward its destination. Instead, the zigzags were arranged in such a way that their cumulative effect was to keep the ship traveling on its base course, at a constant relative speed.

How this was accomplished is probably best illustrated by the Number 8 Zigzag, the pattern most commonly used by the *Queens.* It began with the ship steaming along her base course for four minutes, then altering course twenty-five degrees to port and maintaining that new course for eight minutes. Then she swung to starboard fifty degrees, held that for eight minutes, and turned twenty-five degrees to port again, which would bring her back on her base course, holding that for four minutes. She then made another twenty-five-degree turn, this time to starboard, followed eight minutes later by a fifty-degree turn to port, and eight minutes after that a twenty-five-degree turn to starboard, which brought her back on her base course again. This cycle was repeated every forty minutes, all the way across the Atlantic. A special clock in the wheelhouse chimed whenever the time arrived for another course change. For a U-boat captain trying to track a ship following such a zigzag pattern, a plotting table and torpedo officer would not be sufficient to work out a firing solution—he would need a crystal ball!

Still, there were two times during each crossing that the *Queens* were particularly vulnerable to U-boat attack: as they were leaving port and as they were arriving. This was due in large part to their size. There was only one port in the United States that could handle them: New York. And with Southampton within range of half the Luftwaffe, the only port left to them in Great Britain was Gourock, on the Clyde in Scotland, just below Glasgow. Consequently, there was no hope of trying to deceive the Germans as to where the *Queens* were sailing.

Instead, elaborate measures were taken to keep the date and time of the *Queens'* departures secret—or at least not general knowledge. The ships themselves were heavily guarded at all times to prevent sabotage—the combined military and police contingent in New York numbered 750 men—and the crew members who served on them were carefully screened by both American and British Intelligence. Despite these precautions, there were still incidents that may have been simple acts of vandalism—bottle caps found inside fire hoses, holes in lifeboats—or that may well have been something more sinister. And there *were* some serious attempts at crippling one or the other of the ships: In April 1943, two bombs were found on board the *Queen Elizabeth* during a routine inspection of her machinery spaces. Defused, they were promptly thrown overboard.

When either of the *Queens* was preparing to sail from New York, her captain was never informed of the exact time of departure more than twenty-four hours in advance, nor did he know until the ship was at sea precisely what course he was to take—and the ship never followed the exact same course twice. A set of sealed orders was handed to the captain at the Shipping Office on Cunard's Pier 90, which he was not to open until the ship was past the Ambrose Light. At that time, he would open his instructions and inform the navigating officer and helmsman of the course and speed, as well as the zigzag pattern to be followed.

An escort of four or five of the U.S. Navy's most modern destroyers would accompany the liners until they were 150 miles out of New York, and navy patrol planes or blimps escorted them some distance farther. Once the last escort turned back for New York, the *Queens* were on their own until they were met by their British escorts north of Ireland. No one but a handful of naval officers on either side of the Atlantic, and the men on the bridges of the liners themselves, knew where they were supposed to be, or when they would arrive at their destinations. It was during these solitary passages that the *Queens* would sometimes loom swiftly and unexpectedly out of the mist, sweeping past a solitary patrol vessel or fishing trawler, only to disappear back into the mist moments later, earning the them nickname the "Grey Ghosts."

The possibility of a German attack—from above, on, or below the sea— was always a constant and real fear for the crew and troops alike aboard the *Queens*. Daily gunnery drills were held to keep the skills of the gun crews sharply honed, with prizes sometimes being awarded for particularly smart performance. These drills also did a lot to sustain the morale of the troops, who would be essentially helpless aboard the ships if they were attacked, something the men were acutely aware of. The rattle of the various machine guns, the staccato barks from the twenty-millimeter and forty-millimeter anti-aircraft guns, the bangs of the three-inch guns, and the thunder of the six-inch stern mount were reassurance that if need be, the *Queens* could always bite back—*hard.*

What every GI aboard looked forward to, and every sailor, as well, was the rendezvous with the British escorts. Usually the first to appear was a Sunderland flying boat, part of the RAF's Coastal Command, responsible for patrolling the waters around the British Isles. The Sunderland was a big four-engine aircraft that looked like something like a humpback whale with wings, but was much feared by U-boats and German aircraft alike for its heavy armament: The Luftwaffe aircrews flying their Fw-200 Kondors called the Sunderland "the Flying Porcupine" because it fairly bristled with guns. In June 1943, six Ju-88 fighter-bombers attacked a solitary Sunderland north of Scotland. Three of the German planes were shot down, and although seriously damaged, with several crewmen wounded, the Sunderland was able to limp back to its base. Other Coastal Command patrol bombers included American B-17s, which the British called the Fortress I, II, or III, depending on the model; the B-24, known as the Liberator to the RAF; and the Catalina, which the Americans called a PBY.

The first patrol planes would appear while the *Queens* were roughly six hundred miles from land, the first surface escorts about fifteen hours after that. The rendezvous point was usually somewhere off Bloody Foreland on the northern Irish coast. A squadron of a half dozen destroyers, generally accompanied by a light cruiser for additional antiaircraft protection, was the usual escort, the destroyers taking up formation ahead of the Queens to sweep the waters with their asdic, or sonar, systems, listening for enemy submarines, while the cruiser stayed close to the liners to better protect them from enemy aircraft.

It wasn't always easy. The Royal Navy had more tasks to accomplish than it had ships to accomplish them, and although a large part of the American fleet was serving in the Atlantic, the demands of war in the Pacific meant that most of the cruiser strength of the U.S. Navy had been diverted to the other side of the world. Destroyers were the backbone of antisubmarine defense, cruisers the key to antiaircraft protection. This was because of the great number of relatively light weapons that cruisers were designed to carry. A modern cruiser boasted twenty-millimeter and forty-millimeter rapid-fire cannons, as well as batteries of three-inch or four-inch dual-purpose guns. The Dido-class light cruisers actually had a main armament designed to serve as either surface or antiaircraft guns.

The problem was that there were not enough modern cruisers to go around. Even before the war began, the Royal Navy became acutely aware that its fleet was badly unbalanced, for while its capital ship strength was sufficient to overwhelm any possible European foe (and the possibility of war with the United States, Great Britain's only equal in naval strength, was the least of the Royal Navy's worries), the numbers of lighter units—cruisers and destroyers—were barely enough to meet the requirements of peacetime. Trying to make up for the shortage, the Royal Navy had gone to the Reserve Fleet, a collection of ships that, because of age or design limitations, were no longer suitable for front-line service, but still could be useful in secondary and support roles. Consequently, they were maintained afloat in various navy yards, where they were routinely inspected and kept in reasonably good repair. One example of this type of ship was the "C" class of cruisers, of World War I vintage. Originally numbering twenty-eight, half the class was sold to smaller navies during the early 1930s, while the remaining fourteen were relegated to the Reserve. As the likelihood of war grew at the end of the decade, they were reactivated and refurbished, most of them being modified with up-to-date weapons and range-finding equipment, along with such new inventions as radar. Several of them had been converted to antiaircraft cruisers when their original armament of five six-inch guns, whose mountings did not allow enough elevation to make them effective against aircraft, were replaced by eight four-inch dual-purpose guns, mounted in four twin turrets that allowed the guns to be elevated to seventy degrees. This modification, plus the addition of two-pounder pom-poms along with twenty-millimeter and forty-millimeter Bofors guns scattered about the cruisers' superstructures, made them particularly useful in escorting convoys through the Western Approaches.

But the ships themselves weren't always up to the challenge. No amount of modification could make up for the fact that many of the "C" class cruisers were twenty-five years old and showing their age. Bluntly put, they were not up to the rigors of the North Atlantic: They had been designed to protect the Empire's sea lanes in the more temperate climes of tropical and subtropical colonial service. That they were still in service and had been pressed into front-line duties was the fault of successive short-sighted governments in the years between the two world wars. Determined to keep defense spending to an absolute minimum, Prime Minister Stanley Baldwin and his successor, Neville Chaimberlain, had not merely cut the fat from Great Britain's defense budgets, they had cut them to the bone, so that when the crisis came, the Royal Navy had no choice but to return the aging ships to service. As for their hulls and engines, there was little that could be done; that there would be no catastrophic failures was the best that could be hoped for.

That didn't prevent the cruisers' crews from doing their level best to carry out their duties with as much dedication and professionalism as the crew on any of the newer ships in the Royal Navy. Even if they couldn't be privy to the plans of the Allies' grand strategists—and they weren't—the officers and ratings of the escorts knew they were performing an incredibly important task protecting the *Queens*. In May 1942 the *Queen Mary* brought 9,880 American troops to Gourock; along with the 875 crewmen aboard, this was the first time more than 10,000 people had been carried aboard a single ship. Within a few weeks, the *Queen Elizabeth* was carrying similar numbers. Even greater feats were to follow: On her first crossing in August of that same year, the *Mary* carried 15,125 GIs, an entire division, the first time one complete division had ever been transported on a single ship.

From their very first Atlantic crossings, the *Queens* proved the wisdom of the decisions made by Churchill and Marshall. Captain Bisset, who commanded the *Queen Mary* on nearly three-quarters of her Atlantic crossings during the war, was in a unique position to judge how useful they really were, and in his memoirs concluded: "Together they were equal to a fleet of twenty normal troop transports. That calculation takes into account their high speed, which enabled them to make more voyages in a given time than ordinary liners could make." Their safety and survival soon transcended all other considerations, something Capt. Giles Gordon Illingworth sought to drive home to those aboard the *Queen Mary* in October 1943, when he addressed the passengers and crew:

> I call upon all officers and men to obey my orders to the letter. I have but one task. It is the job of bringing this ship safely to port, and that job, God willing, I *will* do. It is not important that you, numbering some 15,000, arrive safely in the Firth of Clyde, but it is important that the ship be brought safely to anchor there. Remember that. You and I are not indispensable to the successful prosecution of this war, but the ship is. You will keep in mind, therefore, that all your thoughts during the crossing will be directed to her security. Enemy forces will be at work, and the Hun will try every device in his power to bring the "Queen" to harm. Submarines will trail us and aircraft will harass us. They have done it before and we have every reason to believe they will do it again. But the "Queen" will take care of herself. From now until the moment you debark, think in terms of the ship. Treat her gently and do not abuse her. She stands ready to do for you what she has done for thousands who have gone before. Keep her confidence and do not betray her by carelessness or misdeed. Do these things and the ship will bring us to the mouth of the Clyde on Tuesday next—so help us God.

Certainly the Germans shared Captain Illingworth's estimate of the *Queens'* importance to the Allied war effort. Not long after the two liners began ferrying troops across the Atlantic, Adolf Hitler offered a reward of RM 1 million, the equivalent of $250,000, to the U-boat skipper who sank either of them. While no one ever collected the bounty, it was not for want of trying.

Probably the best chance any U-boat captain would have had of collecting this bounty would have been during a seagoing epic that became known as "The Long Voyage." After carrying ten thousand American GIs to Gourock, where she spent ten days while stores were replenished and some minor damage caused by exceptionally heavy seas was repaired, the *Queen Mary* left the Clyde with nearly ten thousand British "Tommies" aboard, bound for Suez. There, an equal number of Australian Diggers replaced the British troops, as the last of the Australian divisions were being returned home. Some thirty-one thousand soldiers were distributed between the five troopships that made up the convoy the *Mary* now joined. They were the *Ile de France,* taken over by the Free French and placed at the disposal of the Allies, the Dutch *Nieuw Amsterdam,* the *Queen of Bermuda,* and the old Cunard warhorse *Aquitania.*

Captain Bisset was designated the commodore of the convoy. As the senior merchant officer, the responsibility for maneuvering and directing the troopships fell on his shoulders. It was, he later confided, "the most anxious voyage that I made in the *Queen Mary,* and the biggest responsibility that I have ever had thrust on me." The convoy departed Suez on January 25, 1943, bound for Sydney. The trip would take just over a month, for the convoy's orders were to stay together, so they were limited by the top speed of the slowest ship, the aging *Queen of Bermuda,* which was eighteen knots. By some miracle of good luck, the convoy was never sighted by enemy submarines or warships, and arrived safely in Sydney on February 27. After a month of refitting, the *Queen Mary* was ready to return to the Atlantic, and with eight thousand American servicemen aboard, she set out for Gourock by way of Cape Town. She arrived in the Clyde on April 22, where Bisset, in need of a well-earned rest, turned command over to Captain Illingworth.

The first time an attack on one of the *Queens* in the North Atlantic was claimed came on October 1, 1942, when the *Queen Mary* was still about a thousand miles west of the British Isles. The *U-407,* commanded by Capt.-Lt. Ernst-Ulrich Brüller, fired a spread of four torpedoes at the *Mary,* but all of them missed. That is, Brüller claimed he fired on the *Queen Mary*—no one on the liner saw anything.

A better-documented incident occurred the next month. Germany's information minister Joseph Goebbels announced that on November 9 the *Queen Elizabeth* had been torpedoed and sunk. She had been sighted by the *U-704* about two hundred miles west of Ireland, carrying a few hundred British government officials and army officers who were on their way to an Allied strategy conference, as well as several thousand women and children who were being evacuated from the British Isles. Capt.-Lt. Horst Kessler, commanding the U-boat, fired a spread of four torpedoes at the *Elizabeth,* claiming one hit. In truth, none did. What appears to have happened was that three of the four torpedoes ran too deep and never came near the liner, but the fourth seems to have slammed into a wave hard enough to set off the warhead. The *Elizabeth*'s crew did report an unexplained explosion near the ship on the afternoon of November 9, but no one aboard the liner saw a submarine. Ironically, the Germans had no way of knowing how close they came to striking what may have been a decisive blow to the Allied war effort that day. Alan Turing, the cryptographic genius behind the Allies' success at unlocking the secrets of the Germans' supposedly "unbreakable" Enigma cypher system, was traveling aboard the *Elizabeth* on this crossing, on his way to the United States to confer with his American and Canadian counterparts. Turing had played a pivotal role in the intelligence attack on the U-boat cyphers, which in 1943 would allow the Allies to decisively turn the tide of the Battle of the Atlantic against the U-boats. Without Turing's contributions, that battle may well have turned out very differently.

The only other chance the Germans ever had at the *Queen Elizabeth* came almost two and a half years later, in March 1945, on one of her last crossings carrying troops to Europe. She had just met up with her inbound escorts off the coast of Ireland, when a signal was flashed to her that two destroyers had picked up the sounds of German U-boats lying astride the *Queen Elizabeth*'s course. The escorts immediately went over to the attack while the *Elizabeth*'s captain, C. M. Ford, resolutely maintained his course and speed. Though the waters ahead of the ship were filled with depth charges exploding on suspected targets, no submarines were actually sighted, and the liner sped on to Gourock.

Three even greater opportunities for the Germans to change the course of the war, had they known about them, were the times Winston Churchill crossed the Atlantic on the *Queen Mary*. The first was in May 1943, when the Prime Minister and his entourage took passage to New York on their way to the Trident Conference in Washington, D.C. The others were for the Quadrant Conference in August 1943 and the Octagon Conference in September 1944, both held in Quebec.

Elaborate security precautions were taken to disguise the identity of the Prime Minister and his party prior to departure, as well as to conceal their presence on board until the ship was on the high seas. Cover stories were concocted by British Intelligence and spread as rumors among the dockyard workers of the Clyde, some claiming that the *Mary* would be transporting high-ranking enemy prisoners of war to special detention camps in Canada, others that exiled European royals were being moved to safety in the United

States. Probably the most successful was the tale that several hundred victims of an unspecified but highly contagious disease were being taken to America for treatment.

Churchill was never mentioned by name on any document relating to the crossing, nor was any member of his entourage; "Colonel Warden and party" was substituted instead, although sometimes the cryptic "239 and party" was used. (No explanation has ever been offered about the significance of the number 239.) The "special party" always boarded the *Queen Mary* after dark, and no one was allowed on any of the upper decks until the ship was well out to sea in the Western Approaches. In a not unexpected departure from the *Mary*'s usual crossings, a large Royal Navy escort of several cruisers and a large number of destroyers accompanied the ship all the way across the Atlantic. Special precautions were taken for Churchill's safety in the event that somehow a U-boat or Luftwaffe bomber got lucky and scored a critical hit on the *Mary.* A lifeboat was reserved for the Prime Minister's exclusive use, and at his instructions, a .303-caliber Vickers machine gun was mounted on it, so that he could, in his words, "actively resist capture" should the *Queen Mary* be torpedoed and sunk. As events would have it, Churchill's marksmanship, which in truth was amazing for someone his age, was never put to the test, but the incident is interesting, as it demonstrates that Churchill's combativeness was not confined to his rhetoric.

The Prime Minister's traveling companions usually included his Chief of Staff, Gen. Sir Hastings Ismay; Gen. Sir Alan Brooke, Chief of the Imperial General Staff; Minister of War Transport Lord Leathers; and always a small horde of cypher clerks, signal personnel, and secretaries (including his own daughter, Mary), as well as a large number of military specialists and advisors. Depending on the agenda of the conference he was attending, Churchill might also be accompanied by Field Marshall Archibald Wavell, commander in chief in India; Admiral of the Fleet Sir Andrew Cunningham, Commander-in-Chief, Mediterranean; or Field Marshall Lord Mountbatten, Supreme Allied Commander, Southeast Asia. The entire Imperial General Staff was brought along for the Quadrant Conference, one of the most critical strategy-making sessions of the war. The Americans and the British didn't always agree on what strategies would best contribute to the defeat of Germany, and Churchill was well aware that his American colleagues would bring their best and brightest experts to argue the military, logistic, and political advantages of their proposals. He was determined to give himself the same advantages.

Consequently, the passage on the *Queen Mary* was never just a pleasantly idle five or six days at sea. Churchill and his staff worked, and worked hard. The Prime Minister had become intimately acquainted with the day-to-day workings of Britain's war effort, and he expected to be as well informed at sea as he was on land and, if the need arose, to be able to intervene in any crisis that might suddenly spring up. Several cabins on the Main Deck were converted to communications centers, cypher offices, map rooms, conference rooms, typing pools, and offices for the various staffs, and according to Churchill himself, "from the time we went on board our work went on ceaselessly."

Coordinating a worldwide war effort required a lot of communication, and that presented a difficulty of sorts for the signal officers on Churchill's staff. Receiving signals was not a problem, but the *Mary* was under strict orders to maintain radio silence at all times, lest the German signals intelligence service, which was arguably the best in the world at the time, home in on her signals and provide patrolling U-boats with the information they needed to intercept her. The solution was to flash urgent signals by Aldis lamp to one of the escorting destroyers, which would then sheer away from the convoy, steam off for as much as 150 miles, and transmit the signals to London.

After the end of the working day, which could be as late as 10:00 at night, Churchill and his staff did relax, and did so in style. Furnishings and fittings for some of the public rooms were brought out of storage, and several staterooms in First Class were restored to some semblance of their prewar elegance. Meals were served with the same standards and etiquette that prevailed before the war, although now the waiters and stewards were Royal Marines clad in scarlet tunics rather than Cunard livery; after dinner, the men enjoyed cigars and brandy in the Smoking Room.

There were a few problems in adjusting the *Queen Mary* to Churchill— and Churchill to the *Queen*. Gen. (later Field Marshall) Alan Brooke wrote in his diary about an infestation of insects aboard the ship that had apparently begun when coolies were unloading equipment from the ship in Suez—and the Prime Minister's reaction to it:

> We were told about the vermin which has resulted from troop movements. It was impossible to clear this entirely without going into dry-dock and a long process, but by a system of gassing, the live insects would be killed, but not their eggs. We should consequently have the period of incu-

bation, about six days, of relative immunity. PM accepted the risk. The last blow however was a heavier one. The ship was "dry"! At this Winston pulled a very long face, but was reassured that the suite occupied by him need not be.

By some sort of strange juxtaposition, while the British were taking every conceivable precaution to keep German submarines and bombers away from the Prime Minister and his staff, on each of the crossings Churchill made aboard the *Queen Mary,* there were thousands of German and Italian soldiers within a few hundred feet of him. They were prisoners of war, being shipped to detention camps in the United States and Canada, and their transport added a new dimension to the wartime careers of the Warrior *Queens.*

With the numbers of Allied troops being stationed in Great Britain increasing monthly, the question of where to keep Axis POWs was becoming a thorny one. There was barely enough room to billet the Allied troops and their equipment, and the burden of feeding tens of thousands of Axis POWs would have strained the resources of the British Isles to the breaking point. The solution was readily at hand, since the British had already been using their transport ships, including the *Queen Mary,* to carry German and Italian prisoners captured in North Africa to Australian detention camps. It simply made sense to do the same with both of the *Queens* once they were transferred to the North Atlantic run. The conversion from troop transport to prisoner-of-war transport was fairly easily accomplished. Both ships had been divided into three sections to better control the movements of the GIs aboard, and it was a simple task to erect barricades at the partitions separating those sections, post armed guards at them, and confine the prisoners to easily patrolled and monitored decks. Additional precautions were carefully placed machine guns that covered the exits from the prisoners' sections of the ships, as well as electric alarms for the guards to summon help instantly if need be.

The POWs mostly were well disciplined and cooperated with their captors, although there were moments of defiance. In his book, *War, Peace, and Big Ships,* Captain Bisset recalled how a group of German POWs were found scrawling anti-British graffiti on the walls of their cabin: "When these were found, the occupants had to clean them off, and were then put in the 'brig' on a bread-and-water diet for a few days. Next, six men in one of the cabins decided to be sarcastic, and wrote 'Rule Britannia' in large letters on the bulkhead. They too were punished, just to show that we played no favorites!"

The *Queen Mary* began carrying prisoners to America in January 1942, the *Queen Elizabeth* a few months later; by the end of 1943 they had carried nearly 170,000 POWs to the United States and Canada. The numbers grew even higher in 1944, following the D-Day invasion, as the Allied armies swept across France and the Low Countries. In September alone, 55,000 German prisoners of war were carried across the Atlantic by the *Queens* and other transport ships. By the end of the year, each of the *Queens* was carrying an average of 5,000 POWs on each westbound crossing.

It has been suggested that the apparent "immunity" that the *Queens* had from U-boat attack was partly because the German Naval High Command was aware that they were carrying German POWs when they were bound for New York or Halifax. It has also been suggested that the prisoners were put aboard the *Queens* for that very reason. If the former were true, it would not only fly in the face of the strategic objectives of the Kriegsmarine, it would also defy the standing operational orders of the U-boat service. If the latter were true, it would merely demonstrate that the Allies had a firmer grasp on the realities of war and the importance of the *Queens* to their plans for eventual victory. By 1942 the Battle of the Atlantic had become ruthless and merciless—the "*Laconia* order" issued by Admiral Doenitz proved that beyond a doubt. For the Germans, the blow that sinking one of the *Queens* would strike at the Allied effort to build up an invasion force, not to mention the devastating effects it would have on Allied morale, would have been worth the lives of a few thousand POWs. The U-boats showed few qualms of conscience about sinking other ships that were clearly transports, westbound with prisoners of war aboard, so there is little reason to believe that they should suddenly develop scruples over attacking one of the *Queens*. The reality of the situation was best summed up when a famous admiral made this observation about U-boat warfare in the First World War: "The essence of warfare is violence, and moderation in war is imbecility." The admiral was the First Sea Lord, Adm. Sir John Fisher.

The Germans were not the only threat the *Queens* faced; sometimes the sea could be just as dangerous. In one of the most frightening episodes on all of the North Atlantic crossings by the *Queens*, the *Mary* was struck broadside by a rogue wave that was so large and powerful, it almost caused her to capsize. In December 1943, while carrying more than ten thousand GIs and a crew of nearly a thousand, the *Mary* was steaming through heavy but not unusually rough seas while still some seven hundred miles west of Scotland. The sky was overcast and there had been intermittent rain all day—in other words, a typical winter day for the North Atlantic. At about 2:30 that afternoon, without warning, one monstrous wave reared up and smashed into the ship's port side. The wave was so huge that it stove in boats on the Boat Deck and smashed windows on the bridge—ninety-five feet above the waterline. As the weight of the wave bore down on the ship, she heeled over to starboard, beginning a roll that more than one person on board thought she would never recover from. Over she went, past thirty degrees, past forty, past forty-five, past fifty, until she finally reached an angle of fifty-two degrees. The wave held her there for some seconds, the starboard lifeboats and Boat Deck railings awash, nothing but green seawater visible though the portholes and windows on the starboard side of the ship. Then, with an agonizing slowness, she began to recover, regaining an even keel some minutes later.

Below decks was chaos. Since there had been no warning for either troops or crewmen, people had been thrown out of bunks, tossed around machinery spaces, flung across decks, galleys, and mess halls. Men had broken arms and legs, cracked skulls and concussions, but amazingly there were no fatalities. Even more amazing, no one topside was swept overboard—if they had been, they would have been lost, since the *Mary*'s orders forbade her stopping or altering her course. For the men in the antiaircraft gun positions, it was a particularly terrifying experience: Normally sitting well over a hundred feet above the water, the men at the port-side guns had the awesome prospect of this mountainous wall of water threatening to break down over them at any moment, while those on the starboard guns had the equally frightening vision of the sea rushing by only a few feet below them.

It was later calculated that the *Queen Mary* had come within three degrees of capsizing. If she had, not only would it have been a huge loss for the Allied war effort, but it would have become one of the great mysteries of the sea, as it is quite likely that she would have sunk without a trace—there would have been little chance for anyone below decks to escape, while those above decks who were lucky enough to get away would have succumbed to the cold of the sea within a matter of hours. The *Mary* was still more than a day out from her rendezvous with the Western Approaches escort, so that even if she had remained afloat for a few hours, some time would have passed before she would have been missed. What would have been the greatest maritime disaster in history had been avoided by the slimmest of margins. It was a chilling reminder that the sea was an ally to no one, and a constant danger.

And sometimes the *Queens* themselves were the danger. . . .

CHAPTER SEVEN

A Royal Tragedy

It was our war-ship ~Clampherdown~,
Fell in with a cruiser light
That carried the dainty Hotchkiss gun
And a pair o' heels wherewith to run
From the grip of a close-fought fight.

—Rudyard Kipling

ON AN UNCOMMONLY BRIGHT MORNING IN AUTUMN 1942, IN WATERS just off of Bloody Foreland, northwest of County Donegal, Ireland, seven ships were steaming eastward in a loose, ever-changing formation toward the Western Isles. They were the *Queen Mary*, with over 10,000 American soldiers of the 29th Infantry Division and a crew of more than 850 aboard, and six escorts—five destroyers and the light cruiser *Curacoa*. It was just 10:00 that morning when the cruiser took up a position roughly five miles ahead of the huge liner, and the two ships wove back and forth in an intricate pattern of zigzags designed to distract and discomfit any U-boat commander trying to line up an approach to get a torpedo off at the *Mary*. Almost immediately a series of incidents and circumstances, unnoticed at the time but glaringly obvious in hindsight, began to fall into place that would lead to the moment when, at 2:14 in the afternoon of October 2, 1942, the eighty-one thousand-ton *Queen Mary* would run down the four thousand four hundred-ton *Curacoa*, knifing the cruiser in two and killing three-quarters of her crew.

How it happened is the kind of mystery that haunts ships at sea and causes captains to have nightmares. Visibility was excellent, and both ships had each other in full view the entire time they were approaching the instant of collision. Both captains were aware of the other ship's speed and course, as well as what each ship's movements, as dictated by the zigzag pattern, would be at any given moment. Both ships' officers and crew did everything right, both did everything wrong. It was almost as if the collision was preordained from the moment the *Queen Mary* and *Curacoa* sighted each other.

HMS *Curacoa* was a "C" class cruiser of World War I vintage, the twenty-second built in a class of twenty-eight. Laid down in the Pembroke Dockyard in Wales in July 1916, she was launched ten months later, on May 5, 1917; fitting out took until February 18, 1918. She was 451 feet in length, with a beam of 43 feet; her displacement was four thousand three hundred tons. She was armed with five six-inch guns and protected by a three-inch belt of armor at the waterline. Since she was designed primarily for scouting duties with the main fleet or, alternatively, protecting friendly shipping in far-flung seas, speed was essential. Two sets of Brown Curtiss geared turbines drove a pair of screws at as much as 280 revolutions per minute, giving *Curacoa* a designed speed of twenty-five knots, although on at least two occasions her engineers pushed her to just over twenty-nine. The turbines were fed steam from six oil-fired Yarrow water tube boilers. Originally, the design of the "C" class cruisers (designated "C" class because all of the ships' names allotted to the class began with the letter "C") had three funnels, but a reworking of the uptakes halfway through construction of the class reduced that number by one, so it was as one of the first two-funneled cruisers in the Royal Navy that *Curacoa* began her service.

As soon as she was commissioned, *Curacoa* joined the Harwich Force, a collection of cruisers and destroyers responsible for protecting the shipping in the English Channel, where she immediately became the flagship of the force commander, Rear Admiral Sir Reginald Tyrwhitt. At the beginning of the Great War, the Harwich Force had been something of a joke, as it was then a motley collection of antiquated ships and superannuated officers, known popularly as "Tyrwhitt's Navy." By the middle of the war, by dint of a lot of drill and hard work, as well as the addition of newer ships and the scrapping of older ones, the Harwich Force had begun to cut quite a dash, dueling with marauding German destroyers and light cruisers that sought out the British convoys steaming up and down the channel, and the name "Tyrwhitt's Navy" had become a source of pride for the crews that served in it. *Curacoa's* wartime service with the Harwich Force was brief, as Germany sued for an armistice less than ten months after the cruiser joined the fleet. She and her crew had the compensation of taking part in the ceremonies when Germany's High Seas Fleet surrendered and was interned at Scapa Flow.

In the decade and a half to follow, *Curacoa* had a varied but generally happy career. She served at various times as a transport for one of the royal families of Europe, as flagship of the Royal Navy's 2nd Light Cruiser Squadron (later the 2nd Cruiser Squadron) of the Atlantic Fleet, and as flagship of the 3rd Light Cruiser Squadron of the Mediterranean Fleet. The crews were drilled constantly, as the officers did their best to prepare them for any contingency, and while there was a certain monotony to the relentless exercises, *Curacoa* gained a reputation for being a smart ship. And the adventures to be had ashore at ports of call as distant in space and culture as the Baltic Sea and the eastern Mediterranean more than made up for the seemingly endless drills.

There were moments of excitement, as well, as in early September 1922, when she was called on to be the "spotter" for four Royal Navy battleships off the Turkish port of Smyrna. The Turks, in violation of a long-standing international treaty, had refused the British permission to enter the port. The British took such treaties very seriously (after all, Great Britain had gone to war in 1914 over just such a "scrap of paper") and were determined to force the issue. *Curacoa,* responsible for spotting and correcting the fall of the shells from the bombarding battleships, had to position herself almost under the guns defending the harbor at Smyrna. Fortunately for all involved, the Turks relented before the warships opened fire, but it had been a tense few hours.

Crewmen who served aboard *Curacoa* between the wars could look back on cruises to Sweden, Norway, Denmark, Bulgaria, Romania, Egypt, Palestine, Greece, Turkey, and the islands of the Aegean. In 1930 she was assigned to the China Station and added such names as Aden, Colombo, Singapore, Hong Kong, Hankow, Nanking, and Shanghai to her list of ports of call. The sun had not yet set on the British Empire, and the Royal Navy was still the Empire's primary instrument of policy. Goodwill cruises and showing the flag were the most popular ways of demonstrating Britain's desire to be on good terms with her neighbors, wherever they were in the world, but always behind the appearance of a ship like HMS *Curacoa* was the subtle reminder of the still-awesome power of the British Fleet and the empire that maintained it.

By 1932, though, *Curacoa* was fifteen years old and beginning to show her age. Recalled to the Mediterranean at the beginning of that year, she started having intermittent problems with her turbines, and at the end of the year she returned to Britain, where she was taken off active duty and placed in the Reserve Fleet. It proved a brief interlude, however; in little more than a year, she underwent a refit at Portsmouth and then sailed to the Far East for a four-month stint in Hong Kong. At the end of July 1933 she returned to Britain and was once more placed in the Reserve. At year's end, she was once more refitted, this time as a training ship at the Gunnery and Torpedo School at Portsmouth, a duty she would perform for the next six years.

Warclouds were unmistakably gathering over Europe in the summer of 1939, and the hopelessly myopic Government of Neville Chamberlain finally began to look to repairing Britain's defenses, which it had so long disparaged and neglected. Chamberlain's penny-pinching throughout the 1930s, first as Chancellor of the Exchequer, then as Prime Minister, had hampered the Royal Navy, allowing only a handful of new ships of all classes to be built in those years. Desperate for cruisers, the navy resorted to keeping the aging "C" class ships on active duty, as well as many of their contemporaries. In an effort to improve their survivability, as well as address the realities of warfare in the age of air power, eight of the "C" class cruisers were earmarked for conversion into antiaircraft cruisers that summer, among them HMS *Curacoa*.

It was an ambitious undertaking. The work was done in the Chatham Dockyard, beginning in June 1939. All five of *Curacoa*'s six-inch guns were removed and were replaced by eight four-inch guns in four twin mounts. These were special high-angle/low-angle mountings that could bring the guns to bear against surface targets, but could also be elevated as high as seventy degrees, allowing them to engage enemy aircraft. In addition, a multiple pom-pom (four two-pounder guns) was mounted forward of the bridge, and a four-barreled, .50-caliber machine gun was installed to port and starboard of the forward funnel. (Later these machine guns were replaced with six twenty-millimeter Bofors guns.) The Air Defense Position, a lookout platform for directing the fire of the antiaircraft guns, was constructed at the base of the foremast, and the bridge structure was enlarged. Two high-angle director tow-ers were added as well, one atop the foremast, the other at the aft end of the superstructure. On January 1, 1940, the refit was complete, and *Curacoa* was placed back in commission and rejoined the fleet.

No sooner was she worked up than she was thrown into the fray. Assigned to the British naval force deployed to forestall a German invasion of Norway in April 1940, *Curacoa* spent barely a week in those cold northern waters. The Norwegian campaign was marked by a great deal of confusion and bumbling on both sides, as they attempted to thwart the strategies of their enemies. On the Germans' part, they had anticipated a token resistance at best, and the unexpectedly fierce opposition by the Norwegians, coupled with the appearance of British ships and troops, threw all of their plans into disarray, so that they were forced to improvise their scheme for conquering the country. As for the British, it appears that from the start they had no real strategic plan, so much of the efforts by the Royal Navy and Army were expended in responding to German initiatives. Many warships' captains on both sides were unhappy at having to take their ships into the narrow, confining fjords, where they had little room to maneuver and were subject to air attacks with little or no warning.

Curacoa fell victim to such an attack at dusk on April 24, 1940, when a Heinkel He-111 dropped three 250-pound bombs on her. Damage was serious, as power was knocked out, and the engines stopped. All of her director gear was also knocked out, making her useless as an antiaircraft ship. The superstructure had been torn open in several places, and casualties were severe—forty-five dead and thirty-six wounded. *Curacoa* was immediately ordered out of Norwegian waters and back to the fleet anchorage at Scapa Flow, where she arrived on April 26. Three days later she set out for the Chatham Dockyard for repairs—a voyage that required her to sail all the way around the British Isles instead of straight down the North Sea and into the English Channel, as the threat of German bombers in those waters was considered far too great to a ship in her crippled condition.

Repairs took five months, and when she returned to service in September 1940, *Curacoa* was assigned to escort duties in the North Sea and the waters around northern Scotland. Her role was to provide extra antiaircraft protection for both inbound and outbound convoys, as German aircraft based in Norway and the Low Countries posed a constant threat to Allied shipping. She would pick up the inbound convoys just west of Scapa Flow, then accompany them down as far south as Rosyth, where the convoys would disperse. Guarding the outbound convoys, she followed this route in reverse. It was repetitive duty and hardly exciting—between September 1940 and July 1942, she escorted some 169 convoys, but only 17 of them were ever attacked by the Luftwaffe. When the attacks came, though, they were swift and furious, and given *Curacoa's* previous experience with being bombed, none of the crew regretted it when the German aircraft were absent.

On August 1, 1942, *Curacoa* was transferred to the Western Approaches, the waters around the Western Isles of Scotland and the north coast of Ireland, to serve as an antiaircraft escort for convoys sailing to and from Gourock, Scotland. She had her first encounter with the *Queen Mary* a week later, as she met the giant liner near Bloody Foreland and escorted her into the Clyde. Four days later, she escorted the *Mary* back out as the liner returned to

New York. There were four more such meetings in the next eight weeks, as well as two similar encounters with the *Queen Elizabeth.*

Escorting either of the *Queens* wasn't an easy task. When they were inbound from New York to Gourock, the escorts first had to make their rendezvous with the liners north of Ireland, which was difficult enough. That particular section of the North Atlantic is famous—some would say notorious—for the unpredictability of its weather, as the relatively warm waters of the Gulf Stream meet the cold arctic currents flowing down from the Norwegian Sea. Fog, squalls, high wind, and heavy seas are normal conditions; good visibility is an exception rather than the rule. The liners had to continue the zigzags they had maintained all the way across the Atlantic and were not permitted to slacken speed. Consequently, the escort vessels had to fall in with them as best they could and adapt their movements to the big ships, searching the waters for U-boats and keeping a sharp lookout for enemy aircraft. For the destroyers, which could work some distance from the liners as they made their antisubmarine sweeps, this was no problem, but for the antiaircraft cruisers, it was a different story.

The antiaircraft cruisers were crucial for the protection of the *Queens*, especially in 1942, because neither of the *Queens* had much antiaircraft armament of their own mounted at the time, and German patrol planes and bombers were taking a heavy toll of shipping in the waters around Great Britain. The antiaircraft cruisers had to make up for that deficiency by staying fairly close to the *Queens* so that their guns could protect their charges. As long as the liner and the escorting cruiser coordinated their movements, the task was simple, though it was not exactly easy, requiring that the crew of each ship keep a careful eye on the movements of the other. Certainly it was a task that demanded the attention of a first-class officer in command on each bridge.

No one would have disputed the fact that Capt. John W. Boutwood was such an officer. He had taken command of *Curacoa* six weeks before her transfer to the Western Approaches, having previously been the commanding officer of the Royal Navy's Gunnery School in HMS *Pembroke.* Born in 1899, he joined the Royal Navy as a midshipman in September 1917; his first shipboard assignment was on the battlecruiser *Inflexible.* At the end of the Great War, Boutwood chose to continue his career in the navy and attended Cambridge University at Admiralty expense, then completed the long and difficult Gunnery Course at the Gunnery School in Chatham. The next two decades saw him rising regularly through the officers' ranks, serving as a gunnery officer aboard a succession of large and medium-size ships in the Atlantic, the Mediterranean, and the Far East. In October 1938 he was given his first command, a destroyer of eleven hundred tons, HMS *Whitley*. A year later he was appointed the "commander" (the Royal Navy term for "executive officer") of the battleship *Iron Duke* at Scapa Flow. In 1941 he was given command of the Gunnery School, where he remained until named the captain of HMS *Curacoa*. While no single command had marked him as an exceptional officer, that he was more than simply competent was demonstrated by his promotion to captain in early 1941, a rank not lightly bestowed in peacetime or war.

Boutwood was remembered as something of a martinet when it came to discipline, although the same officers and ratings who so described him were quick to point out that he was fair and never seemed to hold a grudge. His only real shortcoming in this area was that he often neglected to make clear the reasons for his disciplinary ways, which were for the safety of the ship and her crew, something that prewar regulars knew and understood but that reservists and wartime ratings often failed to comprehend. Once he reprimanded a sailor for putting his arm outside the gunwale of a ship's boat as it was motoring across the harbor. It may have seemed like a trivial offense, but Boutwood knew that the man risked a broken arm or worse if the boat suddenly slammed into the side of a ship or a mooring buoy. He did not bother to explain this to the offending seaman, which made Boutwood's concern appear as little more than petty meddling to the man.

On the other hand, he could be remarkably thoughtful. One seaman, Tom McMeekin, who was serving as Yeoman of Signals on a ship Boutwood commanded, recalled how one afternoon a rather prolonged exchange of signals caused him to miss a meal, and Boutwood invited McMeekin to share his lunch with him. Though Boutwood was never a popular captain—and to his credit, he never tried to be one—it was gestures like this that made him respected by his officers and crew. A handful of those who served with him had some grievance, real or imagined, against Boutwood and remembered him less than charitably, but they were very much in the minority.

There were some lingering doubts about his abilities as a shiphandler, though. Not long after taking command of *Curacoa*, Boutwood brought her hard alongside her dock in Belfast, badly scraping her paintwork and doing some minor damage. While no doubt he had to knock some rust off his seagoing skills after serving for more than two years as an instructor ashore, there is a lingering question about how familiar he had become with the way *Curacoa* handled by the time she had her fatal encounter with the *Queen Mary.*

The man on the bridge of the *Queen Mary* that day was Capt. Giles Gordon Illingworth. Like Boutwood, he took over his new command in June 1942, and like Boutwood, he had spent most of his adult life at sea, although being some ten years older, he had considerably more experience. Like many British Merchant Marine officers, he was a member of the Royal Naval Reserve, and during the First World War he had served aboard a cruiser, a dreadnought, several destroyers, and even a Q-ship, a heavily armed decoy designed to look like an innocent trawler. He spent most of 1917 and 1918 in antisubmarine duties, including several long stints aboard convoy escorts.

After the war, Illingworth went back to Cunard, where in the 1920s and 1930s he held a succession of commands. He was respected within the company as being a conscientious and careful officer, qualities that Cunard always placed a high value on. When the war broke out, he returned to the Royal Navy and was given command of the *Laconia,* a liner converted into a troopship that would eventually earn her own measure of notoriety a few years later. It has been said that Illingworth was not a popular captain with his crewmen and implied that this was somehow a reflection of his competence. Certainly he was disliked by the officers of the Royal Navy, although it is impossible to determine at this remove whether that animosity was due to the collision with *Curacoa* or predated it. No doubt some of it stems from the traditional rivalry—rarely friendly—that always existed between the Royal Navy and the British Merchant Marine. It is difficult to seriously question Illingworth's competence as a captain, since Cunard had entrusted him with the pride of their fleet—a responsibility compounded by the sheer number of lives she was carrying on each of her wartime crossings. It had been with as much truth as wit when, forty years earlier, Mark Twain summed up Cunard's attitude toward their captains when he observed: "The Cunard people would not take Noah as first mate until they had worked him through the lower grades and tried him for ten years or such matter. . . . It takes them about ten or fifteen years to manufacture a captain; but when they have him manufactured to suit at last they have full confidence in him." That standard had never changed.

Nevertheless, there *were* problems that came up between the escorts and their charges, and not all of them were minor. Boutwood had been particularly outspoken about what he regarded as shortcomings in the convoying system, and he wrote a strongly worded report to the Admiralty in August 1942.

He was highly critical of the signaling arrangements between the *Queen Mary* and *Curacoa,* and felt that the signalers aboard the liner were deficient. He also believed that those officers and crewmen manning the bridge aboard the *Mary* didn't pay sufficient attention to the movements or instructions of the cruiser. He went to some length to point out that by requiring her to maintain the same 28.5-knot speed she had held while crossing the Atlantic, no matter how hard the cruiser tried, eventually she would be left behind by the ship she was meant to protect. Even when following a zigzag course, the *Queen Mary's* rate of advance was still 26.5 knots, a full 1.5 knots better than *Curacoa* could muster, as her days of twenty-nine-knot top speeds were long past. Whether he thought through some of the other implications of this speed differential is not known—he did not address them in his report.

Boutwood was right in his assertion that communication between the *Queen Mary* and *Curacoa* left much to be desired; at one point it took two hours to pass a message from *Curacoa* to the *Queen Mary* by signal lamp. And certainly poor communication was the major factor in the looming tragedy—but it was a communication problem of a different kind that doomed the little cruiser. Inexplicably, both Boutwood and Illingworth failed to pass critical information to each other. Both men made certain assumptions about their own ships and each other's that, had they made those assumptions clear to one another, might have averted the tragedy that was about to unfold.

Because the *Queen Mary* had used the Number 8 Zigzag pattern on her previous approaches to the Western Isles, Illingworth apparently assumed that Boutwood, aboard the *Curacoa,* knew that she was following it this time. In point of fact, Boutwood *did not* know this, and why Illingworth never thought to inform him just to be certain has never been explained. Admittedly, when the two captains had met in August, Illingworth mentioned to Boutwood that he preferred the Number 8 pattern, as it suited the *Queen Mary's* handling characteristics very well, and that conversation may have been the basis for Illingworth's assumption. But even then, Illingworth should have informed *Curacoa* what leg of the zigzag the *Queen Mary* was on, allowing the cruiser's officers to plot her future movements and plan their own accordingly. Boutwood's failure to inquire what pattern the *Mary* had adopted, or what leg of the zigzag she was on, is just as difficult to understand.

Equally baffling is why the two commanders never conferred about their interpretations of the "Rules of the Road," specifically concerning which ship should be regarded as the overtaking vessel for determining which would have the right-of-way. This was no trivial consideration, since the handling characteristics of the two ships—the *Queen Mary* being big, ponderous, and clumsy, slow to answer her helm compared with the light and nimble *Curacoa*—differed so vastly that in the event of an emergency situation such as an air attack or a U-boat threat that might require swift and violent maneuvering by *Curacoa,* it would be vitally important for each captain to know what was expected of his ship as well as the other.

Even in the ordinary maneuvering that *Curacoa* undertook in performing her escort duties, the question of right of way was important. As the *Queen Mary* moved back and forth on the various legs of her zigzag, *Curacoa* was required to move to a station where her guns could best protect the liner. This sometimes meant the cruiser had to move back and forth from one side of the *Mary* to the other, sometimes across her bow, sometimes across her stern. This presented the problem of which ship would have to give way to the other should their courses bring them uncomfortably close to one another.

As it was, Illingworth assumed that because the *Queen Mary* was the convoy, and that the standard practice in the North Atlantic was to give the convoy the right-of-way, that practice would be followed by Boutwood's escort squadron. In the Atlantic, the escort vessels, which were often twice as fast as the slow and ponderous merchantmen they shepherded, were free to dart in and out among the ships in the convoy, but it was their responsibility to keep clear and give way to the merchantmen, which always had the right-of-way. Even though the *Mary* never crossed with an escort, and was actually faster than the escorting ships that had rendezvoused with her, Illingworth acted on the belief that the same practice applied to his ship and her escorts.

Boutwood, on the other hand, saw the situation in exactly the opposite terms. The "Rules of the Road" were very specific about which ship had to give way when two were approaching one another or steaming on parallel courses at different speeds: The faster ship always had to give way to the slower vessel, regardless of size or circumstance. That the *Queen Mary* was decidedly faster than *Curacoa* Boutwood was very much aware. Consequently, he believed that his ship had the right-of-way in any situation where *Curacoa* or the *Queen Mary* might have to give way to the other.

Thus both captains believed they had the right-of-way, each thinking the other ship was obliged to keep well clear of their own. It was a situation rife with disaster. It would take exactly five hours and twelve minutes for that disaster to come about.

So it was that the morning of October 2, 1942, found HMS *Curacoa*, accompanied by the destroyers *Bulldog, Skate, Saladin, Bramham, Cowdray,* and *Blyskawica*—this last being a Polish ship with a fearsome combat record—steaming steadily to the west roughly forty miles off the north coast of Ireland, waiting to make their rendezvous with the *Queen Mary*. It had been a bit of a rough crossing, if not particularly uncomfortable, and the *Mary* was two hours behind schedule as a consequence. The liner was finally sighted at 9:00 A.M., and the destroyers quickly deployed ahead of her to begin their sonar sweeps, looking for German submarines. *Curacoa* turned around and began to work up to her maximum speed of twenty-five knots, and by 10:00 A.M. she had taken up what Captain Boutwood felt was a satisfactory position just over five miles ahead of the *Queen Mary*.

Nobody knew it at the time, but a situation was taking shape that was leading both the *Queen Mary* and *Curacoa* into danger. The cruiser could do a maximum of only 25 knots, but the liner's rate of advance was still an inexorable 26.5 knots: In four hours the *Queen Mary* would overtake *Curacoa*, and Captain Boutwood lacked the information that would let him know exactly where the liner would be when that happened. As time passed and the ships began to draw abreast of each other, Boutwood would not know when the *Mary* was due to change course, or what that change would be. If his ship was in the wrong place when that happened, there might not be time or room enough to get out of the way. . . .

Up on the bridge of the *Queen Mary,* eighty feet above the water, the situation seemed well in hand. The escorts made their rendezvous at the right place and the right time, and visibility was good. Every few minutes, the clock chimed to remind the helmsman of another course change. The only possible cause for concern was that the heavy seas were causing the bow to yaw back and forth as ship drove on, which required the helmsman to pay particular attention to those course changes to make certain that the *Queen Mary* settled on the proper course. The yawing also made it difficult for observers on either ship to be certain when the other vessel was actually turning or when it was just being pushed about by the sea.

At noon the watch changed. The Junior First Officer, Stanley Wright, handed over to the Senior First Officer, Noel Robinson. Wright informed Robinson of the *Mary's* course and speed, the zigzag pattern she was following, what leg she was on, and the position of the cruiser—all the usual details of a formal exchange of watch-keeping duties. At this point, *Curacoa* was just off the liner's starboard bow, just over five cables distant (a cable is a nautical unit of measurement equal to roughly two hundred yards), maintaining a course parallel to the *Queen Mary*'s base course.

Joining Robinson on the bridge was the Third Officer, Albert Hewitt, who was kept busy in the charthouse plotting the liner's course and position, and the Junior Third Officer, William Heighway, who was taking sun sightings for Hewitt. Quartermaster John Lockhart was at the helm in the wheelhouse. As required, each time the zigzag clock chimed, Lockhart would inform Robinson that a course change was due and wait for Robinson's confirmation before putting the wheel over. At 12:30 *Curacoa* signaled, "I AM DOING MY BEST SPEED 25 KNOTS ON COURSE 108. WHEN YOU ARE AHEAD I WILL EDGE IN ASTERN OF YOU." Robinson passed this message on to Captain Illingworth, who was in the chartroom.

Just after that signal was sent, Captain Boutwood left *Curacoa*'s bridge and went below to his quarters to have an early lunch. He returned to the bridge at 1:00, noticing immediately that though the two ships' base courses were supposed to be parallel, on the legs where the zigzag took the *Queen Mary* away from the cruiser the distance between them kept growing. He had no way of knowing—and no one knew it on the *Queen Mary* at the time—that the liner's compass was off by 2 degrees: What was supposed to be a course of 108 degrees was actually 106. Trying to bring the cruiser closer to the *Queen Mary*, Boutwood ordered *Curacoa*'s course changed, first to 105 degrees, then to 100 degrees, cutting across the liner's bow.

At the same moment that Boutwood was giving the new course to his helmsman, the zigzag clock in the *Queen Mary*'s wheelhouse chimed. It was 1:32, and Quartermaster Lockhart requested permission to change course from Senior First Officer Robinson—this time a fifty-degree turn to port. Robinson gave him the go-ahead, but kept a close eye on the cruiser. The liner had just cut across *Curacoa*'s wake as the cruiser had passed from starboard of the *Queen Mary* to a position off her port bow. She was less than four cables away, and Robinson was uncomfortable—he thought that she was much too close to the liner. Now, as Lockhart spun the wheel and the *Queen Mary* began to swing to port, it was apparent that the liner was overtaking *Curacoa*. Robinson, fearing running up onto the cruiser's stern, told Lockhart to hold the ship steady when she was only halfway through her turn; he intended to complete the course change when he judged *Curacoa* to be safely clear.

At this moment, Wright reappeared to allow Robinson to go get a quick lunch. Robinson informed him that the *Mary* was on the fifty-degree port leg of the zigzag, but that he had halted the turn until the cruiser got clear. With that, Robinson went below. Wright took a look at the cruiser and decided that there was enough room for the *Mary* to finish her turn, and informed Lockhart accordingly. No sooner had she completed it than Wright saw that *Curacoa* was still off on the *Mary's* port bow, and preparing to cut in front of the liner again. Deciding that the cruiser was too close, he suddenly told Lockhart, "Hard a-starboard!" intending to open up some sea room between the liner and the cruiser, and allow the cruiser to draw away before the *Queen Mary* resumed her zigzag.

When Captain Illingworth heard Wright call out, "Hard a-starboard!" he instantly came out of the chartroom to see what the urgency was. Wright quickly explained what had happened and what he planned; Illingworth went out on the port bridge wing and took a look for himself. Though the cruiser was close, she was not as close as his First Officers believed her to be—at least, not in his opinion. There seemed to be enough room behind *Curacoa's* stern for the *Mary* to pass by safely. Coming back into the bridge, he told Wright, "That's all right. Put your helm amidships and come back on the port leg [of the zigzag]." Wright promptly passed the order to Lockhart, who brought the ship around onto her proper course.

Illingworth and Wright talked for a few minutes about ship's business, then Illingworth went back to his interrupted lunch. As he did so, he reassured Wright about *Curacoa*: "You needn't worry about her. These fellows know all about escorting. He will keep out of your way." Illingworth was very confident of that: After all, that was the way it was done in the North Atlantic convoys. But he had never confirmed that with Captain Boutwood, and a tragic price was about to paid for that failure.

Two opposing concerns were determining how Boutwood was maneuvering his ship. The first was that *Curacoa's* primary responsibility was to protect the *Queen Mary* from air attack, and to do that she had to stay relatively close to the liner. The other was that the cruiser was slower than the ship she was supposed to be escorting. This made keeping station with the *Queen Mary* not only difficult, but dangerous as well. Still, the tactics Boutwood devised as a compromise seemed to be working. As the liner gradually overtook the cruiser, she remain under *Curacoa's* guns, and as she passed the cruiser and pulled away from her, she would be drawing closer to the screen of destroyers and their protective antiaircraft umbrella.

At the same moment that Captain Illingworth was reassuring his First Officer that the cruiser would keep well clear of the *Queen Mary*, Captain Boutwood was standing on *Curacoa*'s bridge, gazing at the liner looming ever larger off his port quarter, slowly overtaking his ship, confident that as the slower vessel, *Curacoa* would be given the right-of-way, as outlined in the "Rules of the Road." He had lookouts posted in the Air Defense Platform on the mainmast above his head, and there is every reason to believe his officers were taking bearings and plotting the *Queen Mary*'s movements, though how much of this information they actually passed to Boutwood remains unclear. Although the two ships had closed until they were less than three cables apart, Boutwood was satisfied enough with the situation to be turning his attention to coordinating the *Queen Mary*'s arrival in the Firth of Clyde, where his escort responsibilities would end. At 1:55 he sent a signal to the *Queen Mary* asking, "PLEASE GIVE ME YOUR ESTIMATED TIME OF ARRIVAL AT TOWARD POINT."

At 2:00, in the wheelhouse of the *Queen Mary*, Q. M. John Leydon relieved Quartermaster Lockhart at the helm. No sooner had he done so than the wheelhouse clock chimed, indicating that it was time for a twenty-five-degree turn to starboard. Wright confirmed the course change, and the *Mary*'s bow began to swing to the right.

Boutwood watched the liner's bow begin to move, although given how much both ships had been yawing back and forth in the heavy seas, it was not immediately clear that she was actually making a course change. There appears to have suddenly been some confusion on the bridge of *Curacoa*, as Lt. Tony Johnson, her navigating officer, who was responsible for keeping track of the liner's position as well as that of his own ship, seemed to be unsure of the *Queen Mary*'s intentions. Noting the movement of the liner's bow, he commented to Captain Boutwood, "I think she's turning now—or it another yaw?"

At 2:04 the *Mary*'s wheelhouse clock chimed once more, and Quarter-master Leydon called out to Wright for permission to change course. This one was a twenty-five-degree swing to starboard. Wright, noticing that the *Curacoa* was now only a little more than two cables away, was disturbed by her proximity and the fact that this turn would be *toward* the cruiser, but reassured by his captain's words that "he will keep out of your way," he told Leydon to go ahead and execute the turn. A few minutes later, Robinson reappeared on the bridge, and Wright quickly handed over the watch, disappearing into the chartroom to answer a summons from Captain Illingworth.

The relief seems to have been somewhat perfunctory, for neither Robinson nor Wright later recalled mentioning anything to each other about the closeness of the cruiser. Robinson quickly took stock of the situation, noting that the *Queen Mary* was now closing rapidly on *Curacoa,* and that she was now less than two cables distant from the liner—dangerously close. Junior Third Officer Heighway reminded Robinson of Captain Illingworth's instruction that all legs of the zigzag be completed in full, but Robinson still ordered Leydon to "port a little," hoping to open up some room between the two ships. He was concerned, but the situation didn't appear to have gotten out of hand yet: Robinson, like Illingworth, was convinced that the cruiser would give way if the two ships got too close.

Robinson stepped into the wheelhouse a few moments later to satisfy himself that the *Queen Mary* had resumed her proper course, then returned to the bridge to look for the cruiser. What he saw was terrifying: She was so close now that when she rolled he could see down her funnels. The two ships were still closing. There was less than a cable between them.

Turning toward the wheelhouse, Robinson yelled, "Hard a-port!" and Leydon spun the wheel as fast as he could, but the sheer bulk of the *Queen Mary* meant that she would turn too late. A lifetime too late. More than three hundred lifetimes too late.

The officers and crewmen on *Curacoa's* bridge and upper works were admiring the *Queen Mary.* So was a gathering crowd of seamen on the cruiser's quarterdeck. Rarely had they been this close to the great liner, and even in her dull wartime gray, she made for an impressive sight. As Captain Boutwood watched her, he was still wondering if she was yawing again or turning to starboard. Had he known that she was following Number 8 Zigzag pattern and apprised himself of which leg she was on, he would have known that she was due to make a fifty-degree turn to port momentarily. Just to be safe, he ordered, "Starboard 15," intending to put some extra distance between his ship and the *Mary.* Telegraphist Allin Martin, a radio operator on the cruiser's lower bridge, later recalled how quickly the impressive visage of the liner turned nightmarish:

> The upper bridge speaking tube clanged and my "oppo" [opposite number–partner] indicated that if any camera was to hand a particularly good view of the *Queen Mary* was

available. Unclipping the bulkhead door, I stepped outside, where, to my horror, I saw the enormous bulk of the *Queen Mary* bearing down on our port quarter at about fifty yards range. Her huge white bow wave seemed as tall as a house and it seemed inevitable that we were within seconds of being torn apart. I dived for my lifebelt.

Like Robinson's order to Leydon on the *Queen Mary's* bridge, Boutwood's "Starboard 15" was just too late. Too much time would have to pass before the cruiser could begin to respond, and time had run out. It was 2:12 P.M.

It was over in barely a second. The *Queen Mary* struck *Curacoa* 140 to 150 feet forward of her stern, at an angle somewhere between twenty and forty degrees. Impacted by the incredible momentum of eighty-one thousand tons of steel moving at 28.5 knots, the cruiser never stood a chance. The liner knifed through the belt of three-inch-thick armor as if it were not there; split the cruiser's hull wide open from side to side; crushed through decks, bulkheads, machinery, and crewmen as if they were little more than tissue paper; then shunted the two halves of the ship aside and continued to thunder on, her speed not abated a whit.

The impact rolled *Curacoa* over on her starboard side so far that it seemed she would turn turtle. The crash of the collision was instantly followed by the screech of tearing metal and the scream of escaping steam, as every steam line in the ship gave way, and a huge cloud of vapor and smoke surrounded her. The stern section did roll over completely, the cruiser's two bronze propellors spinning lazily as that half of the ship quickly sank. The forward part righted itself momentarily, causing Captain Boutwood to hope for an instant or two that he might somehow save his ship.

On board the *Queen Mary,* Captain Illingworth and Junior First Officer Wright were working out an answer to the cruiser's query about the liner's estimated time of arrival at Toward Point when they felt a bump. Illingworth's first thought was that the ship had been bombed. Rushing to the wheelhouse, he asked the quartermaster, "Was that a bomb?"

"No, Captain," Leydon replied, "we hit the cruiser."

Below decks and in the engine room, the collision was felt as hardly more than a bump, as if the *Mary* were butting through a large wave. On deck it was a different story, though, as hundreds of American soldiers watched in horrified fascination as the *Queen Mary* cut the cruiser in two. Many of the

GIs began tossing their own lifebelts into the water, along with any life rafts that were handy, but they had only seconds to react as the *Mary* thundered on, rapidly leaving *Curacoa's* wreck in her wake.

The reaction of Philip Levin, an American sergeant, was typical of many of GIs aboard the liner:

> I was in the office on the main deck at the time and felt only the slightest rattle and vibration. Actually it seemed quite normal. But word of the collision spread quickly like wildfire through the ship. I raced to the open upper decks and looked aft to see the two halves of the *Curacoa* drifting in our wake and then rather quickly sinking. . . . The *Mary* simply continued, uninterrupted and at relatively high speed.

One of the *Queen Mary's* crewmen, A. W. Masson, recorded his observations in his diary:

> The cruiser took station ahead of us . . . at 2:10 p.m. when passing from starboard to port we rammed and sank her. She sank in less than ten minutes. Georgie Reed and I were just leaving the weather deck, when we felt the bump (which incidentally was very slight). We rushed out on deck, and I was just in time to see the cruiser's quarterdeck and after turret passing down our starboard side. It was covered in oil and there was no one to be seen. I rushed aft and saw both parts of the cruiser, her stern sticking up, looking for all the world like the *Indefatigable* at Jutland! The forepart of the ship was at a distance to the right. The cruiser had been rammed just aft of the after funnel. It was covered in a heavy pall of smoke and steam, then slowly it sank by the bows, then it reared its bow perpendicular—and with a little water foaming round her, she quickly sank. I did not notice what happened to the afterpart. Much later two of the escorts went racing toward the scene. We did not slacken speed at the time of the accident but later on we cut down to about 15 knots.

Back up on the bridge, Captain Illingworth could see both halves of the cruiser falling quickly astern. There was nothing he could do for her at this point: His first and overriding responsibility was the safety of the *Queen Mary* and the more than eleven thousand lives aboard her. Before anything else was done, he had to determine how badly the collision had damaged his own ship.

Staff Captain Harry Grattidge had been asleep in his day cabin when the collision occurred. The jolt woke him up. He grabbed his duffle coat and helmet, and ran up to the bridge. He got there just in time to watch what was left of *Curacoa* sink.

Arriving at almost that same moment was a damage report from the Bosun. The stem of the ship had been crushed somewhat, and she was making water, but the situation was not dangerous. Wanting to be sure of this, Illingworth sent Grattidge below to inspect the damage, then ordered the liner's speed reduced to ten knots. When Grattidge reached the forepeak, he found the situation much as the Bosun had described it:

> The speed was still on the ship when I reached the forepeak. By the light of a torch I could see the water racing in and out of the forepeak, a great column of it forming a kind of cushion from the collision bulkhead, the watertight reinforced steel wall that rises from the very bottom of the ship to the main deck. If that bulkhead were weakened I did not like to think of the *Mary*'s chances. I sweated through my silent inspection. But finally, not a crack. Not a break. I turned to the Bosun and the carpenter: "Get every length of wood you can find, Bosun. Get it down here and strengthen that collision bulkhead as much as you possibly can. I'll report to the Captain." . . . I was sick at what we had done, yet I marveled, too, at the strange and terrible impregnability of the *Queen Mary.* It came home to me that she had no equal anywhere in the Atlantic, perhaps not anywhere in the world.

Reassured of the *Mary*'s safety by Grattidge's report, Illingworth now had to make what was probably the most agonizing decision in his life. Really, the decision was out of his hands: His orders were explicit and left no room for interpretation. The *Queen Mary* was not to stop, for any reason, once she had left New York until she reached Gourock. No true seaman will willingly leave another to die in the water, but Illingworth had to put the safety of his ship and the 11,000 men aboard her ahead of the 439 men of the *Curacoa*'s crew; the good of the many had to outweigh the good of the few. He ordered the escorting destroyers to turn around and pick up any survivors they could find, then abandoned the zigzag and increased speed to thirteen knots, bound for Gourock.

The commander of HMS *Bulldog* gave the four older, slower destroyers, *Saladin, Skate, Bramham,* and *Cowdray,* the task of rescuing any they could of the *Curacoa's* crew, while his ship and the Polish destroyer *Blyskawica* continued to escort the *Mary.* It would take more than two hours for the four little ships to reach the site of the collision and begin plucking from the water the fortunate few who survived.

Lt. Patrick Holmes was the Air Defence Officer aboard the *Curacoa,* and his action station was in the Air Defence Position (ADP) on the cruiser's mainmast. He had an unparalleled view of the unfolding tragedy as the *Queen Mary* bore down on his ship, and his recollections are vivid, sometimes frightening:

> It was thrilling to watch the "grey ghost" as the *Queen Mary* was nicknamed because of her wartime camouflage. She gained on us slowly, sometimes over a mile-and-a-half away on our port quarter, and at other times more or less dead astern on the starboard leg of her zigzag. There is no finer sight in the world than a great passenger ship at full speed in a heavy sea, if the passengers were close-packed American troops—over ten thousand of them.
>
> By 2 p.m. she was nearly level with us about a mile away on our port side and steaming parallel with us. Then she turned slowly towards us and that turn of 25 degrees was at first misinterpreted on our bridge as merely a yaw to starboard. We got a magnificent view of her as she approached— her bow wave gleaming in a slant of sunlight, her decks crowded with GIs, wisps of smoke streaming from her three funnels.
>
> Suddenly my admiration turned to fear, and looking over my right shoulder down to our bridge I saw the captain take over the conning of the ship. I saw him speak down the voicepipe to the helmsman below, look back at the *Queen Mary* and speak again.
>
> By now the sharp bows of the *Queen* were heading directly at us in the ADP and a few seconds before she crashed through a hundred feet abaft us I shouted "Hang

on!" But even so two of the lookouts disappeared over our starboard side as we were knocked over 70 degrees or more. The noise of escaping steam from severed steam pipes was deafening. The forepart of the ship slowly returned to nearly upright. As I looked astern I saw what I thought at the time was a U-boat sinking, until I realized it was our own stern about half a mile away.

Captain Boutwood's illusions about saving his ship were quickly dispelled, as the forward half of *Curacoa* began settling rapidly. He shouted out, "Abandon ship!" although it was doubtful that anyone who was not standing next to him heard the order over the noise of the ruptured steam lines. In any case, it was unnecessary: Men all over the wreck began diving into the water, as it was clear that what was left of *Curacoa* was not going to stay afloat long. Telegraphist Martin scrambled out of his ruined radio room and, along with Leading Signalman Donald Eaton, dashed toward the stern. Suddenly the two men were confronted by the fact that the stern wasn't there—the ship ended abruptly at the after funnel. Martin hesitated only a few seconds before diving into the water. Eaton balked at jumping, and by the time Martin came to the surface, he had been swept some distance from the wreck and never saw Eaton again.

Great gouts of thick, black fuel oil from the cruiser's ruptured fuel tanks began floating to the surface, coating anything and everything they came into contact with. Wooden boxes, furniture, oil drums, loose equipment all began bobbing up on the water, just the sort of debris that hundreds of men struggling to stay afloat could have used in their bid for survival—there had been no time to launch any of *Curacoa*'s lifeboats, and only a few Carley rafts floated free of the ship. But the oil made the debris slick and slippery, and the men had trouble holding on. A few "flotanets"—heavy rope mesh supported by cork floats—were spread out on the sea, but often the oil made even them too difficult to keep a grip on.

Kenneth Clarkson was one of the lucky ones able to hang on to a flotanet. He had been asleep in the Stokers' Mess at the time of the collision, and when he tried to make his way to his duty station in the after boiler room, he was met by a rising flood of water in one of the ship's passageways. Fighting to stay ahead of the incoming sea, he barely made it to the upper deck before he was washed off the ship. After a while he found the flotanet, got a good grip on it, and waited, hoping some ship would come to the rescue.

William "Joe" Murray was another who found a flotanet and was able to hang on. Like Clarkson, he had been asleep on the mess deck when the *Queen Mary* struck *Curacoa*. Quickly putting on his lifejacket, he inflated it as he made his way topside, then slid down the ship's side into the water. Turning to watch the wreck of *Curacoa,* he saw one of the ship's lieutenants—he couldn't tell who it was—fall into the sea from one of the cruiser's gun positions, and then caught a momentary glimpse of another officer, this one a sublieutenant, struggling to stay afloat. Murray lost sight of both of them seconds later; neither of the officers survived.

In fact the only officers who survived the collision were Captain Boutwood and Lieutenant Holmes. Holmes had managed to stay in the Air Defence Position as *Curacoa* fell over onto her starboard side when she was struck, then righted herself moments later. After seeing that all the remaining lookouts had left the position, he scrambled down the ladder to the bridge, then made his way to the main deck. He and his best friend, Lt. John Maxwell, jumped into the sea together, but Holmes never saw Maxwell again. He always believed Maxwell went back to the wreck to see if there were any more crewmen left behind, and was trapped when it went under. One officer who definitely stayed behind to make sure as many of his men as possible got off the ship was the Engineer, Cmdr. Douglas Robertson. But Robertson cut it too close himself and was taken down by the cruiser as she sank.

Holmes swam away from the rapidly sinking ship, then turned to watch *Curacoa's* last minutes. Telegraphist Martin, who was nearby, did the same. They watched as the bow reared skyward, standing almost vertically, then began sliding downward into the sea. As water rushed into the hull, it forced air pockets out of portholes and hatches, creating a deep, almost organlike moan as the ship slid under. One particularly large air pocket split the foredeck open with almost explosive violence, then the bow disappeared. *Curacoa* was gone; it was 2:24.

Captain Boutwood had tried to save his ship, but there was nothing that could be done. He stayed aboard *Curacoa* until he saw that as many men had gotten off the bridge as possible after he gave the order to abandon ship. When the bridge went under, he floated off.

Fred Dennis had been one of the lookouts in the Air Defence Position with Holmes and was able to scramble down from the platform onto the bridge. He went over the starboard side of the ship and into the water, where he found a wooden box floating by. For the next two hours, he and a shipmate clung to the box, until the destroyers appeared and began picking up the survivors. Dennis Hearn, a signalman, was fortunate enough to find one of the Carley rafts that had floated free, and shared it with three other crewmen as they waited to be rescued. Geoffrey Carter, who had been on the bridge, was another survivor who was able to reach one of the Carley rafts.

So was Sgt. Sid Dobbs of the Royal Marines. The Marine detachment aboard *Curacoa* was almost wiped out: Twenty-eight out of thirty of them died, including their Captain, John Cole, and their senior sergeant, Edward White. The only other Marine who survived was twenty-one-year old Eric Bower, who came within inches of being trapped below decks by the rising water as the ship started to sink.

Exactly how many men were able to get off the sinking *Curacoa* before she went under has never been determined—it may have been as many as two hundred. But scores of men were trapped below, and either died in the collision or else were taken down with the ship. Only one crewman from either engine room survived. No one from the severed stern section survived. Without a doubt, most of the men who had gathered on the quarterdeck to watch the *Queen Mary* were crushed in the collision, and the stern section sank too quickly for anyone else to escape. What survivors there were clung grimly to their Carley rafts, flotanets, or whatever bits of debris and wreckage they had, waiting anxiously for a rescue that they could only pray was coming.

On the bridge of the Queen Mary, Captain Illingworth knew that he had done all he could for whatever survivors there were from Curacoa by ordering the destroyers to pick them up. Now came the unappealing task of informing the Admiralty of what had just happened. At 2:20 he sent a signal to Whitehall: "HMS Curacoa RAMMED AND SUNK BY Queen Mary IN POSITION 55.50N 08.38W. Queen Mary DAMAGED FORWARD. SPEED TEN KNOTS." A few minutes later, he flashed to Bulldog by Aldis lamp: "IT WOULD APPEAR THAT Curacoa ATTEMPTED TO CROSS MY BOWS WHEN COLLISION OCCURRED. AM REDUCING SPEED TO ASCERTAIN EXTENT OF DAMAGE AND HAVE CEASED ZIGZAG. WILL KEEP INFORMED." It was shortly after that that Illingworth received Grattidge's report that the collision bulkhead was holding, and ordered the Queen Mary's speed increased to thirteen knots. Within a few hours she was steaming up the Clyde and tying up at Gourock.

It was almost two and a half hours after the collision that the destroyers *Skate, Bramham, Cowdray,* and *Saladin* reached the survivors. Intensive searching by the ship's whaleboats in the heavy swell discovered the clusters of survivors clinging to scattered flotanets and Carley rafts, as well as the occasional individual floating by himself. Captain Boutwood was one of the latter, pulled only half-conscious from the water by *Bramham's* whaleboat. As quickly as possible, *Curacoa's* surviving crewmen were brought aboard the rescuing destroyers and given medical attention where necessary, followed by a change of warm clothing and a quick tot of rum, the Royal Navy's cure-all for four hundred years. The captains of all four destroyers quickly began taking names and preparing a muster of what was left of *Curacoa's* complement of officers and ratings.

Of the 439 men of *Curacoa's* crew, only 101 were saved. No one would ever know how many went down with the ship, though doubtless scores died in the collision itself, and many more were lost to the cold of the sea or washed off into the encroaching darkness, beyond the vision of the searching destroyers. Of the 338 who died, the bodies of 21 eventually washed ashore, either on the Isle of Skye or the Scottish coast. Two cemeteries on Skye—one at Portree, the other at Strath—and one on the mainland at Arisaig hold all the recovered remains of the lost crewmen of the cruiser *Curacoa*. The sea held on to the rest.

The news of the collision and the sinking was suppressed in Great Britain until the war was over. In June 1945 a formal Court of Inquiry was convened to determine responsibility for the disaster, as the Admiralty and Cunard each held the other to blame. The hearings lasted for eighteen months, and the presiding officer, Justice Sir Gonne St. Clair Pilcher, eventually ruled that the *Queen Mary* was free from any blame in the incident, and that the collision was due entirely to negligent navigation on the part of the captain and officers of the cruiser *Curacoa.* The Admiralty appealed the decision, and eventually the case went before the House of Lords for final adjudication. In the end, their lordships revised the findings of the inquiry and determined that the blame for the disaster should be apportioned two-thirds to the cruiser, one-third to the liner. Lawsuits against Cunard by families of the crewmen lost aboard *Curacoa* dragged on for another five years.

But something seems wrong in allowing attorneys and judges to have the last word on the *Queen Mary's* royal tragedy. Both Captain Boutwood and Captain Illingworth were good officers; under different circumstances, their oversights and errors would have been minor annoyances, not the causes of a disaster. The gulf between the abstractions of a warm, dry, quiet courtroom in peacetime and the realities of the bridge of a warship on the high seas in wartime is almost beyond imagination. The judgment of Boutwood's and Illingworth's peers is perhaps more fair and more important than the opinions of any barristers or judges. The only other surviving officer of *Curacoa*'s crew, Lt. Patrick Holmes, rendered what is probably the most honest assessment of how the two men should be judged. In his account of the disaster, *Queen Mary and the Cruiser*, he wrote: "The terrible responsibility was, of course, in the final count, that of the two captains. One went on to be knighted and become commodore of the Cunard Line, the other to win the DSO [Distinguished Service Order] and command minesweepers in the Mediterranean. Both men had a heavy burden of grief to bear for the rest of their lives."

CHAPTER EIGHT

Life Aboard a Troopship

Troopin', troopin', give another cheer—
'Ere's to English women an' a quart of English beer.
                              —Rudyard Kipling

THE PHRASE "CONVERTED TO A TROOPSHIP" IS SOMEWHAT DECEPTIVE. IT conveys none of the complexity involved in the work that was undertaken, to say nothing of the painstaking planning that was done before the work began. Nor does it hint of the meticulous organization that had to be implemented once the conversion work was complete, so that the ship could function properly and actually meet the needs of the troops it was meant to carry.

Before any work could begin, the ship in question had to be surveyed. In nautical parlance, "surveying" means inspecting a ship for the soundness of its structure, the condition of its machinery, its general seaworthiness, and its habitability. Ships with structural defects, unreliable engines, or spaces below decks with little or no ventilation were as much a threat to the troops they might carry as an enemy warship would have been.

Conversion required more than just setting up several thousand bunks and hammocks throughout the ship. Not only did arrangements for the troops' sleeping quarters have to be made, which was the most obvious part of the conversion process, but the extent of the facilities required for their hygiene—toilets and showers, certainly, laundries in some circumstances— had be calculated and space found for their installation, and the capacity of the ship's freshwater supply augmented or increased to handle the additional demand. Likewise with feeding the troops: Shipboard galleys had to be able to produce enough meals to feed the troops aboard the ship at least twice a day, and space was needed for the men to be able to sit down and eat their meals.

Even after all of these determinations were made, and the ship's facilities modified to meet the requirements, the job was not over. Several thousand men could not all shower at once, or eat at once, or take a stroll on the deck at once. A methodical routine of access to the ship's facilities, as well as the mess halls, had to be worked out. In order to prevent the men from getting lost below decks, a system of coordinating and directing their movements had to be established. It was all a very complex and time-consuming process, even under the best of circumstances. Under the pressure of wartime exigencies, that such an undertaking was attempted, let alone accomplished successfully, is nothing short of astonishing.

With the *Queen Mary* and the *Queen Elizabeth,* that is exactly what happened. Working round the clock in the Boston Navy Yard, U.S. Navy surveyors and architects worked with the builders' drawings of the two ships, as well as taking thousands of measurements of their own, to determine which spaces were to be utilized for berthing, where extra toilet facilities would be located, and how the mess halls should be set up for feeding the troops. Often there was no time for detailed drawings to be prepared, and sometimes there was no need: When the work to be done was relatively straightforward, markings and measurements were chalked on the decks for construction crews to follow when they came on board a few days later.

In one significant aspect, the conversion work on the *Queen Elizabeth* was a simpler job than it was on the *Queen Mary.* The absence of many of her interior furnishings and much of her decor meant that greater use could be made of her large public rooms, and modifications were considerably simpler to those decks that were given over to staterooms. While carpets could be rolled up and furniture removed from the *Queen Mary,* removing fixtures and furnishings from many of her public rooms wasn't feasible, and the architects overseeing the conversion work simply had to adapt and make do. This resulted in some rather startling incongruities, such as a pharmacy housed in the Tourist-Class cocktail bar on the main deck, complete with bar, barstools, and brass footrail, with pharmaceuticals lining the shelves behind the bar that had been designed for the finest brands of whiskey and spirits. The installation of the bunks created some lasting images of their own. Soldiers who sailed aboard the *Queens* later likened the appearance of some of the larger public rooms, with their rows upon rows of standee bunks, to the shelves of a supermarket.

Because much of the work already done by the Australian shipwrights at the Cockatoo Yard in Sydney on both *Queens* anticipated the American requirements, it took less than two weeks for all of the additional bunks, latrines, and storerooms to be installed and finished. In a real sense, that was the easy part. While it is true that together the *Queen Mary* and *Queen Elizabeth* moved an entire army from America to Britain, what is not always appreciated is that it took another army—or at least its numerical equivalent—to make it happen.

Every convoy, every troop movement that crossed the Atlantic had to be coordinated with every other Allied troop movement and all other Allied shipping in order to prevent bottlenecks and minimize confusion at both the port of departure and the port of arrival. The overall responsibility for this lay with the British Admiralty, working through its Trade Division, which had ultimate charge over all British-flagged merchantmen, regardless of which country exercised local control; the Operational Intelligence Center, which kept tabs on the movements of German U-boats and surface ships; and the Naval Control Service, which kept track of all non-British shipping. Escort assignments on both sides of the Atlantic had to be worked out, with the British Home Fleet and the Western Approaches Command in British waters, and the U.S. Navy's Atlantic Fleet and the Royal Canadian Navy in American waters. Courses and speeds, as well as rendezvous points and times, had to be determined. On both sides of the Atlantic, road-transport services, airlines, railways, docks, and shipyards all had to be coordinated to make sure that the *Queens* sailed on time.

In Great Britain, sufficient motor transport had to be arranged to take the troops away from the docks and to a railway station as soon as they left the ship, where a waiting train would take them to whatever locale in Britain their unit would be calling home. This in turn allowed the maintenance crews to begin their work with a minimal amount of delay, so that the time the *Queens* spent sitting in the still-vulnerable Clyde would be as brief as possible. All of this meant that the exertions of thousands of men putting in thousands of man-hours of effort had to be carefully dovetailed to ensure that each component of the operation arrived at the right place at the right time, ready to do the right job. Much ado has been made over the years about the enormous amount of staff work that was done to ensure the success of Operation Overlord, the D-Day landings on June 6, 1944, but that effort pales in comparison to the staff work that was carried out, day after day, for five long years to make the Atlantic convoys succeed.

The first time all of these arrangements were put to the test was on May 11, 1942, when the *Queen Mary* left New York with units of the American 1st Armored Division and the 34th Infantry Division aboard, along with artillery and hospital units, just over ten thousand men in all, arriving at Gourock on May 16. The process had been so thoroughly worked out that despite a few minor problems, the entire operation went smoothly enough that no major changes or modifications had to be made. By May 22 the *Mary* was ready for sea again, this time taking ten thousand British soldiers to Suez.

Within a few months the whole system was functioning so well that the Americans felt confident enough to ship the entire 1st Infantry Division ("The Big Red One") across to Great Britain. With a total strength of 15,125 officers and enlisted men, this was the first time that an entire division had been carried aboard a single ship. There would be many more to follow.

Part of all of this planning and coordination was devoted to creating well-thought-out, careful procedures for getting the *Queens* ready for sea and loading the troops. Each eastbound crossing actually began in the Allied Combined Shipping Operations Office. Located in what had been the German consulate in New York, the Shipping Operations Office was one of two centers for controlling the Allied convoys on the North Atlantic (the other was in the Admiralty building in Whitehall, in London). This was where the *Queens'* captains were briefed on the details of troop loading and escort procedures for each convoy—and for administrative reasons, the *Queen Mary* and the *Queen Elizabeth* were each considered a complete convoy in itself.

In addition to the captain and any of his officers whose attendance he felt necessary, representatives from the British Ministry of Transport and the U.S. Army Transportation Corps would be present, along with liaison officers from the Royal Navy, the Royal Canadian Navy, and the U.S. Navy. Everyone present was briefed by an intelligence officer, who gave estimates of the location of German U-boats, as well as the rare surface raider. At the end of the briefing, the captain was handed a set of sealed orders, to be opened only after the ship was well at sea, that would reveal to him the course and speed he was to follow.

While this briefing was taking place, and for some time after the captain returned to his ship, the crew members made their own preparations for getting under way. Depending on the requirements of the voyage, the crew of either *Queen* could range from 850 to 1,000 men, divided into four departments: the Engineering Department, which was responsible for the engines and machinery aboard the ship; the Catering and Purser's Department (sometimes called the Victualing Department), which had the primary task of feeding the troops; the Deck Department, which took care of the navigation, handling, and operations of the ship; and the Permanent Military Staff, which was responsible for loading and unloading the troops to be embarked, as well as all discipline aboard.

Because the *Queens'* primary defense against enemy attack was their speed, the boilers and engines were always the first priority on both ships. They were maintained by the Engineering Department, which consisted of about 270 Assistant Engineers and assorted Engine Room Artificers—the stokers, boiler tenders, and machinists who kept all the machinery functioning—all working under the supervision of the Staff Chief Engineer and the Chief Engineer. The *Queen Mary* had twenty-four boilers, but the *Queen Elizabeth's* boilers were much larger, and she required only twelve. Both ships burned roughly a thousand tons of fuel oil a day, so before each crossing, as much as eight thousand tons of oil would be loaded into their bunkers, a task that the Engineering Department was responsible for overseeing. The boilers provided steam for the four sets of turbines that propelled each ship, as well as turning the generators that provided the ships with electricity and also worked much of the machinery, including the refrigeration plants for the cold storage rooms in the galleys. It was a tribute to the quality of the Scottish engineers and workmen who designed and built the *Queens* that in six years of war and nearly a million miles of steaming, neither ship suffered a failure of any of their engines or boilers.

The galleys were the bailiwick of the Catering and Purser's Department, which had probably the busiest role of any of the departments on either of the *Queens.* The Purser's Department on each ship consisted of 350 men, who worked round the clock from the day before the ship left New York to the day after she docked at Gourock. Feeding 15,000 soldiers (and nearly 1,000 crewmen) two meals a day required a lot of planning and preparation, as well as hard work. The typical load of stores brought aboard for a six-day crossing included 155,000 pounds of meat; 124,000 pounds of potatoes; 76,000 pounds of flour; 53,000 pounds of eggs, butter, and powdered milk; 31,000 pounds of canned fruit and an equal amount of coffee, tea, and sugar; 29,000 pounds of fresh fruit; 20,000 pounds of bacon and ham, as well as a similar amount of jams and jellies; and 4,600 pounds of cheese. Although water usage was strictly rationed, 6,500 tons of fresh water was pumped aboard. To stock the nine troop canteens scattered about the ship, where soldiers could buy personal items, 50,000 bottles of soft drinks, 5,000 cartons of cigarettes, 400 pounds of candy, and varying amounts of razor blades, soap, shampoo, shaving cream, and other toiletries were brought aboard as well. For obvious reasons, no chewing gum was sold aboard either ship.

The Deck Department was made up of the seamen and officers who actually worked and sailed the ship: the Captain, Staff Captain (a position something akin to the "executive officer" in the U.S. Navy or the "commander" in the Royal Navy), watch-standing officers, navigators, radio operators and signalmen, quartermasters, bosuns, trimmers, lookouts, and able-bodied and ordinary seamen. Professional seamen all, these were the men who were charged with taking the ship across the Atlantic and delivering the thousands of GIs aboard safely to the British Isles.

The Permanent Military Staff, 120 strong on both the *Queen Mary* and the *Queen Elizabeth,* was an assortment of British, American, and Canadian personnel, both officers and enlisted men. They acted as liaisons between the officers and senior NCOs of the units embarked and the senior staff of the crews. The senior officer, styled the Commandant of the Permanent Staff, was usually a major, and the complement of his department was made up of gunnery and ordnance specialists, who were responsible for the antiaircraft and deck guns on each ship, the medical personnel who worked in the ship's infirmary, the Military Police detachment, and a handful of Red Cross workers. The Military Staff was responsible for passing along any day-to-day orders from the captain, enforcing the standing orders and ensuring that the troops aboard complied with all security and blackout regulations, and assigning work details throughout the ship. The Military Police were responsible for handling any serious breaches of discipline, although minor offenses were usually taken care of within the offender's own unit.

The methods created to load, house, and feed fifteen thousand men during the six-day crossing were nothing less than a work of genius, a demonstration of that peculiarly American talent for organization and application of assembly-line techniques to human resource problems. The regimens imposed on the two ships were virtually identical. Each ship was divided into thirds, the sections labeled from bow to stern "Red," "White," and "Blue." Every GI embarked on the ship was given a button in one of these three colors, to be worn at all times. Troops were embarked on all three areas simultaneously and, once aboard, were restricted to their designated area of the ship, unless they were assigned to a work detail, in which case they were free to go anywhere their duties required.

The GIs would start boarding the ship the day before she sailed. Each man brought with him his rifle, helmet, canteen, cartridge belt and webbing, field pack, and a duffel bag with his spare uniforms and any personal belongings he chose to bring along—a burden of just over a hundred pounds for each man to carry.

The experience that nineteen-year-old Jerry Cerrachio had aboard the *Queen Mary* was typical. Cerrachio was from Elizabeth, New Jersey, and had enlisted in the Army Air Corps six months after the attack on Pearl Harbor. By December 1942, having been promoted to sergeant and completed the Air Corps radio operator training program at Madison, Wisconsin, he was assigned to the 459th Air Transport Command, one of several units scheduled to set sail aboard the *Queen Mary* on December 8. His unit was embarked the night before she left New York. Once the men reached their berthing areas, they were under strict orders not to move from that area until given permission to do so by the ship's captain.

Sergeant Cerrachio dumped his duffel bag in a section of the deck set aside for them, then made his way to his designated tier of bunks. As he zeroed in on the bottom "rack," as the standee bunks were soon nicknamed, a friend called out behind him, "Don't take that one, Sarge—if one of the guys above you throws up, it'll wind up all over you!" Instantly seeing the wisdom of this observation, Cerrachio instead took the top rack—a bit more difficult to reach and to get into or out of, but definitely safer!

The troops made themselves as comfortable as possible, which admittedly wasn't much, while they waited out the remaining hours for the *Mary* to pull away from the pier and make her way down the Hudson River and through New York Harbor. Once past the Verrazano Narrows Bridge, the captain gave the all-clear, and the troops were allowed to move about within their areas of the ship. Not that it was particularly easy to do so—the passageways were often crowded, and the men were usually encumbered by some of their equipment. Sergeant Cerrachio recalled that he carried his weapon (a .30-caliber M-1 carbine instead of the heavier, bulkier M-1 rifle) with him everywhere he went, and that most of the men, particularly the infantry, did the same.

Even after the captain gave the all-clear, movement within the ship was carefully controlled, mostly to prevent the men from getting lost in the rabbit warren of passages and ladders below decks. A system was put in place such that the starboard passageways were used only for forward movement, port-side passageways for moving aft. Traffic control was the responsibility of the Military Police detachment, and probably their single most important function.

Once aboard, each soldier was given a copy of the ship's Standing Orders, which covered emergency procedures in the event of an air attack, abandon-ship drills, and fire precautions. In addition, Daily Orders were published by the Permanent Staff every morning and posted throughout the ship. The Daily Orders announced work assignments, religious services, any entertainment being provided, and general news about developments in the war. They always ended by informing the reader that "ignorance of these regulations will not be accepted as an excuse in any case of breach of discipline."

Though each soldier was assigned a bunk, he didn't always have to sleep in it every night he was aboard, which could be as many as six or seven nights, if he was one of those unfortunate souls whose units were among the first to board and the last to leave the ship. Since the total number of "standee" bunks aboard each of the *Queens* was only 12,500, when either ship was carrying an entire division of troops, some fifteen thousand strong, a rotation was worked out so that in the summer months each man would sleep "topside" on the open upper decks for two nights, twenty-five hundred men at a time. Far from being a hardship, a berth on the upper decks was coveted by many of the soldiers, and understandably so: In most places below decks, there was only about eighteen inches between one bunk and the next above it, cramped and claustrophobic by anyone's standards. Also, a lot of GIs believed, not unreasonably, that men who slept topside had a better chance of escaping the ship should she be torpedoed. Of course, sleeping on the upper decks was allowed only in the summer months—winters on the North Atlantic were far too cold.

When the men were not sleeping, they were eating or else had very little to do. Work details kept some of the men busy, as there were decks to scrub, paint to touch up, and common areas to be kept clean. The ship's staff, as well as the officers of the units being transported, did their best to find ways of keeping the men occupied. There were always a number of individuals who imagined themselves as future stars of stage and screen, ready to present comedy routines or impromptu concerts, and sometimes there was a regimental band aboard that would give a series of concerts throughout the ship. The Canadians were the best off in this respect, as they always traveled with their regimental bands; Americans, less traditionally inclined, usually didn't. Both *Queens* had a small library of films aboard and showed movies several times a day. The limited number of choices made little difference to the soldiers, since none of them would be on board long enough to go through the entire catalog of films carried aboard either ship, but the rather sparse selection did become something of a hardship for the crews; it is recorded that one crewman aboard the *Queen Mary* saw *Pride and Prejudice* 120 times.

And there were always lectures: lectures on tactics, on equipment, on personal hygiene. There were also lectures—to which most of the troops, to their credit, paid close attention—about getting along with the British, soldiers and civilians alike. Every soldier was given a copy of the U.S. Army Special Services Division's leaflet "A Short Guide to Britain," which articulated some of the most crucial "do's and don'ts" about everyday life in the British Isles. Among the more memorable passages was this collection of some very sound advice:

> You are higher paid than the British "Tommy." Don't rub it in. Play fair with him. He can be a pal in need. It isn't a good idea to say "bloody" in mixed company in Britain—it is one of their worst swear words. To say "I look like a bum" is offensive to their ears, for to the British this means that you look like your own backside. The British are beer drinkers—and they can hold it.

However entertaining the movies and lectures were, the most popular form of entertainment aboard both of the *Queens* was also strictly forbidden: gambling. Barely had the troops found their billets aboard the ship than scores of poker, blackjack, and crap games would commence. A watchful eye was kept for wandering MPs who patrolled the ship, their sole purpose being to break up these illegal games, as the GIs set up their makeshift gaming tables. There is a sense that a large part of the attraction of these games was the fact that they *were* illegal. Some of them would go on for the entire six days of the crossing, players drifting in and out as their fortunes were made or lost. Certainly they helped the men pass the time on what was otherwise a tedious crossing.

The officers and crews did their bit as well. Often the crewmen were the first "foreigners" that many GIs had ever met. For more than one young American, meeting a British sailor face-to-face brought the reality of the war home to him as nothing had done before, with the people who had been the targets of Nazi bombs and U-boats suddenly becoming very human indeed. Sometimes the crewmen were able to turn the tables on the Germans with a typically British display of humor. On one crossing, the captain of the *Queen Mary* made an announcement over the ship's public-address system, informing those aboard that the ship had just been sunk. A German propaganda broadcast to that effect had just been picked up, apparently made in the hope that the *Queen Mary* would break radio silence in order to assure the Admiralty that it was untrue. The Germans wanted to get a radio fix on the liner that way and set up an ambush with their U-boats, but the captain, in this instance Commodore Bisset, wasn't about to fall for so transparent a trick and violate his standing orders. He did, however, have the unique pleasure of announcing his own greatly exaggerated demise on four successive days, as the Germans kept repeating their broadcast in the vain hope that Bisset might fall for their ruse.

Daily lifeboat drills and inspections of all the berthing areas did their bit to help relieve the boredom as well, and some commanding officers organized calisthenics on the upper decks for their units. These could be rather awkward, since the ships' standing orders required the men to wear their life jackets at all times and to put on their steel helmets anytime they were above deck. Regulations were regulations, of course, although the real usefulness of the life preservers was a bit questionable, especially in the winter months. A comment made by one of the *Queen Mary's* crewmen to Sergeant Cerrachio drove the point home. "I'll tell you something about that thing, Yank," the crewman confided, pointing to Cerrachio's life jacket. "If the Jerries sink this ship, you're not going to need that!" At the very least, the life preservers made fairly serviceable pillows.

The most popular drill was the daily practice firings of the *Queens'* anti-aircraft batteries. The *Queen Mary's* guns were controlled from a director platform set up on the Verandah Grill at the aft end of the Boat Deck; the *Queen Elizabeth's* director was positioned just behind her second funnel. Since the gun crews were made up of British and American troops, the Gunnery Officers often staged competitions between crews of different nationalities to see who were the swiftest in bringing their guns into action. One of the most enduring memories for soldiers who crossed the Atlantic on either of the Queens was the number of guns they carried and the din those guns made when they were fired.

Two meals were served to the troops each day, breakfast in the morning, beginning at 6:00 A.M. and running until 11:00, and dinner, from 3:00 P.M. until 7:30. Enlisted men took their meals in what had been the First Class Dining Room, now converted to a cafeteria-style mess that seated twenty-five hundred men at a time. The men ate in shifts, each section allowed forty-five minutes to get their meal, eat it, and clean their mess kits. Even this mundane chore had been carefully regimented. Each soldier had two lengths of wire, one of which he looped through holes in the handles of his knife, fork, and spoon, the other through the D-rings of his mess kit. He would then dip and swirl them around in a succession of four vats, first in one filled with soapy water, next in one full of boiling fresh water, the third with boiling disinfectant, and the fourth a saltwater rinse. Schedules were so carefully set up and dovetailed that as the last men of one shift were leaving the mess, those of the next were just taking their seats. As the men left the mess, they passed by tables laden with ham-and-cheese and roast beef sandwiches, which they would take with them to fight off hunger pangs until the next meal.

The Officers' Mess was the Tourist Class lounge. The officers did not have to queue up to be served, instead enjoying the luxury of sitting at proper tables and having a steward bring their meals to them. Many of the officers had the added comfort of being berthed in staterooms with only one, two, or three other officers, unlike the enlisted men, who had to share their quarters with as many as twenty others. The officers also had stewards to clean their quarters and maintain their kits, responsibilities that enlisted men had to take care of themselves. There was a price for these services, beyond that of the added burden of responsibility that officers bore. At the end of each crossing, the officers were expected to tip the bedroom and table stewards who had looked after them, much as would have been done in peacetime. The expected gratuities ranged from $1.00 for single officers to $1.50 for an officer who had been given permission to bring his wife with him; British officers of the rank of major and above were expected to tip their stewards five shillings each, while the rate for captains and lieutenants was four shillings, sixpence.

The single most highly anticipated event of every crossing was the first sight of land. The *Queens* would normally be met by an escorting antisubmarine bomber or patrol plane while still about a day out of Scotland, the surface escorts—usually a half dozen destroyers and an antiaircraft cruiser—arriving ten to twelve hours later. The Western Isles began to loom over the horizon—Uist, Benbecula, Barra, Tiree, Coll, then Islay, Kintyre, and Arran, as the escorts shepherded the big liners into the Firth of Clyde. As many men as possible would crowd onto the decks of the *Mary* or the *Elizabeth* to get what was often their first glimpse of a foreign land.

The River Clyde had been home to one of Britain's great seaports for more than a century, but during the Second World War it achieved much greater importance than it had ever known before. The dock complex at Gourock was the only one in the British Isles that could berth the *Queens* in reasonable safety. Even in 1944 the Luftwaffe's bombers posed too great a threat to the docks at Southampton from their bases in France to risk sending any of the big troopships there, but the Clyde was beyond the reach of all but the longest-ranged German aircraft. The additional distance also gave the

Royal Air Force more warning time and allowed fighter patrols to scramble aloft to meet the raiders, something the short distance Southampton sat from the French coast did not permit. James LaForce, an airman in the Royal Canadian Air Force, was witness to a remarkable reminder of the RAF's presence one October morning in 1943 aboard the *Queen Mary*. As the ship was entering the Firth of Clyde, a Spitfire flew alongside her so low that LaForce, who was standing on the Promenade Deck, some seventy-five feet above the water, was able to look *down* at the fighter as it went zooming past.

Through the docks, piers, and wharves spread out for miles along the banks of the Clyde, from Greenock to Glasgow itself, flowed the manpower and materiel that the Allies would use to tip the balance against Nazi Germany. Mixed in among them were nearly eighty shipyards of varying sizes, where every sort of ship was built or repaired, from huge battleships and aircraft carriers to tiny corvettes and destroyers. It was an awesome display of sea power and industrial might.

It certainly made an impression on Daniel Marien, a private in the U.S. Army's 87th Infantry Division. When the *Queen Elizabeth* docked at Gourock, his first glimpse of Scotland was a stunning view of "a very green hill, on which the morning sun was falling, with what appeared to be a castle along the top." Then he looked around, amazed at the incredible number of ships of all sizes and descriptions, merchantmen and warships alike, riding at anchor in the Clyde. It was quite an experience for a nineteen-year-old who had never been outside of New York City until he joined the army. It was a bit more disconcerting for Jerry Cerrachio. He remembers getting worried once the *Queen Mary* stopped at Gourock and the troops began to disembark into the waiting tenders, thinking, "Holy Hell! What if the Germans try to sink us? They've got to know we're here!"

The soldiers didn't have much time for sightseeing once the docking preparations began. Early in the *Queens'* service as transatlantic troopers, the dock at Gourock was not yet finished, so the troops had to debark into tenders that then took them ashore. By mid-1943 that problem had been solved, so that once the *Queen Mary* or the *Queen Elizabeth* drew herself up into the Clyde, a half dozen tugs would take her in tow and gently nudge her alongside the dock. Gangways would be brought up to A, B, and D decks in each of the "Red," "White," and "Blue" sections of the ship. Long strings of trucks waited at dockside to take the troops away as soon as they got off the ship. These motor convoys wound their way through the streets of Glasgow, taking the troops to waiting trains or sometimes directly to their camps.

As soon as the last of the soldiers were away, an army of cleaning and maintenance people boarded the ship. Provisions for the crew and anyone else making the return trip to New York were brought aboard, along with any special supplies or equipment that might be needed on the crossing. As the war progressed, the *Queens* were used more and more frequently to evacuate severely wounded or disabled servicemen back to the United States and Canada, and in some cases special provision had to be made for their care. If any POWs were being transported, their rations had to be loaded, and the guard posts and security barricades that kept them confined set up as well. Freshwater tanks were filled, fuel bunkers were topped up, and the engineers worked round the clock to bring their maintenance up-to-date on the boilers, engines, and machinery.

To give the ship a good cleaning, 120 or so Glasgow women would be mustered, and they would spend the next three or four days scouring, polishing, sweeping, and scrubbing from one end of the ship to the other. Like all of the work done on the ship in Gourock and New York, their labors went on under the watchful eyes of security personnel and Military Police, ever alert for any hint of sabotage. Unless there was some special work or repairs that needed to be finished, the ship would be ready to leave for New York within four or five days of her arrival at Gourock.

It would be both untrue and unfair to create the impression that crossing the North Atlantic on board either of the *Queens* was a sort of six-day holiday for the troops aboard them. In point of fact, those six days could be miserable, and often were, for a variety of reasons. Even though some thought had been given to the general comfort of the troops for the duration of their time aboard, necessity was the overriding consideration. Transportation aboard one of the *Queens* was a means to an end, not an end in itself: The troops were aboard for the sole purpose of getting them from New York to Gourock, and nothing else. Thus it was taken as a given that they could put up with a certain degree of temporary inconvenience and discomfort. After all, it was wartime, and many of those young men would come face-to-face with much worse before it was over.

One of the most obvious problems was seasickness: Most of the soldiers the *Queens* carried to Britain had never been aboard a ship before; many had never even seen the ocean. The *Queen Mary* rolled heavily in anything more than a moderate seaway, which made the problem worse for those with already sensitive stomachs. The *Queen Elizabeth,* her hull design having the benefit of thousands of tank tests, was not anywhere near as lively, although the North Atlantic, a notoriously fickle and vicious ocean, could produce winds and seas any time of the year that would make any ship bob and pitch like a cork. Harold Butler, an Able-bodied Seaman during the war, still spoke feelingly fifty years later when recalling how the Atlantic could produce waves big enough to bury the bow of a ship one day, and be as smooth as glass the next.

Consequently, many of those meals served to the troops, as well many of those between-meal sandwiches, didn't always stay down after they had been eaten. For troops who were fortunate enough to be on the upper decks and reasonably close to a side rail, or near a toilet if they were below decks, the problem was minor, but for those not so lucky, the remains of their breakfasts or dinners wound up on the decks. The ventilation systems on the *Queens*, designed to meet the demands for circulating fresh air for three thousand people, were badly overtaxed when called upon to deal with the assorted odors produced by ten thousand or more men kept in close confinement for a week. Showers were available for officers, but not for the enlisted men; even had they been, most of the men would have abstained. They had been told over and over again that in an emergency, they would have to be instantly ready to make their way topside. No one wanted to run the risk of being caught in the middle of taking a shower when the signal sounded for an "abandon ship" drill—or worse, the real thing! By the time the ship was a day or two out of Gourock, the stale air below decks would have become ripe with a mixture of the odors of sweat, combat boots, and unwashed bodies and clothing, tinged now and then with a whiff of fuel oil, and overlaid with reminders of rejected breakfasts and dinners.

Despite the best efforts of their officers, as well as the crews aboard the *Queens*, boredom was widespread, and with it came anxiety. The enforced inactivity of the six or seven days a soldier was compelled to spend aboard the ship was a stark contrast with the hectic pace of training that had gone on for months before, and the bustle and rush of troop trains carrying the men to New York, followed by the controlled chaos of boarding. Suddenly the GIs had a chance to be alone with their thoughts, as an endless panorama of gray sea sped by. For the first time in the lives of most of them, they were cut off from everything familiar, surrounded by the artificial environment of the army, one that they had found themselves involuntarily, if willingly, thrust into. They were being borne toward a war about which many of them had only a superficial understanding, and of whose realities they had no real conception, only romanticized fantasies. Though many of them would never see combat, thousands of them would, and in doing so would experience conditions that no amount of education or training, nor anything they had ever experienced up to this point, could ever prepare them for. Whether he was an infantryman, cook, mechanic, clerk, or radio operator, the six-day journey across the Atlantic drove home to each man in a way particular to himself that he was about to undergo an experience that would change his life forever, sometimes for better, sometimes not, but a change that was inevitable. It was a realization that would come to each man at a different time in a different way, but it had the power to turn the most facile men momentarily thoughtful.

And there were other factors as well, some of them not tangible, that could make a crossing on one of the *Queens* an ordeal. David Olsen, who served with the 87th Armored Field Artillery, recalled how the exigencies of war created a situation that was memorable for its apparent callousness. The 87th had been training at Fort Knox, Kentucky, until it was moved to Camp Shanks in New York in November 1943, in readiness to be shipped to Great Britain. On December 20 the men were driven to New York City, where they were loaded aboard the *Ile de France.* Mechanical troubles kept the old French liner from sailing the next day as scheduled, so the 87th was taken back to Camp Shanks on Christmas Eve. A week later the unit was back in New York, aboard the *Queen Elizabeth,* sailing on New Year's Day. Several of the men in the unit felt that, considering the unsettling week they had just spent at Camp Shanks, being given sailing orders on what should have been a holiday was particularly coldhearted. It seemed to emphasize even more strongly just what the young men in the unit were leaving behind, and the uncertainty and danger of the future they were facing.

At the same time, Olsen was able to demonstrate that quintessentially American gift for finding a few moments of humor in almost any circumstance. In a unit history of the 87th Armored Field Artillery, he recalled that some of the battalion's junior officers shared a compartment aboard the *Queen Elizabeth* that was next to a cabin assigned to a half dozen army nurses. A door connected the two compartments, an arrangement that in peacetime would allow them to become part of a suite. The nurses had carefully locked the door, much to the disappointment of the young officers next door, and adding insult to injury, they had blocked up the keyhole. There was some bantering back and forth between the nurses and the lieutenants, but the artillerymen came out very much the worse in the exchange: One of them, a second lieutenant by the name of Cantwell, asked one nurse "if her mother had any children?" The nurse, who got this artilleryman's range very quickly indeed, shot back, "The more I see of you, the more I believe in birth control." As Olsen put it, "The conversation definitely went downhill after that."

Not all of the units that were shipped to Great Britain aboard the *Queens* were ground combat units, nor were all of them American. The buildup of Allied forces required not only tens of thousands of combat troops, but also tens of thousands of support personnel. In particular, the American air forces in Britain required thousands of crewmen to fly the thousands of aircraft (each B-17 Flying Fortress or B-24 Liberator had a flight crew of ten men), but just as urgently needed were the ground personnel who maintain the airplanes. The Americans' standard operating procedure was to have the aircrew fly their aircraft across the Atlantic from New York via Newfoundland, with a refueling stop in Iceland or the Azores on the way. The ground personnel, crew chiefs, mechanics, armorers, and ordnance experts were brought over on troopships, including the *Queens.*

The option of flying across the Atlantic was open only to the large, multiengine aircraft. Single-engine fighters such as the P-47 or the P-51 simply lacked the range—not to mention the pilots lacking the endurance—to make such long hops. The Army Air Corps' solution was to crate up the aircraft and ship the entire fighter group by sea, such as the 78th Fighter Wing, which sailed on the *Queen Elizabeth* in November 1942, or the 67th Fighter Wing, which the *Elizabeth* carried to Gourock in August 1943. The numbers of personnel carried in these movements were as large as any of the division-size army units the *Queens* carried—more than fifteen thousand men each.

Large numbers of Royal Canadian Air Force personnel also were carried to Great Britain aboard the *Queens.* The Canadians did things a little differently than the Americans, though. Since the RCAF used British equipment and flew British aircraft, the aircrews trained in Canada, but rather than fly their airplanes across the Atlantic to bases in Great Britain, the Canadians would use equipment and aircraft the British already had awaiting them. Consequently, the Canadian aircrews found themselves on troop transports like the *Queens.*

Regardless of where they came from, their nationality, or what service they belonged to, these young men whom the *Queens* were carrying beyond the shores of their homelands for the first time were on their way to what would become the great adventure of their lives. Like all adventures, there would be danger, laughter, boredom, fear, courage, tragedy, and triumph. Not all of them would return, and not all of those who returned would be whole.

But they were about to become part of the greatest military force ever assembled, one that was gathering its strength and slowly clenching like a titanic mailed fist, poised to strike a devastating blow at the most evil regime the world had ever known. Those bored, hungry, lonely, seasick kids huddled aboard the *Queen Mary* and the *Queen Elizabeth* were about to become men, the young soldiers and airmen who would achieve the Allied victory.

CHAPTER NINE

Triumph!

*This embattled shore, portal of freedom,
is forever hallowed by the ideas, valor and sacrifice
of our fellow countrymen.*

—Monument inscription on
the Normandy coast

THE GREAT THUNDERCLAP OF DOOM THAT BURST OVER THE THIRD REICH
sounded on June 6, 1944, when Operation Overlord successfully landed
175,000 soldiers and fifty thousand vehicles on the Normandy shores. They
were supported at sea by a naval force of more than five thousand ships and in
the air by more than eleven thousand aircraft. It was an operation that had
taken two and a half years of planning, entailed tens of thousands of hours of
staff work, demanded the creation of new weapons and new tactics, and
required endless days and nights of training for soldiers and airmen who
would carry out the assault.

Twenty-six Allied divisions, two American air forces, and two Royal Air
Force commands were committed to the D-Day landings, their support, and
follow-up. It was a concentration of men and materiel the likes of which the
world had never seen before, and that the Germans could never hope to turn
aside. The one chance the German Army had of staving off defeat was to stop
the Allied invasion at the water's edge; once the American, British, and Canadian armies had made it ashore, all the Germans could do was buy time and
try to inflict enough casualties on the Allies that they would be compelled to
make a separate peace, allowing Germany to turn all of her waning strength
to face the advancing Russians in the east.

So while almost all of the senior German officers in the west realized that
the war was lost for Germany after D-Day, that did not mean that the German

Army was about to roll over and play dead. Instead, whenever possible, the Germans fought tenaciously. There were many and varied reasons for this: professional pride, delusion, a sense that they were protecting and shielding the civilians at home, and sometimes just sheer bloody-mindedness. Whatever the reason, after the initial success of the D-Day landings, the Allies found that instead of the steady, methodical advance they had planned, they were bogged down in the Normandy hedgerow country for the remainder of June and all of July. It was a campaign where casualties were heavy, particularly among infantrymen, and advances were measured in yards instead of miles.

It wasn't until the breakout at St. Lô at the beginning of August that the Allied armies, in particular the U.S. Army, were able to execute the swift, sweeping war of movement and maneuver that Allied planning had envisaged. What had been a stubborn and systematic withdrawal by the German Army suddenly turned into a rout. German units disintegrated as they ran pell-mell for their border, allowing the Allied forces to roam almost at will across France.

The Luftwaffe, all but driven from the skies by the combined strength of the U.S. Army Air Corps and the Royal Air Force by August 1944, lost their bases in France to the advancing Allied armies, so what little fighter and bomber strength it still possessed in the west was pulled back into Germany. This meant that Southampton was no longer a potential deathtrap for Allied troopships, allowing many of the smaller liners to bid farewell to Gourock for the remainder of the war and disembark their troops in southern England. This simplified the process of getting replacements and reinforcements to the combat units in France, since it was no longer necessary to transport all of the incoming troops south by rail from Scotland, something that had always created a bit of a bottleneck for Allied staffs. The *Queens* continued to dock at Gourock, though, as it was the considered opinion of the Allied staffs that sending them into Southampton would be tempting fate—and the Germans. In any case, the flow of replacements and new units was simplified, and as events transpired, it could not have come at a better time, for the services of the *Queens* and their compatriots were soon to be needed more desperately than ever.

Operation Overlord, as successful as it was, had not been the strategy that the Americans had wanted to follow. To General Marshall and the Chiefs of Staff, it seemed only reasonable to exploit the strengths of the United States— phenomenal industrial capacity and a large manpower base—and bring them to bear against the Axis powers with the methodical, almost businesslike approach to war that has been the hallmark of the American military since the Civil War. The Americans' approach differed vastly from that of the British, who were facing a very different set of problems. Great Britain's pool of available manpower was a very finite resource, and the British Army wasn't organized, equipped, or trained to bludgeon its way to victory, a concept inherent in the American way of war.

Marshall and the Chiefs of Staff wanted to invade the Continent at the earliest possible moment—1942, if feasible, 1943 at the latest. The British were aghast at the idea. Churchill had never lost sight of the political consequences of the Allies' military actions and advocated a strategy of avoiding direct confrontation with the Wehrmacht where it was strongest, but eroding its strength and sapping its will to fight though a series of operations around the periphery of the Third Reich, where Allied mobility and sea power could be exploited to their maximum. Churchill also worried about the consequences of the Red Army advancing into Central Europe as they drove the Nazi invaders from Russian soil, and hoped to persuade President Roosevelt to adopt a strategy that would put the Anglo-American armies in a position somewhere in the Balkans, so that they could serve as a buffer and a brake to the Russians. Churchill's worst nightmare was seeing Germany crushed between the Allies advancing from the west and the Red Army advancing from the east. It wasn't the defeat of Germany that bothered him—the destruction of Adolf Hitler and all that he stood for was a cause dearest to his heart—but he *was* frightened of the specter of Eastern Europe being occupied by the Soviet Union, the "liberated" nations becoming so many Soviet puppets.

As it turned out, Churchill and the Imperial General Staff were able to impose some of their strategic thinking on their American allies, and in 1942 there was no invasion of Europe. President Roosevelt had promised Comrade Stalin, the chairman of Russia's Communist Party and *de facto* dictator of the Soviet Union, that the U.S. Army would engage the Germans in 1942, apparently with a landing somewhere in France in mind. Instead, the Americans landed in North Africa—Morocco and Algiers—where they confronted the waning strength of the Panzerarmee Afrika, successor to the Afrika Korps. This campaign was essentially foisted on the Americans by the British, who politely but firmly pointed out to General Marshall and his colleagues that at this point in the war, at least, the majority of resources devoted to the operation were still British. The Americans were supplying the landing force, but little more. The Americans had wanted to prepare for a cross-channel invasion of France in an operation code-named "Roundup," to take place in the summer of 1943, but the British made it clear that they wouldn't cooperate with such a strategy, and that the North African assault was the Americans' only choice if they were to make good on Roosevelt's promise to Stalin. The burden on Allied resources to carry out the Operation Torch landings meant that a cross-channel assault in 1943 would be out of the question as well. Neither of the *Queens* were involved in Operation Torch, but the attack did have an effect on their subsequent wartime careers—not to mention the Allied command structure.

Good peacetime soldiers do not always make good wartime soldiers, particularly in the case of officers, although it is impossible to tell beforehand which officers will be competent, or better, and which ones will be mediocre—or worse. The battles fought in Tunis between the green, undertrained Americans and the grim, tough German veterans exposed flaws and weaknesses in American organization, doctrine, and leadership at every level. Though the men fought bravely and were led with courage by their lieutenants, captains, and majors, bumbling by the higher levels of command led to disasters in the field where even the stoutest units were forced to retire—and some to even break and run. The worst offender was an American major general named Lloyd Fredendall, who had been a highly regarded officer in peacetime, but in combat became the physical embodiment of all those parodies of military incompetence. Lt. Gen. Dwight Eisenhower, who had commanded the Torch operations and was to become the Supreme Commander Allied Expeditionary Forces, and lead the invasion of Europe, began ruthlessly purging the ranks of the U.S. Army of incompetent officers, beginning with Fredendall, and replacing them with fighting men like the flamboyant George Patton and the quiet but highly capable Omar Bradley. At the same time, Eisenhower began cleaning house in his own staff, ensuring that the failures of the North African campaign would not happen again.

Operation Torch almost certainly did the Allies a favor, for the very thought of Lloyd Fredendall trying to lead a landing on the French coast is chilling. It also meant that any such attempt would not take place until 1944, by which time the United States had replaced Great Britain as the senior partner in the Western Alliance. American strategy, if not American tactics, would prevail in the invasion of Europe.

Thus the *Queen Mary* and the *Queen Elizabeth* spent all of 1943 ferrying American and Canadian soldiers and airmen to Great Britain. Those voyages were the ultimate vindication for the men who three years earlier had decided to spare both ships for transport duties. The British strategy of forcing the Germans to disperse their increasingly limited resources to defend the periphery of their empire by small-scale attacks and operations went by the board, as the American concept of victory through brute force became the strategic foundation of Operation Overlord. The assault on occupied France would be massive and brutal—there would be no subtlety once Overlord began. The Allies were not interested in simply outfighting the Germans: They were going to overwhelm and overpower the Wehrmacht. The *Queens* were the keystones of that strategy—they would provide the margin of manpower that would make the strategy work.

Statistics can sometimes be incredibly boring, and an endless tally of how many troops each of the *Queens* carried on each of its crossings would soon become mind-numbing. But there are times when the sheer power of numbers can be staggering. This is especially true of the *Queen Mary* and the *Queen Elizabeth,* which together brought to Great Britain, by April 1944, over four hundred thousand American and Canadian army and air force personnel. A remarkable comparison gives a sense of scale to the magnitude of this accomplishment: In early 1942, when the U.S. Army's 34th Infantry Division was sent from New York to Belfast, it required a convoy of twenty-one ships and took eleven days. Eight months later, when the 1st Infantry Division was sent from New York to Gourock, one ship—the *Queen Mary*—accomplished the same feat in half the time. Of the twenty-six Allied divisions committed to the D-Day landing and its immediate follow-up, more than half of them had been brought to Great Britain aboard just two ships—the *Queens.* Each crossing the *Queens* made freed a score of other ships to carry vital supplies and equipment. Put another way, the thirty-eight combined crossings from New York to Gourock made by the *Queen Mary* and the *Queen Elizabeth* between May 1942 and April 1944 was equal to the combined crossings of *eight hundred* ordinary transports and merchantmen.

The reopening of the port of Southampton in the fall of 1944, though the *Queens* continued to dock at Gourock, was a godsend to the Allies, because it made the task of getting replacement troops to the front much simpler. As the Allied armies advanced across France, they began to outrun their supply lines, and as soon as they did so, their advance slowed to a crawl. This allowed the Germans to get one step ahead of the Allies, and the German officers began to gain some control over the headlong rush of their troops toward the German border, so that the rout became a retreat and the retreat an orderly withdrawal. The Wehrmacht began organizing the defenses of the western German border in September, which then stopped the Allies cold in October. What had been almost a whirlwind tour of France for the Allies suddenly became a battle again, as the Germans finally stood their ground and fought back.

The stiffening German defense and the corresponding rise in Allied casualties made the *Queens* as indispensable to the continued advance of the Allied armies as they had been to the buildup of troops for D-Day. Between May 1944 and April 1945, the *Queens* carried more than quarter million soldiers to Europe. These replacements were critical, as the Allies were facing the beginnings of a manpower crisis in late 1944. Great Britain had run out of replacement troops by this time (an eerie echo of 1918), while the number of trained infantrymen arriving from the United States was falling below the needs of the units at the front. Training schedules were stepped up at boot camps across the country, and the U.S. Army scoured its ranks for personnel who could be transferred to combat units.

To satisfy these demands, the *Queens* kept up as feverish a pace as they had during the buildup for Overlord. In July 1943, during that buildup, the *Queen Mary* had carried 15,740 troops on a single crossing; along with her crew of 943, this was the greatest number of people ever embarked on a single ship at one time. While that was an exceptional instance, on every subsequent crossing she made until the end of March 1945, she carried at least 12,000 people. The *Queen Elizabeth* never quite matched that single voyage record, but she carried, crossing for crossing, roughly the same numbers as the *Mary*. These were critical voyages, for the replacement troops and new units the *Queens* were carrying would become the spearhead of the Allied drive into Germany in 1945, bringing fresh strength to regiments and divisions exhausted by the ordeals of Operation Market-Garden, the struggle for the Hurtgen Forest, and the Battle of the Bulge.

One question that has never been fully answered is how significantly decisions made and actions taken to protect the *Queens* were influenced by Ultra. The code name for the British intelligence operation that successfully cracked the Germans' "unbreakable" Enigma cypher system, Ultra was fanatically guarded. It was a carefully utilized asset that allowed the Allied military leadership clandestine access to the operational—and sometimes tactical—planning of the German armed forces, as coded signals were sent via radio from the various command centers to units at the front or ships at sea. Though it sometimes took days to decypher a signal, there were occasions when they were read by the Allies as fast as or faster than their German recipients.

The information Ultra disclosed had to be used with extreme care, lest the Allies' reaction to German operations give away the secret to the Germans that the British and Americans were "reading their mail." More than once during the war, the security of German signals and cyphers was called into question by one or another of the branches of the German armed forces, but investigations by the various German security services never turned up sufficient evidence to suggest that the Enigma system had been compromised. Admittedly, it would have been hard to believe that it had: The arrangement of cypher keys, switches, and coding wheels in the Enigma machine allowed for a possible 150,000,000,000,000,000,000 substitutions for each letter typed into it, with no letter ever receiving the same substitution twice in a row. While the Germans did not deceive themselves into thinking that the codes could *never* be broken, they were convinced that the codes were unbreakable in any reasonable amount of time to be of any use to the Allies: Breaking the codes to extract information that was weeks, even months, out of date would have been a pointless waste of resources.

Winston Churchill took it upon himself to oversee the dissemination and utilization of Ultra intelligence personally and was quite prepared to make great sacrifices to protect its secret. It has been suggested, plausibly if not compellingly, that he went so far as to allow the Luftwaffe to bomb the English city of Coventry in April 1941—a raid that he knew of in advance, courtesy of Ultra—without giving the defenses any advance warning or taking any extra measures to protect the city. He believed, it has been said, that had he done so, it might have tipped the Germans to the knowledge that the British were reading German signals and caused them to seek a new cyphering system that would take the British years to break—if ever.

If Churchill were willing to sacrifice an entire city to protect Ultra, then it is fair to wonder if he would have been willing to sacrifice one of the *Queens* for the same purpose. Fortunately, it was a question that was never put to the test; on the balance, though, it seems doubtful that Churchill would have risked either of the *Queens* in order to save Ultra. The ability to read the German cyphers was of incredible value to the Allies; the *Queens,* on the other hand, were absolutely indispensable—and irreplaceable. Not only that, but should the *Mary* or the *Elizabeth* be sunk by a U-boat, the loss would have been such a propaganda coup for the Germans, as well as a devastating psychological blow to the Allies, that it was a risk the British and the Americans could not dare to run. The political consequences of losing one of the *Queens* are frightening to imagine. The death of most, if not all, of twelve to fifteen thousand soldiers and sailors aboard at a single blow—not lost in battle, from which the American and British people could derive some consolation, but instead destroyed by an unseen, undetected foe, without the means or opportunity to strike back—would have sent shock waves coursing through both nations. While it would be too much to suggest that either the British or American people would have clamored for a separate peace with Germany, it is not difficult to believe that they could have compelled their leaders, civilian and military, to rethink their strategies. With their troop transport capacity drastically curtailed, the Allies may well have been forced to postpone the invasion of Europe until 1945—by which time the Manhattan Project would have borne fruit. It may well have been that the first city to fall victim to an atomic bomb would have been Berlin, not Hiroshima, with a death toll in the millions rather than the tens of thousands.

The almost absolute immunity from U-boat attack that the *Queen Mary* and the *Queen Elizabeth* shared was almost certainly the result of a judicious use of operational intelligence garnered from Ultra intercepts. Knowing where and when Admiral Doenitz would be concentrating his U-boats would give the Admiralty planners the ability to plan courses for the *Queens* that would take them out of the threatened areas of the Atlantic.

While the existence of Ultra and the uses (real and imagined) made of it have garnered quite a bit of attention from historians in the last two decades, the fact that the Germans had made deep and potentially disastrous penetrations into British naval cyphers is not as widely known. For four years prior to the beginning of the war, the Beobachtungsdienst (German Naval Intelligence, usually shortened to B-dienst) had been monitoring British naval communications, eventually cracking the basic naval cypher, Number 2, in all but its highest-level variants. Though this was not a particularly dangerous state of affairs in peacetime, when war broke out in September 1939, the Royal Navy, in an incredible oversight, continued to use variants of this cypher, none of which long resisted German attempts to penetrate them. This was the cypher that the merchant fleet used, and almost all convoy signals were transmitted in it. The ability to read Admiralty signals gave the U-boats several significant advantages, not the least of which was foreknowledge of the course and speed of the convoys. The information on a convoy's composition was invaluable as well, as it allowed the U-boats to intercept convoys that were transporting particularly critical materials or equipment. Tankers were always a favorite target, since Britain had to import every gallon of gasoline, every ton of fuel oil.

Consequently, the B-dienst listened very carefully to every wireless transmission made by every ship on the North Atlantic. The British tried to keep all transmissions to a minimum—though they were unaware of the vulnerability of their cyphers, they did realize that every signal made by a convoy could provide the Germans with a position fix, which could prove deadly enough. But there was no way to eliminate such transmissions altogether: Changes in departure dates or times, escorts, or rendezvous points; additions to a convoy; reports of breakdowns or stragglers; details of enemy attacks—all had to be reported, providing the Germans with a goldmine of information about almost every Allied convoy, except for the *Queens.*

That there were none of these loopholes for the B-dienst to exploit in the security arrangements surrounding the *Queens* was due to their huge size. Given the number of troops each liner could carry, each sailing of either of the *Queens* was designated a convoy in itself. Their speed made escorts unnecessary, which eliminated one complication, and the fact that the "convoy" consisted of a single ship did away with the others. As a result, there were no last-minute alterations or additions made to their sailing orders that would require them to break radio silence and send a cyphered signal that the Germans could intercept and decode. The details of sailing dates, routing, and escort arrangements were kept secure by passing them between London, Washington, and New York via cable, which the Germans were unable to tap, as all of the terminals were in Allied hands. They were reduced to such transparent ruses as having one of their U-boats signal that it had torpedoed and sunk the *Queen Mary* or the *Queen Elizabeth,* in the hope that the Admiralty would demand an answer from the *Queen* in question, which would have allowed the Germans to get a fix on her radio signal. The Admiralty, whatever their other faults may have been, were never stupid enough to fall for that trick, and the strict observance of radio silence was reiterated and reinforced to the captains of both *Queens* with each sailing, so they were never tempted to fall for the ruse either. On the contrary—some of them, like Commodore Bisset, seemed to take an almost perverse delight in the repeated number of times their ship had been "sunk."

It wasn't long before the British suspected that there was a leak in the Admiralty somewhere, but they were unsure of its source—was it espionage or compromised cyphers? There was no point in changing cyphers if the source was an enemy spy in Whitehall or New York. The latter was a distinct possibility, as the American FBI was never as successful at catching German spies as the British XX Committee. Eventually, though, the British were able to accumulate enough evidence to show that the Germans were reading the Number 2 cypher almost at will, and when the Number 3 cypher replaced it in late 1941, the successes that the U-boats had been enjoying at the expense of the convoys began to decline dramatically. As for the *Queens,* their security apparently was never compromised during the course of the entire war, as the few times a U-boat encountered one of them were entirely chance events. In terms of its effect on the war, it was a security triumph every bit as great as that of the Manhattan Project.

There was another side to the coin of victory, however, one that military historians are often wont to gloss over, shunt aside, or, worst of all, ignore completely, and yet it was in many ways the most intimate and personal facet of the war—and of the service of the *Queens.* In his 1946 masterpiece, *The Best Years of Our Lives,* film director William Wyler presented a profoundly realistic portrayal of three American servicemen returning home for the first time after the war. The most memorable of the three was Homer Parrish, who had lost both hands in an explosion on the ship he was serving aboard. The actor who was given the part of Parrish, Harold Russell, had been selected for the role because, as a sergeant in the Canadian Army, he had lost his hands in a training accident. Russell and the character he played gave a very human face to the plight of thousands of soldiers who survived the war, but at a price: sometimes a simple wound, sometimes a disfigurement, sometimes the loss of a limb or other disability.

As the Allied armies advanced across Western Europe and up through Italy, then drove deep into Germany, the constant flow of troops eastbound from America to Great Britain was matched by a corresponding flow westward, one of fewer numbers but equal importance: wounded troops being taken back to the United States for treatment and convalescence. The Wehrmacht, though it knew after D-Day that defeat was inevitable, could still put up a skillful, sometimes fierce, always costly, defense.

Properly treating and caring for casualties was a priority for the Allies. Whole books could be written describing the medical services the Allies developed during World War II, from the medic in the field to the huge base hospitals in Great Britain. By mid-1944 the methods for evacuating a wounded soldier from of the front line, getting him back to an aid station, a clearing station, a field hospital, and ultimately to Britain, if necessary, were so carefully worked out that if a casualty made it back to the aid station alive, he had a 90 percent chance of survival.

Early on, the medical services developed a procedure that was used to assign priority to casualties, called "triage." A popular concept of triage is that of a ruthless system of deciding who will live without immediate treatment, who will die without immediate treatment, and who will die regardless of treatment. In practice, it was far less brutal: As applied by the Allies' medical services, triage was used at each facility to determine which casualties could be adequately treated there, which ones required treatment more specialized or sophisticated than the current facility could provide but were in no immediate danger, and which casualties needed to be sent farther back for proper treatment but whose wounds demanded immediate attention if they were to survive the journey.

Ultimately, almost all of the seriously wounded soldiers found themselves in a hospital in Britain, but before long, overcrowding in British medical facilities became a serious problem. The American Surgeon General and the Army Transportation Corps began casting about for ways to alleviate the crowding by evacuating increasing numbers of wounded men to the United States, beginning with modifying Liberty ships, turning their cargo holds into hospital wards that could hold as many as five hundred patients on each westbound crossing. While it was a help, this was a far from ideal solution, as there were problems with the Liberty ships that were difficult to overcome. The sanitary conditions of the holds were not the best, and adequate ventilation was a major concern. Also, few of those ships had anything approaching a properly equipped operating theater, an absolute necessity and not the sort of facility that could be thrown together in a few days.

On first thought, using the *Queen Mary* and the *Queen Elizabeth* as medical transports may have seemed an obvious solution to the problem, but there were significant problems with their suitability as well. Though each ship had been built with a small but comprehensive hospital, and both had additional troop dispensaries added while they were being converted for trooping duties, those really were not the sort of facilities needed to tend to several hundred or even several thousand seriously wounded men. The dispensaries were meant to treat the odd broken bone, sprained ankle, or bloody nose that would occur on the rougher crossings, and the hospitals were designed to meet emergency needs—appendectomies and the like. They were never intended to supply care for hundreds or thousands of seriously injured soldiers or sailors at one time.

Nevertheless, the need for medical transport became so urgent that the decision was made to utilize the *Queens* after all. In October 1944 both ships were surveyed in New York, and together the British Ministry of War Transport, the U.S. Surgeon General's office and the U.S. Army's Transportation Corps drew up plans to accommodate a thousand stretcher cases and seven hundred ambulatory patients in each. The conversion work took less than two weeks for each ship, essentially turning the ships' superstructures into huge hospital wards. Laboratories were added, several of the larger staterooms were given over areas where patients could exercise or receive physical therapy, and kitchens were installed that would cater to those patients with special dietary requirements. The permanent medical staffs were increased from thirty-five doctors and orderlies to over three hundred.

In late October both the *Queen Mary* and the *Queen Elizabeth* began bringing seriously wounded soldiers back to the United States, carrying an average of sixteen hundred patients on each trip. On several of these crossings, Canadian units being rotated out of Italy were embarked and carried to New York, where they boarded trains bound for Montreal. In January 1945 both ships had their medical facilities expanded to accommodate two thousand stretcher cases and a thousand ambulatory patients each. One of the unexpected consequences of that modification was that in order for some of the Canadian troops to reach their mess hall, they had to pass through part of the hospital area. Soldiers everywhere will always talk to other soldiers, and soon the Canadian lads and the wounded Americans began to strike up conversations. When they learned that the Canadian troops had been fighting there, the Americans soon were anxiously inquiring about the war in Italy.

The timing of the decision to utilize the *Queens* for medical evacuation was fortuitous, for the fall and winter months brought the Allies their heaviest casualties of the entire Western European campaign. The battle for the Hurtgen Forest, a wet, miserable, pointless campaign fought for an essentially worthless tract of land, lasted for ninety days and cost the American First Army more than twenty-four thousand combat casualties, three-quarters of them wounded. In addition to those losses, another nine thousand soldiers were victims of trench foot and disease. Barely two weeks after the Hurtgen Forest battle petered out, the Germans launched their Ardennes Offensive, which Americans came to know as the Battle of the Bulge—the Wehrmacht's last, desperate attempt to win a decisive victory in the West. By the time that campaign was officially declared closed, at the end of January 1945, almost eighty thousand American soldiers had become casualties to enemy fire or the bitter cold. Almost half of the reinforcements brought to Europe by the *Queens* between May 1944 and January 1945 were needed to replace these losses. The *Queens* were as vital as ever.

Eventually, though, the day came when the *Queens'* eastbound crossings, laden with troops destined for combat, came to an end: It was in March 1945 that both the *Queen Elizabeth* and the *Queen Mary* made their last runs to Gourock with troops aboard. By this time, the Third Reich was collapsing almost faster than the Allied armies could overrun it. The westbound crossing carrying wounded and invalid soldiers continued until June. In the meantime, the British and the Americans were drawing up detailed plans for using the *Queens* to bring American GIs back from Europe to the United States, where they would have a chance to rest and refit, and be trained to fight the Japanese in the Pacific.

The *Queen Mary* began this process on June 10, 1945, when she left Gourock for New York, with 14,777 GIs aboard, arriving in New York Harbor ten days later. She received a welcome of magnitude more tumultuous than her maiden voyage. Decked out in flags from stem to stern, the *Mary* found herself surrounded by hundreds of harbor craft, from fireboats throwing up sprays of water to small powerboats and sailboats that looked like the tiniest of minnows next to the greatest of whales. Every ship in the harbor sounded their whistles and horns in salute to the *Mary* as she passed, which she returned with almost constant blasts on her horn. The troops crowded the upper decks, straining to catch a glimpse of the Statue of Liberty and the New York skyline. Overhead, helicopters buzzed the ship, while a pair of blimps kept up a more stately escort. As the *Queen Mary* was eased against the Cunard pier, thousands of people leaning out of the windows of skyscrapers along the Hudson River, along with other thousands lining the docks, cheered wildly. At the pier, a brass band played continuously, unheard among the din. The troops began to disembark almost immediately, to be swallowed up in a heroes' welcome.

It wasn't to be a unique experience: New York accorded the same sort of welcome to the *Queen Elizabeth* later that month, and to both liners as each made another four crossings bringing GIs back to the United States. Similar welcomes awaited the *Queens* when they returned to Britain, for they brought with them nearly ten thousand Britons, expatriates returning home for the first time in almost five years, including thousands of children who had been evacuated to Canada during the dark days of 1940. It was altogether a very happy time for both ships.

The need for all those soldiers to be sent to the Pacific to fight the Japanese evaporated in early August 1945, when the Americans dropped atomic bombs on the Japanese cities of Hiroshima and Nagasaki, and the Rising Sun took a backward topple into the sea. When the news of the Japanese surrender was announced on August 14, the *Queen Elizabeth* had just delivered twelve thousand GIs to New York, while another fifteen thousand were in the middle of embarking on the *Queen Mary* at Gourock. Suddenly, these troops were not going home only to be shipped out again to fight another foe in another war—they were going home to stay!

By October 1945 the *Queens* brought almost 150,000 GIs home from Europe, an accomplishment that made the American public happy but was a source of some bitterness among the British. While the war was still being fought, no one questioned the wisdom of allowing the *Queens* to remain under American control, but now that the fighting had ended, many Britons, in and out of the Government, began to wonder out loud why they were being used to transport Americans home from Europe, rather than bringing British soldiers home from India and the Far East. Prime Minister Clement Atlee (who had replaced Churchill at No. 10 Downing Street in May) sent a cable to President Truman in October, bluntly telling him, "With so many of our troops overseas awaiting repatriation after nearly six years of war and separation from their families, I cannot justify to the British public the use of our three biggest ships [the *Aquitania* was also being used by the Americans] in the American service." Atlee went on to say that while he was not actually demanding the immediate return of the three ships, he did expect the United States to make a sufficient number of other ships available to the British to equal the capacity of the *Queens* and the *Aquitania*. Truman immediately ordered the Army Transport Corps to work out an equitable arrangement with the British Ministry of War Transport. Peacetime inertia had not yet set in for the bureaucracies involved, and in less than a week it was decided that the *Queen Mary* would remain under American authority and continue to bring the GIs home from Europe, while the *Queen Elizabeth* and the *Aquitania* were immediately returned to British control.

Originally, the U.S. Army Transport Command had worked out a schedule to have all of the GIs who were eligible to return to the United States brought back home by the end of January 1946. Following President Truman's directive, this was rapidly revised, and the details were carefully worked out to reshuffle the assignments and routing of a large number of ships, so that all of the GIs originally scheduled to return home would still be able to do so, even without the *Queen Elizabeth* and the *Aquitania*. The intricacies of the operation were lost on the American public, who could see only that two of the three largest troopships being used to return the GIs from Europe were suddenly being taken out of American service and given to the British. Newspapers across the country echoed that sentiment, adding their own editorial bleatings about how unfair it was that the British were being given preference over American boys and questioning the right of the British to demand the return of their own ships! It was all very unreal, but fortunately the ruckus was a tempest in a teapot that rapidly blew over, as it became apparent with each passing week that the original schedules were being maintained, even without the *Queen Elizabeth* and the *Aquitania.*

Ironically, the *Elizabeth* continued to sail between Gourock and New York until January 1946, bringing Canadian troops home from Europe, rather than GIs. It didn't matter—the cheers of the people greeting her arrival were just as loud and long as if the soldiers had been Americans: The people were simply delirious with peace. Once the Canadians disembarked, they were taken to Grand Central Station, where they waited for the trains that would take them to Montreal. American Red Cross volunteers working at the station plied them with coffee and doughnuts, and showed as great an interest in Newfoundland soldiers who were just returning from Italy or a Winnipeg regiment coming home from a year's combat in the Netherlands and the Lower Rhine as they did any American unit that had served with Patton's Third Army. These volunteers were fondly remembered for providing each soldier with a small khaki bag, nicknamed a "housewife," that contained shaving gear, a toothbrush and toothpaste, and a sewing kit, small treasures for which the soldiers were grateful, using them to make many a field uniform, as well as the man wearing it, look smarter on the last leg of the journey home. Some of the Canadian soldiers kept theirs for years afterward.

January 1946 found both *Queens* carrying their last contingents of troops. In a space of almost six years, they had traveled over a million miles, carried almost one and a half million soldiers, airmen, VIPs, POWs, and wives and children. The exact numbers will never be known, as many of the records for the first three years of the war were lost or incomplete. What is beyond dispute is their impact on Allied strategy and planning, and hence the course of the war itself. Without them, victory would have been far more costly, not only in terms of human lives, but in the price paid by humanity for that victory; with them, the Allies were able to bring the most evil empire history has ever known crashing to ruin. Sir Winston Churchill expressed it best in his tribute to the *Queen Mary* and the *Queen Elizabeth:* "Built for the arts of peace and to link the Old World with the New, the *Queens* challenged the fury of Hitlerism in the Battle of the Atlantic. Without their aid the day of final victory must unquestionably have been postponed."

CHAPTER TEN

Peace

Peace and rest at length have come
All the day's long toil is past,
And each heart is whispering, "Home,
Home at last."

—Thomas Hood

"THE PROBLEM WITH YOU YANKS IS THAT YOU'RE OVERPAID, OVERSEXED, AND over here!" It was an observation that had begun as a good-natured gibe when the numbers of American soldiers and airmen stationed in Great Britain began to grow to appreciable totals in mid-1943, but as the months passed, a note of asperity began to creep into it.

It had begun in October 1942, when the 29th Infantry Division was brought to Great Britain aboard the *Queen Mary*, the same voyage on which the *Mary* rammed and sank the cruiser HMS *Curacoa,* hardly an auspicious beginning for the American presence in Britain. At this point, Allied plans and objectives were still in a state of flux, and nobody knew what to do with the 29th. A somewhat desultory and apparently pointless training regimen was begun, but the division's morale eroded as the war seemed to be passing them by. Other units arriving in Britain began suffering the same decline— even the U.S. Army Air Corps, which at least had the ability to strike at the Germans, was confronted with serious morale problems when casualties began rising to frightening levels in the 8th Air Force's bombing raids over Germany.

The British, though certainly not hostile, were understandably perturbed that many of their "Tommies" were off to Africa or Italy to fight the Germans, or India and Burma to fight the Japanese, while ever-increasing numbers of American soldiers appeared to be doing nothing but sitting in their camps. At least it could be seen that the airmen were fighting. For the most part, the British accepted the situation with their typical phlegmatic poise, touched by a dash of humor, but the undercurrent of strain was always there.

When Gen. Dwight D. Eisenhower was appointed Supreme Commander of the Allied Expeditionary Forces in December 1943, things began to change. One of his first directives was to immediately initiate a program of extremely intense training for all Allied units, believing, with some justification, that training could be so intense and strenuous that the troops would become convinced that combat could not be any worse. It was greeted with something less than enthusiasm, though, to say the least, as all it seemed to do at first was add to the overall misery of the troops. Field exercises in the notoriously fickle British weather left the GIs exhausted, wet, and wretched. Adding homesickness to the mix only made it worse—the Americans were thoroughly unhappy.

After a few months, though, that began to change. The troops became more fit than they had ever been, and as their skill and proficiency improved, they gained a confidence and poise that they had never known before. Disciplinary problems declined as they took more pride in themselves, and as their self-pity evaporated, they began to look around them at the beautiful country to which they had been posted, and discovered the wonderful people among whom they were living.

Suddenly it was a situation almost akin to an invasion by a friendly army of occupation. The Americans discovered local pubs, local dances, and local girls who had been living—courtesy of the German U-boat fleet—under an austere regime of rationing and doing without. If there had been the slightest hint of malice in the GIs' actions or motives, the entire Western Alliance might have collapsed, but the Americans represented themselves to be exactly what they were: lonely young men, many of them not even out of their teens, who were a long way from home and just wanted the company of a friendly face.

If that face happened to be female, young, and pretty, so much the better. The British girls could hardly be blamed for being overwhelmed by the abundance of candy, chewing gum, cigarettes, and food from army and air corps mess halls. The young ladies' parents no doubt had their worries about their daughters and the intentions of their "Yank" friends—though that rarely stopped them from accepting the gifts of canned ham or fruit, ground coffee, or other delicacies, long vanished from wartime Britain, that the GIs brought along as a peace offering to "Mum and Dad."

And it wasn't just the American boys: The First Canadian Army, which the Overlord planners had designated as part of the invasion force, mustered a strength of nearly one hundred thousand men. At the same time, tens of thousands of other young men in the Royal Canadian Air Force were flying Lancaster, Mosquito, and Halifax bombers from bases scattered across the British Isles. The advances on the hearts of Britain's young ladies was an international, two-pronged assault.

The results were inevitable: American and Canadian boys fell in love with English and Scottish girls left and right, and the local priests and clergy were soon making regular visits to commanding officers all over Britain with requests for permission to marry one of the local girls to one of the officer's young men. The officers knew that their charges were often caught up in the throes of wartime passion, but they also knew that the men were liable to get married whether permission was forthcoming or not, so many a Solomonlike interpretation of Army Regulations resulted. And with all this going on, the Yanks couldn't let that initial barb go unrepaid. Before long, GIs were responding with typical American cheek: "The problem with you Limeys is that you're underpaid, undersexed, and under Eisenhower!"

When VE-Day arrived, and the GIs who weren't required for occupation duties in Germany began to be shipped back to the States, an intriguing situation developed—one that had no previous parallels. When the servicemen returned home, they were very vocal in demanding of their governments in Washington, D.C., and Ottawa that their brides be allowed to join them—and quickly. Similarly, the anxious new wives were clamoring for His Majesty's Government to make arrangements for them to join their husbands in the United States and Canada. Before the Japanese surrender in September 1945, bringing these "war brides" and their children to their new homes was a low priority, for obvious reasons. By the end of 1946, though, when most of the American troops scheduled to return from Europe were back home, Congress and both Parliaments cooperated in setting up "Operation Diaper," which would bring sixty thousand war brides and children to the United States and Canada.

The U.S. Army Transportation Corps took responsibility for the project and, in January 1946, announced that thirty ships would be taking part. The British Government, anxious to put both *Queens* back into passenger service as quickly as possible, at first resisted the idea of allowing either ship to be used for carrying the war brides and children to America and Canada, preferring that some of the older liners be used instead. The Americans were insistent, however, and eventually a compromise was reached: His Majesty's Government agreed to allow the *Queen Mary* to remain under American control for another six months, while the *Queen Elizabeth* would return to Britain so that she could finally be finished as the passenger liner she was always meant to be.

Before she could become part of what the American press soon dubbed the "bride and baby fleet," the *Mary* required substantial modification from her troopship guise in order to make her a satisfactory transport for young wives and small children. On January 14, 1946, returning to Southampton from her final run to New York carrying GIs, she entered the King George V dry dock, where she was the scene of sixteen frantic days of round-the-clock activity. First to go were the thousands of standee bunks, followed by the latrines and showers that had been temporarily installed throughout the ship. Next, over the side went all of the military equipment and fittings: the splinter shields over the bridge windows, the thousands of sandbags packed around vital areas of the upper works, the gun mounts on the decks, the radar tower behind the bridge, the Gunnery Officer's position on the Verandah Cafe, the gun tubs atop the ventilators—all were removed as quickly as possible. The last of the barbed-wire coils and barricades that had been erected throughout the ship when she was carrying German prisoners of war went over the side as well. The degaussing coil remained in place, though, as there was still a danger from floating mines. The hull was scraped of marine growth and corrosion, and the engineers examined the boilers and engines, replacing any parts that were worn or in questionable condition.

While all this was going on, crews were holystoning (scrubbing with a soft sandstone) the upper decks and scraping and polishing fittings all over the ship. Inside the *Mary,* workers painted the interiors, refurbished the decks, and six relatively comfortable bunks were installed in each of the staterooms. They restored the ship's nursery to its prewar condition, set up playpens in the smoking rooms, and, once the standee bunks were removed, strung the swimming pool on D Deck with clotheslines, the pool having been designated as an area for drying diapers. In anticipation of babies being born in midocean, call bells connected to the ship's hospital were set up in those cabins designated for expectant mothers. The dining rooms that had been turned into mess halls for thousands of soldiers became dining rooms once again, as the tables, chairs, linens, and tableware were brought out of storage and returned to the ship. During the last year of the war, most of the interior furnishings—carpets, furniture, murals, glassware, dishes—that had been removed in New York in early 1940 had been shipped to Southampton in anticipation of the day when they would be restored to their rightful places, and that day had arrived.

By January 30 the *Queen Mary* was judged ready to join the "bride and baby fleet" and was eased out of the dry dock to a place alongside the Ocean Dock, where her pantries and refrigerated rooms were stocked, her stores replenished, and her bunkers topped off. On February 5, 1946, she set sail for New York, with 1,706 brides and their 604 children aboard, the first of six crossings the *Mary* would make to New York as part of "Operation Diaper." There were five of these Southampton–to–New York voyages by the end of April 1946, which all told brought 12,886 young British women and their children to the United States. For everyone aboard, passengers and crew alike, these were happy voyages.

The American and British governments tried to be as fair as possible in determining which women would have priority in being brought to the United States. A handful of women who were deemed "hardship cases" because of special circumstances were given preferential treatment and allowed to come the United States before "Operation Diaper" actually began. One of ten such women aboard the *Queen Mary* when she left Southampton on December 29, 1945, was Mrs. Emily Glass, whose husband, Robert Glass, was a sergeant in the Army Medical Corps. Her special circumstances were named Shawn, Stephen, and Robert, Jr.—seven-month-old triplets. Traveling with her were eighty-eight hundred men of the 82nd Airborne Division, who took up a collection of $1 a man for the children to be used as a college fund. All eighty-eight hundred GIs became instant uncles as well, Mrs. Glass recalled, saying, "The American soldiers were so wonderful. They did just about everything." With one notable exception: Like most men, the soldiers managed to find ways of avoiding laundry duty, leaving Mrs. Glass to wash thirty-six diapers every day.

Joyce Beck was crossing with her fifteen-month-old son, David, in July 1946. Not a good sailor—it was the first time she had ever been aboard a ship—she suffered greatly from seasickness. Her first meal aboard the *Queen Mary* was her most memorable—and her only one. What made it memorable was the white bread. After five years of eating bread that had been grayer in appearance every month, as bleached flour became a wartime luxury, white bread became symbolic to Joyce—and thousands of other young British women who traveled on the "bride and baby fleet"—of not only the end of the war, but also the amazing new country and new life she was sailing to.

Joan MacKelden remembered the bread as well as the oranges—an unknown luxury in Britain for over five years.

Joyce Beck wasn't the only one who was seasick on that crossing. In fact, most of the wives and children were—and it wasn't always the fault of the sea or the *Mary*'s notorious roll. Capt. Giles Illingworth traced the source to something else: "The poor dears had been starved for chocolates. When they found the canteens loaded with sweets, I'm afraid they overindulged." It was a malady that would be repeated on subsequent crossings, as no one had the heart to close the canteens.

These crossings were as much fun for the crew as they were a fascination for the young women and children. During the day, there were lectures on life in the United States, cooking and sewing classes, and instruction on child care and nutrition. In the evenings there were dancing lessons, bingo games, and movies. (It is not recorded whether *Pride and Prejudice* was still being shown.) The ship's carpenter and his assistants built toys, rocking horses, and doll-houses for the children. The women took tours of the ship and saw firsthand how many of their husbands had come to Great Britain. The general consensus of the crew was that the children were noticeably better behaved than their fathers had been.

When the *Mary* arrived in New York at the end of her first crossing carrying war brides, the welcome she received was even warmer and louder than any of her arrivals carrying returning GIs. Every fireboat that could be spared escorted her into New York Harbor, throwing up sprays of water in salute, while hundreds of smaller ships and pleasure craft surrounded the huge liner and dozens of aircraft buzzed overhead. Once the *Mary* was tied up at Pier 90, gangways were swung into place, and a steady stream of young women and very small children began to flow down them. The immigration officials had set up what they thought was an efficient, sensible system for processing the young wives as they came off the ship. Each woman, and her children if she had any, was directed to an enclosure labeled with the name of the state that would be her ultimate destination; they would be processed in alphabetical order.

What the officials hadn't counted on was the reactions of the husbands, many of whom hadn't seen their wives for as much as a year, some of whom had never seen their children. The ex-soldiers and airmen soon ran out of patience and began swarming over the enclosures, pushing past gates and barricades, breaking down doors, doing whatever it took to be reunited with their loved ones. Soon a happy chaos overtook the whole scene, as officials gave up trying to maintain any semblance of order, and hundreds of couples and families were soon gathering each other up in loving embraces.

Sometimes, though, there wasn't a happy ending. Annie Smith was coming to America with her daughter, Joyce Elizabeth. She was one of the lucky ones who were able to secure passage on the *Queen Mary*'s first "bride and baby" crossing in 1946, and she celebrated her birthday on the second day of the voyage, February 6. Ultimately she was bound for Texas City, Texas, the hometown of her husband, Corp. Robert F. Smith. It was a "homecoming" tinged with sadness—Smith had been a tailgunner in a B-17 of the 535th Bomber Squadron, 381st Bomber Group, a plane nicknamed *Spamcan*. On May 24, 1944, *Spamcan* failed to return from a mission over Berlin. Initially Smith had been reported as missing, but by January 1946, the truth was known: He had been killed when his plane went down. Annie eventually reached Texas, where she met her late husband's family, who took her and little Joyce in while she set about trying to build a new life in the shadow of what might have been. Sad as her plight was, in a way Annie was lucky: She had a family waiting for her. Many an English girl or Scottish lass waited in vain for a Yank bomber to return or received a telegram informing her that her GI in France would not be coming back, cried her quiet tears and then carried on, never seeing America, never meeting the family of the boy she loved and lost.

While the *Queen Mary* was kept busy with brides and babies, the *Queen Elizabeth* was undergoing a transformation inside and out. When she left New York on February 21, 1946, the American government returned her to Admiralty control, which then promptly "demobbed" (demobilized) her and turned her over to Cunard when she arrived in Southampton five days later. That same day, the *Elizabeth* was guided into the King George V dry dock that the *Mary* had vacated three weeks earlier, and a small army of dockworkers and shipwrights descended on her to bring her to the glory she would have known back in 1940 had the war not intervened. Hundreds of workers chipped away the layers of wartime gray and applied thirty tons of new paint to dress her in the Cunard livery that she had never worn before: black hull, white superstructure, and Cunard-red funnels with black tops.

Fifteen hundred craftsmen came down to Southampton from the John Brown yard to finish the *Queen Elizabeth*'s interiors, among them 120 women who had mastered the art of applying a French polish finish to fine woodwork. All of the furniture and furnishings that had been prepared for her but had spent the last five years in storage were taken out of the warehouses and brought aboard: fifteen hundred wardrobes and dressing tables; four thousand mattresses; three thousand sets of curtains and bedspreads; forty-five hundred tables, armchairs, and settees; and more than six miles of carpets. When the work was finished, she had cabins for 823 First Class, 662 Cabin Class, and 798 Tourist Class passengers.

One of the more hotly debated aspects of the project was the fate of the handrails throughout the ship. Countless thousands of GIs, Canucks, and Tommies had left reminders of their presence behind on those railings in the form of names, initials, hometowns, regimental names and numbers, and bits of artwork carved into them with bayonet tips or penknives. Some thought that they should be left as they were, as a reminder of the great service the *Elizabeth* had performed during the war. Cunard, on the other hand, felt that there were already enough reminders and remembrances of the war throughout Britain, and their new flagship did not need to be one more. The rails were either planed smooth or, when necessary, replaced entirely.

Of a more practical matter, the *Queen Elizabeth*'s powerplant was given a thorough overhaul, her first in six years. While the dockyard workers were scraping the accumulated marine growth off the bottom of her hull, the *Elizabeth*'s engineers, along with a special team from John Brown, inspected her boilers, uptakes, turbines, and condensers, replacing boiler tubes, turbine blades, and shaft bearings wherever necessary. Her four great screws were removed and remachined to restore them to their proper balance, and her propellor shafts were drawn out and inspected, along with the packing of the shaft housings.

The British Government had decided that getting the *Queen Elizabeth* into service as quickly as possible should be a national priority. Understandably, there was some outcry among the Britons, who were still living under wartime rationing six months after the war had ended (rationing would continue in Britain for five more years) and resented the special exemptions the Government issued to Cunard for materials and workers, simply so the company could put a luxury liner to sea for the pleasure of the British aristocracy and American plutocrats. Cunard countered by pointing out that refitting the *Queen Elizabeth* would provide jobs in a battered British economy, and because the fixtures and furnishings had all been acquired before the war began, nothing was being taken away from the needs of British citizens. The Government believed that a refurbished *Queen Elizabeth* would be proof to the world that Great Britain was prepared to resume her rightful place in world affairs and was successfully putting the war behind her.

On October 16, 1946, the *Queen Elizabeth* finally set out from Southampton on her maiden voyage as a passenger liner, with Cmdr. James Bisset in command. King George VI, along with his two daughters, Princesses Elizabeth and Anne, had paid a visit to the ship a few days earlier while she was running speed trials. Princess Elizabeth, dutifully manning a stopwatch, timed the ship along the measured mile, noting a time of 2 minutes, 1.3 seconds, just a tick of the clock under thirty knots. For reasons known only to God and the laws of physics, despite having a theoretically better hull form and fractionally more power, the *Queen Elizabeth* would always be a shade slower than the *Queen Mary*. The King and his daughters spent the night aboard as the liner returned to Southampton and began final preparations for her long-delayed maiden voyage. The next morning, as he was leaving the First Class Dining Room after breakfast, the King was seen slipping a few of the white-bread rolls into a paper bag to take with him. During the war years, the Royal Family had chosen to live with the same rationing restrictions as the rest of their subjects, and white flour had been as hard to come by at Buckingham Palace as it had been in the East End.

The *Queen Elizabeth*'s first crossing as a passenger liner was booked solid. Among those aboard were several people who had booked passage on her eight years earlier for the maiden voyage that never took place. Two passengers in particular seemed rather out of place aboard her; at least, they were not the sort of passengers normally found in such monuments to capitalist decadence: Vyacheslav Molotov, the Soviet Union's Foreign Minister, and his deputy, Andrei Vishinski, were bound for the first session of the newly formed United Nations. At one point during the crossing, Commodore Bisset invited Comrades Molotov and Vishinski to tour the bridge, where Molotov, grinning like a schoolboy on holiday, took a stint at the ship's helm. It was later reported that he steered somewhat to the left.

Certainly, the two commissars had ample opportunity to sample the delights of western decadence. The dinner served the first night out was positively sybaritic, especially compared with the bland fare that Britons had grown accustomed to during the war:

Grapefruit au Kirsh
Hors d'Oeuvres Variés
Soup:—Consommé Royal, Cream of Mushroom
Fish:—Red Mullet Meunière, Halibut, Sauce Mousseline
Entrées:—Croquette of Duckling, Tête de Veau Vinaigrette

Joint:—Leg and Shoulder of Lamb with Mint Sauce
Vegetables:—Green Peas, Cauliflower
Potatoes:—Boiled, Roast, Snow, and Gaufrette
Relève:—Roast Turkey, Chipolata Sauce
Grill:—Devilled Ham and Succotash
Sweets:—Orange Soufflé Pudding, Coupe Monte Carlo,
Macedoine of Fruit Chantilly
Ices:—Vanilla, Strawberry, Lemon with Petit Fours

Cunard, to forestall any awkward questions about whence these delicacies had suddenly appeared, quickly pointed out in a press release that all of the items on the menu had been purchased in the United States for express use on the *Queen Elizabeth*. There was a minor note of panic when Sir Hugo Cunliffe-Owen, a tobacco magnate and major power in the London Stock Exchange, collapsed after dinner the first night out, but the fears of investors were quickly dispelled when it was reported that Sir Hugo was merely a victim of his own overindulgence and would make a full recovery. His system, accustomed to the bland fare of the war years, had simply succumbed to the richness of that first dinner. More than any other single malady, including seasickness, the consequences of overeating kept the ship's surgeons busy during that first crossing.

While the *Queen Elizabeth* was undergoing her refit, the *Queen Mary* was now being kept busy with a Canadian version of the "bride and baby fleet." From the beginning of May to the end of September 1946, she brought a total of 16,883 young women and their children from Southampton to Halifax, Nova Scotia, as the brides who had wed Canadian soldiers and airmen were reunited with their husbands. Though perhaps a bit more subdued, in keeping with the Canadian way of doing things, than the reactions the *Queen Mary*'s arrivals witnessed in New York, the welcomes at Halifax were every bit as warm and heartfelt. When the *Mary* steamed majestically into Halifax Harbour, her presence created as much of a sensation as the precious cargo she was carrying: She had stopped at Halifax only once during the war, in September 1944, when she brought Prime Minister Churchill and his entourage to Canada for the Octagon Conference. Arriving at nightfall, she was gone with the dawn the next day, and many Haligonians never knew she had been there. So when she arrived in May 1946, it was the first glimpse most of Halifax ever had of her, the largest ship the city had ever seen, or ever would see.

With the last of the British brides gone and the stores and fuel replenished, the *Queen Mary* bade farewell to Halifax for the last time on September 24. Captain Illingworth had been informed that the ship would be returning to civilian control as soon as he returned to Great Britain, happy news he gladly shared with the crew. Once the *Mary* reached open water, he rang down "FULL AHEAD" on all four engine telegraphs and left them there for the rest of the voyage—they were going home at last! Even the *Mary* herself seemed to sense that she was on her way back to the life she had been built for, as she made her fastest crossing of the Atlantic ever—three days, twelve hours, forty minutes, with a *sustained* speed of over thirty-two knots—a time that would stand as the second fastest crossing of the Atlantic by any passenger ship ever.

On September 29, two days after she arrived in Southampton, the Admiralty officially handed the *Queen Mary* back to Cunard. During her service in "light sea grey," she had traveled more than six hundred thousand miles and carried nearly eight hundred thousand people of all descriptions. The *Queen Elizabeth* had traveled more than five hundred thousand miles and carried almost seven hundred thousand souls. With none of the midwinter refits and layups that would have marked their civilian service, the two ships had steamed over a million miles without a major mechanical failure or breakdown. They never missed a sailing, never arrived more than a few hours late. If the quality, pride, or care that John Brown's Scottish shipwrights put into their workmanship were ever questioned, here were the answers.

A ten-month-long refit of the *Queen Mary,* which was as comprehensive as that given to the *Queen Elizabeth,* was undertaken at Southampton. Once again entering the King George V dry dock, her hull was once more scraped and inspected, while her wartime coat of gray was chipped away and replaced with her resplendent Cunard livery. A similar debate to that waged over the GI-scarred railings of the *Queen Elizabeth* broke out over the equally scarred railings of the *Queen Mary.* This time, the decision was made to repair or replace them immediately, but at least one of the yard workers, whose name has been lost to history, decided to save some of the sections of railing, a thoughtful act for which future generations would be grateful. One detail that was attended to, which the urgencies of war had never left time for, was a permanent repair to her bow. The concrete substitute that had been fitted after the *Mary*'s tragic collision with the *Curacoa* was removed, and a new cutwater frame, forged in Glasgow and shipped down to Southampton, was fitted, along with new shell plating. All of her interior fittings and furnishings had been returned to Southampton from Sydney and New York, and soon the *Queen Mary's* interiors were restored to their prewar splendor. Some modifications were made to the passenger accommodations, allowing her to carry 711 First Class, 707 Cabin Class, and 577 Tourist Class passengers, 1,995 in all. An added bonus was that air-conditioning was fitted throughout the ship, something Cunard had overlooked for the *Elizabeth,* an amenity she wouldn't have until 1950.

The *Queen Mary* returned to service on July 31, 1947, sailing from Southampton to New York. The *Queen Elizabeth* left New York Harbor the following day, finally making the Cunard line's dream of a two-ship weekly transatlantic express service a reality. The next decade and a half would be a golden time for the century-old company, as the line had twelve ships in service, including the two greatest ships ever to sail the route, and completely dominated the transatlantic trade. Incredibly profitable during these years, the *Queens* were routinely booked solid on most voyages. With commercial air travel still in its infancy, the ocean liner was still, in John Maxtone-Graham's felicitous phrase, "the only way to cross."

And astonishingly, so many of those making that crossing had, only a few short years before, journeyed across the Atlantic in those same ships, carrying rifles, wearing uniforms and steel helmets. Now, with their new wives on their arms and children in tow, they went back to Europe to reminisce with old friends; drink beer in fondly remembered pubs; stroll in peace along streets where once they could only crawl in safety; gawk at cathedrals that they had only glimpsed through bombsights; gaze out across beaches still choked with burned-out hulks of tanks, trucks, and landing craft; or spend a few silent moments in one of those vast fields of white crosses, saying a last farewell to buddies who would forever be left behind. Peace had come at last.

The Hand of Fate

Though much is taken, much abides. . . .
—Tennyson

SO THE WAR FINALLY ENDED FOR THE WARRIOR QUEENS, AND ENDED WITH shouts of joy and a fanfare of trumpets. Oh, the shouts were real enough, and if the fanfare was more imagined than heard, it was all the more real for that. The *Queen Mary* and the *Queen Elizabeth* would spend the rest of their days proudly wearing the colors of the Cunard line, never again donning war paint or mounting guns. But they could rightly take their place alongside the great warships of history because, on their decks, history was made.

How can that be said? What made the *Queens* more than just two gray behemoths endlessly plying back and forth between the United States and the United Kingdom? They never fired a shot in anger, never sank an enemy ship or submarine, never destroyed an enemy aircraft, never took part in an invasion fleet. Was the signal made by the captain of an escorting destroyer to the captain of the *Queen Mary*, "Tramdriver!" really just a barbed encapsulation of the truth? Many liners, French, American, Italian, British, served as transports during World War II, so why should the *Queens* be singled out and glamorized, when there was nothing fundamentally different about them but their size?

It was their size that made all the difference. It gave them the capacity to carry more troops at greater speeds than had ever been transported at one time before. Between them, the *Queen Mary* and the *Queen Elizabeth* brought an average of sixty thousand American and Canadian soldiers to Great Britain every month—and did so for three years! Ultimately, they transported more than one and a half million men—the greatest ongoing mass movement of troops in history—and it changed the history of the world. They allowed Britain and the United States to build up the strength to launch the invasion of Europe at precisely the right moment, when it would mean the beginning of the end of the Third Reich. The decisive battle of World War II in Europe—D-Day—was only made possible by the accomplishments of the Warrior *Queens.*

Without them, the Allied invasion of Europe would not have been possible before 1945, which would have granted a year's reprieve to the Nazis, a year in which they could have achieved their reorganization of Germany's industries, completed the design and testing of new weapons, finished the defenses of the Western Wall. The Soviet lunge into Central Europe in the summer of 1944, which destroyed so much of the Wehrmacht's power that the Germans never recovered, would have become instead a long, bloody slog against a better-armed and -equipped foe. While the Allied victory may only have been postponed, that postponement would have spelled death and destruction for millions more, civilian and combatant, innocent and guilty alike.

Instead, the British and American divisions went ashore on June 6, 1944, and eleven months later, the Thousand Year Reich lay in ruins. It happened because the Allies depended on the Warrior *Queens,* which never let them down. They brought to Europe the margin of manpower that proved decisive. Their place is assured not only in maritime history, but in military history as well, crystallized in the words of Sir Winston Churchill: "Built for the arts of peace and to link the Old World with the New, the *Queens* challenged the fury of Hitlerism in the Battle of the Atlantic. Without their aid the day of final victory must unquestionably have been postponed."

Their accomplishments left a lasting impression on both the Royal Navy and the U.S. Navy. While the United States has never quite grasped the concept of sea power as fully as Great Britain, the strategic capabilities that the *Queen Mary* and the *Queen Elizabeth* gave the Royal Navy were not lost on its American counterpart. When the decision was made in 1952 to build an American superliner that would wrest the Blue Ribband from the British, every feature of the new ship's design was subordinated to the requirements of her expected wartime role, that of a troopship. When the SS *United States* entered service in 1955, she was every bit as fast as expected, taking the Blue Ribband away from the *Queen Mary* with an average speed of more than thirty-eight knots, a record that, however valiantly she might try, the *Queen Mary* could never hope to surpass. Yet the veil of elegance the *United States* wore was transparent: Features worked into her design to accommodate her wartime role left an impression on the amenities that she offered to her passengers, none more so than the extensive fireproofing throughout the ship. Aluminum was everywhere, wood was not to be found, save for the butcher blocks in the galleys and the grand pianos in the lounges. Except for the linens on the beds in the passengers' cabins and on the tables in the dining rooms, every fabric was fiberglass, from the carpets to the draperies. The *United States* was a technological tour de force but lacked the charm and warmth of the *Queens*—as more than one passenger was quick to remark, for all her veneer of civility, it was never difficult to see that she was really just a warship in disguise.

Her usefulness as a troopship was never put to the test, although the day would come when she would be sorely missed. More than one senior American officer privately bemoaned that the U.S. armed forces lacked her capabilities in 1990 and 1991, when the buildup of forces for Operations Desert Shield and Desert Storm took months and strained the airlift capacity of the American military and civilian air transport systems nearly to the breaking point. Had the *United States* still been in service, the buildup that took five months could have been accomplished in half the time, at a fraction of the cost.

That the Royal Navy never lost sight of the need for troopships was dramatically illustrated during the Falklands War of 1982. Carrying on the proud tradition of her Cunard forebears, the *Queen Elizabeth 2,* accompanied by the P&O Line's *Canberra,* transported nearly five thousand British soldiers to the South Atlantic, then served as a support ship during the four weeks of combat operations, a vital component of the swift and relatively bloodless British victory. It was an effort worthy of the original Warrior *Queens.*

Sadly, though, by then they were gone. Age and wear eventually caught up with them, and the growing popularity of air travel reduced their usefulness from an expensive necessity to merely a costly luxury. Revenues fell as passenger lists declined, while operating expenses mounted, until Cunard was compelled to make the choice it dreaded, but knew was inevitable, and drew up plans to withdraw them both from service. One *Queen* eventually was consigned to permanent immobility within sight of the ocean, becoming a floating hotel and tourist attraction. The other suffered the ignominy of being turned into a monument to one man's ego and self-promotion, then was destroyed by a fire that was never adequately explained.

The *Queen Mary* was the first to go. In 1966 Cunard lost more than £3,000,000, much of it due to the operating costs of the two Queens. Sadly, the line announced that the *Mary* would have to be sold, and in 1967 a deal was concluded with a group of developers in Long Beach, California, where the *Mary* was eventually permanently berthed and turned into a hotel and convention center. On October 31, 1967, as tens of thousands of people watched from the shore and hundreds of small craft surrounded her, she steamed proudly out of Southampton for the last time, flying a paying-off pennant 310 feet long—10 feet for every year of service. It was as she was leaving Southampton that one last salute was paid to her in honor of her wartime career.

HMS *Hermes*, one of the Royal Navy's most modern aircraft carriers, as well as one of its most powerful ships, was entering the harbor as the *Queen Mary* was departing. *Hermes*'s skipper, Capt. Terrence Lewin, always the gentleman, thought it fitting and proper to acknowledge the *Queen Mary*'s passing, not only for her greatness as a liner, but also as a warship. *Hermes*'s complement of Buccaneer bombers and Sea Vixen fighters took to the air to perform a fly-by for the old liner, while the aircraft carrier's crew manned the port side of the flight deck to give three rousing cheers to the departing Queen. Thirty-nine days later, the *Mary* arrived at Long Beach, where she became a permanent reminder of the lost glories of the great transatlantic liners.

For the *Queen Elizabeth,* the end was far more melancholy. Retired in 1969, she was sold to a group of Florida investors who hoped to imitate the *Queen Mary*'s success by similarly ensconcing the *Elizabeth* in Fort Lauderdale. For two years, the last of the great, traditional British liners sat desolate and neglected off the coast of South Florida, as plan after plan was devised for turning her into a paying proposition, but none was ever carried out. Finally, a Hong Kong businessman, C. Y. Yung, who had a bank account to match his ego, purchased the rapidly aging *Queen Elizabeth* and sailed her to Hong Kong Harbor. There she underwent a renovation of sorts, becoming the Seawise University, meant to be a sort of floating institution of higher learning, although exactly how that was to come about was never really explained. The sly reference to the owner's name in the new identity of the *Queen Elizabeth* reinforced the opinion of those who believed that Yung had bought her simply in a fit of the most conspicuous consumption ever displayed. Whatever his real plans for her, the *Queen Elizabeth* never fulfilled them. On the night of January 9, 1972, a fire broke out in one of the ship's kitchens, and within two hours, it had raced through the ship, gutting her completely. By morning, her stability lost as her structural integrity failed, the *Queen Elizabeth* rolled onto her starboard side, her superstructure collapsing within minutes. It took the Hong Kong Harbor Fire Department three days to put the fire out. Two years later, the wreck was scrapped.

Though they were gone from the oceans they once ruled, the *Queens* did not depart without a fanfare of their own, nor without a chance to offer each other one last salute. The time was just past midnight, September 25, 1967, the place somewhere in the middle of the North Atlantic. The two great ocean liners, the *Queen Elizabeth* westbound for New York, the *Queen Mary* eastbound for Southampton, were about to pass one another. The *Elizabeth* had crossed the Atlantic with almost clockwork regularity for over twenty years, the *Mary* for more than thirty, and there had been dozens of such meetings in that time. But this midocean encounter of the two ships was different from any other: it would be their last such meeting, ever. Once the *Queen Mary* reached Southampton, she would be withdrawn from service and retired. The *Queen Elizabeth* would follow her within a year. After a decade and a half of valiant struggle by the great ships, the airplane had finally sounded the death knell of the transatlantic passenger liner.

Word of the encounter had been spread about both ships, and notices reminding the passengers had been prominently posted. Yet when the time came, only a few dozen hardy souls on either *Queen* were willing to brave the cold winds and late hour to watch the two sisters pay a final salute to each other. Anxious eyes on the bridges and upper decks of both ships watched as first one, then two masthead lights edged over the horizon, then suddenly what had been just a blur in the darkness began to take shape as a black-and-white ocean giant. At a word from each ship's captain, the upper decks of both the *Queen Mary* and the *Queen Elizabeth* were illuminated, the red and black of their funnels glowing above their gleaming white superstructures. The ships were each racing at nearly thirty knots, closing with breathtaking speed. As they passed port side to port side, each captain—Capt. John Treasure Jones on the *Mary*, Cmdr. Geoffrey Marr on the *Elizabeth*—stepped out onto the bridge wing to lift his hat in salute to the other. The great steam whistles bellowed out their own acknowledgment, but their stentorian accolade was as much a dirge as it was an honor. . . .

Then, as suddenly as it had come, the moment passed, and the ships sped away from each other toward their uncertain futures. The notes of their whistles faded into the night, their deck lights were darkened. Within half an hour, they were almost out of sight of one another, and those few souls perceptive or romantic enough to understand the meaning of what they had just witnessed broke from their reveries and began to drift off to their cabins. Soon the masthead lights vanished over the horizon, leaving each ship alone on the ocean, bound for destinies that none of the men who built them could have imagined, let alone foreseen as inevitable. The day of the Warrior *Queens* was finally over.

Facts About the *Queens*

	Queen Mary	*Queen Elizabeth*
Launch date:	September 26, 1934	September 27, 1938
Gross tonnage:	80,677	83,673
Length:	1,019 ft.	1,031 ft.
Beam:	118 ft.	118 ft., 6 in.
Draught:		
Designed:	36 ft.	36 ft., 6 in.
Deep:	44 ft.	44 ft.
Number of funnels:	3	2
Number of masts:	2	2
Number of boilers:	24	12
Engines:	single reduction turbines (4 sets)	single reduction turbines (4 sets)
Horsepower:	160,000 shp	160,000 shp
	(both ships were later rerated to 200,000 shp)	
Propulsion:	quadruple screw	quadruple screw
Service speed:	29 knots	29 knots
Top speed:	32.66 knots	32.2 knots
Passenger accommodations:		
First class:	776	823
Cabin class:	784	662
Tourist class:	579	798
Crew:	1,035	1,280

ACKNOWLEDGMENTS

WARRIOR QUEENS WAS AN INTRIGUING BOOK TO RESEARCH, AS WELL AS TO write. I have always had a strong interest in ships and the sea, and in particular, the great liners of the twentieth century. Two of them, the *Titanic* and the *Lusitania,* became the subjects of my first two books, *"Unsinkable": the Full Story of RMS* Titanic (1998), and *The* Lusitania*: The Life, Loss, and Legacy of an Ocean Legend* (2000), both published by Stackpole Books. In the course of my research for those books, I kept encountering bits and pieces of the stories of the two ships that were the ultimate achievements of the British shipbuilders' art, the *Queen Mary* and *Queen Elizabeth.* So I guess it was somehow inevitable, then, that my attention—and my pen—should eventually turn to those great ships. And just as the focus of *The* Lusitania was very different than that of *"Unsinkable,"* so is that of *Warrior Queens* different from the first two books. More than all those years of grand crossings of the Atlantic in peacetime by these two stately ships, with their great black hulls, gleaming white superstructures, and towering red funnels, the most fascinating chapters of their long and storied lives were those years when they wore the Royal Navy's "light sea grey" and became the "Grey Ghosts"—pounding across the North Atlantic, defying Hitler's submarines and bombers, on their way to changing the course of history. It was out of those images that *Warrior Queens* was born.

A surprising number of contributors, separated by time and geography, made *Warrior Queens* possible. While a complete listing of the various institutions where some part, great or small, of the research for this book was carried out can be found in the Sources listings, some deserve special mention. That research began at John Brown Engineering, the successor to John Brown and

Company, Shipbuilders, which in the closing days of the 1990s occupied a fraction of the banks of the Clyde that the great shipyard covered when the *Queen Mary* and the *Queen Elizabeth* were built. Sadly, as the last chapters of *Warrior Queens* were being written, the final pages of the story of John Brown and Company were already writ. On December 31, 2000, the firm closed its doors forever, and one of the last remaining links to the glory days of British shipbuilding was reduced to memory.

The Mitchell Library in Glasgow is a veritable treasure trove of information about the great ships built on the Clyde. The library's filing system does take some getting used to, but the pages and librarians were always models of courtesy and patience. The same can be said for the staff of the Glasgow Museum of Transport. At the shipyard, the library, and the museum, I was always received with typical Scottish hospitality and helpfulness, proving to me that the phrase "dour Scot" was a jealous invention of their southern neighbors.

The next step was the National Maritime Museum in Greenwich, England, where I was received with the courtesy and professionalism I've come to always associate with that institution. No museum in the world can surpass the National Maritime for the breadth and depth of resources or the accumulated nautical knowledge that it makes available to a historian. It is staffed by men and women who truly know ships and the sea, and so can give insights and perspectives on a subject that might otherwise escape an ordinary historian. The British are, of course, still justly proud of the *Queens*, and the staff of the museum, from its director, Dr. Stephen Deuchar, on down to the receptionists at the front desk, made that pride evident with their unstinting helpfulness.

If there is an equivalent to the National Maritime Museum in the United States, it would have to be the Mariners' Museum of Newport News, Virginia. I would be remiss if I failed to acknowledge my debt to its staff, men and women who know and love the lore of ships and the tales of the sea: Their collective knowledge of American maritime history (which the saga of the Warrior *Queens* is unquestionably a part) has no equal anywhere else in the United States.

Logistics is rarely glamorous, but it wins wars. If anyone doubts that fundamental truth, a visit to the U.S. Army Transportation Corps Museum at Fort Eustis, Virginia, will certainly set them straight. The museum's archives and displays tell an eloquent story of the usually unsung but nevertheless herculean efforts that were required to enable the monumental battles about which most military historians favor writing to be fought. Anyone who wants a true appreciation for the accomplishments of the *Queens* during the war years will be more than amply rewarded by a visit to the museum and a discussion with its staff.

Tales of the *Queen Mary*'s visits to Halifax can be found in the Public Archives of Nova Scotia and the Maritime Museum of the Atlantic, both located in Halifax, Nova Scotia. My association with those two institutions, as well as the city of Halifax, goes back many years, to when I began my research on the *Titanic*. It is, in my opinion, one of the friendliest cities in the world, and if the people of Halifax should ever decide to make me an honorary Haligonian, I'll be pleased to claim the title!

The Michigan University Library System was invaluable, as I worked through the library of Grand Valley State University in Allendale, Michigan. In Florida, two library systems are worth mentioning: the Orange County Library and the Broward County Library, both of which could serve as models for public library systems throughout the country. And though no great contribution was directly made to this book by Michigan's Lapeer County Libraries, I have to acknowledge a very real debt: It was in what is now the Marguerite DeAngelis Library in downtown Lapeer that, as a ten-year-old boy, I discovered books and all the worlds they could unlock for me, and unknowingly set myself on a course that would one day lead me to become a contributor to the library's contents.

A special thanks is due to the officers and ratings who escorted me through HMS *Caroline,* a Royal Navy light cruiser permanently moored as a training ship in Belfast, next to the Harland and Wolff Shipyard. *Caroline* is the last of the "C" class cruisers, and the sister ship of HMS *Curacoa*. My visit aboard her gave me an excellent insight into what serving—and living— aboard *Curacoa* was like, as well as an increased respect and appreciation for *Curacoa*'s crewmen.

Particular mention is reserved for certain individuals whose contributions to this work were so unique or so specific that they merit singling out. James Krogan, marine architect and president of James S. Krogan & Co. of Miami, offered his professional expertise, as did Matthew McLean, a retired Bosun of the British Merchant Marine who now lives in Pembroke Pines, Florida. Jerry Cerrachio, of Elizabeth, New Jersey, a former sergeant in the U.S. Army Air Corps, gave generously of his time as he willingly shared his memories of his crossing on the *Queen Mary.* CPO Ivan Harris, RN (ret.), was a goldmine of information on the Royal Navy, and his recollection of the *Queen Mary*'s departure on her final voyage was priceless. Lt. Cmdr. Alan Young, RN (ret.), shared freely of his memories of service in the Royal Navy during the Second World War.

Harold Butler, of Davison, Michigan, who was an Able-bodied Seaman in the American Merchant Marine during World War II, provided advice on nautical terminology, usage, and equipment. He is also my father, and the source of my interest in ships and the sea, so if someone doesn't particularly like any of my books, blame him, not me! His brother, Robert Butler, of Greensburg, Pennsylvania, served in the 15th Air Force during the Second World War, while a third brother, Edwin Butler, of Lapeer, Michigan, served in the Ordnance Corps of the U.S. Army. Though none of the three had any direct experience with either the *Queen Mary* or the *Queen Elizabeth,* they provided a wealth of personal details about the lives of enlisted soldiers and seamen in World War II, and in doing so provided a color and texture that made the stories of the men who sailed aboard the *Queens* much more real and tangible. For that, and for so much more, I salute all three Butler brothers.

A special word of thanks is due to Capt. Tony Crompton, retired Master Mariner, and Ilya McVey, an officer in the British Merchant Marine. These two gentlemen have, in a correspondence lasting for almost four years, offered many insights and real-life examples of how the realities of life at sea differ from the ideals cherished by regulators and academics. It's been an eye-opening experience, to say the least.

Last, my unending thanks to Trish Eachus, of Jacksonville, Florida, best friend and fellow author, who volunteered considerable time and effort to locate source material and research obscure topics. (If she keeps it up, I may have to take her on as a full-time employee.) Trish also did yeoman work in reading this book while it was still in manuscript form, offering her insights, comments, and criticisms—and taking mischievous delight in pointing out the worst of my run-on sentences!

To all of these individuals and institutions, I offer my thanks, however inadequate the words may seem. In every case, they supplied me with information or support of some kind. How I used it is my responsibility, and I hope I haven't done any of them a disservice. If I have, the fault is entirely mine.

SOURCES

BOOKS

Ambrose, Steven. *Citizen Soldiers: The U.S. Army from the Normandy Beaches to the Bulge to the Surrender of Germany, June 7, 1944–May 7, 1945*. New York: Simon & Schuster, 1997.

———. *D-Day: June 6, 1944: The Climactic Battle of World War II*. New York: Simon & Schuster, 1994.

Behrens, C. B. A. *Merchant Shipping and the Demands of War*. From *History of the Second World War: United Kingdom Civil Service*. London: HMSO, 1955.

Bisset, Cmdr. Sir James. *Commodore: War, Peace and Big Ships*. London: Angus & Robertson, Ltd., 1961.

Brinnin, John Malcolm. *The Sway of the Grand Saloon*. New York: Delacorte Press, 1971.

Bryant, Sir Arthur. *The Turn of the Tide*. New York: Doubleday & Company, 1958.

Churchill, Sir Winston S. *The Second World War*. Vols. I–VI. Boston: Houghton Mifflin Company, 1948–1953.

Grattidge, Capt. Harry. *Captain of the Queens*. London: Oldbourne Press, 1956.

Harding, Stephen. *Gray Ghost: The RMS Queen Mary at War*. Missoula, MT: Pictorial Histories Publishing, 1982.

Keegan, John. *Six Armies in Normandy: From D-Day to the Liberation of Paris*. New York: Penguin Books, 1983.

———. *The Second World War*. New York: Viking Penguin, 1990.

Lewin, Ronald. *Ultra Goes to War*. London: Hutchinson, 1978.

Maddocks, Melvin. *The Great Liners.* Vol. 4 of *The Seafarers.* Alexandria, VA: Time-Life, 1978.

Manchester, William. *The Last Lion: Winston Spencer Churchill—Visions of Glory, 1878–1932.* Boston: Little Brown and Company, 1983.

Maxtone-Graham, John. *The Only Way to Cross.* New York: MacMillan Company, 1972.

Miller, William H., and David F. Hutchings. *Transatlantic Liners at War: The Story of the Queens.* New York: David & Charles, 1985.

Padfield, Peter. *An Agony of Collisions.* London: Hodder & Stoughton, 1966.

Roskill, Capt. S. W. *The War at Sea.* Vols. 1 and 2 of *History of the Second World War: Unied Kingdom Civil Service.* London: HMSO, 1954 and 1956.

Stevens, Leonard A. *The Elizabeth: Passage of a Queen.* New York: Alfred A. Knopf, 1968.

Thomas, David A., and Patrick Holmes. *Queen Mary and the Cruiser: The Curacoa Disaster.* Annapolis, MD: Naval Institute Press, 1997.

Van der Vat, Dan. *The Atlantic Campaign: World War II's Great Strugle at Sea.* New York: Harper & Row, 1988.

Winter, C. W. R. *Queen Mary: Her Early Years Recalled.* London: Hodder & Stoughton, 1986.

NEWSPAPERS

Boston Globe
Glasgow Herald
Halifax Chronicle-Herald
London Times
New York Times
Toronto Globe
Wall Street Journal
Washington Post

ARCHIVES AND COLLECTIONS
Australia
The Australian War Memorial, Canberra

Canada
The Canadian War Museum, Ottawa
The Maritime Museum of the Atlantic, Halifax

The Public Archives of Canada, Ottawa
The Public Archives of Nova Scotia, Halifax

United Kingdom
Cunard Archives, Liverpool and London
John Brown Engineering, Ltd., Clydebank
Naval Historical Branch, Ministry of Defence, London
Public Records Office, London
University of Liverpool Archives, Liverpool
The Imperial War Museum, London
The National Maritime Museum, Greenwich

United States
The Eisenhower Center, University of New Orleans
The Library of Congress, Washington, D.C.
The Mariners' Museum, Newport News, Virginia
The National Archives, Washington, D.C.
The U.S. Army Military History Center, Washington, D.C.
The U.S. Army Quartermaster Museum, Fort Lee, Virginia
The U.S. Army Transportation Coprs Museum, Fort Eustis, Virginia
The U.S. Naval Historical Center, Washington, D.C.

INDEX

Admiral Scheer, DKM, 70
Andes, RMS, 50
Aquitania, RMS, 4, 22–23, 44, 91, 154–155
Athenia, RMS, 26, 62, 73
Atlee, Clement, 154
Australia, HMAS, 50

B-17 (bomber), 87
B-24 (bomber), 87
Baldwin, Stanley, 51, 89
Beck, Joyce, 161, 162
Belfast, HMS, 53
Berengaria, RMS, 6
Bismarck, DKM, 70, 71
Bismarck, SS, 4, 6
Bissett, Cmdr. James, 60–61, 62, 89–90, 91, 95, 131–132, 149, 165
Bloody Foreland, Ireland, 88, 99, 103
Blyskawica (Polish destroyer), 109, 117
Boston Navy Yard, 124

Boutwood, Capt. John W., 104–106, 106–107, 111, 112, 114, 118, 119, 121–122
Bower, Pvt. Eric, 120
Bramham, HMS, 109, 117, 120
Bremen, SS, 9, 21, 27, 62
Britannic, RMS, 4, 6
British Merchant Marine, 60, 106
Brooke, Gen. Sir Alan, 93, 94–95
Bruller, Capt.-Lt. Ernst-Ulrich, 91
Bulldog, HMS, 109, 117
Butler, Able Seaman Harold, 136

Campania, SS, 2, 4
Canadian Army, 145, 159
Canberra, SS, xiv, 171
Cape Town, South Africa, 49, 51
Cappellini, HIMS, 76
Carpathia, RMS, 60
Carter, Seaman Geoffrey, 120
Cerrachio, Sgt. Jerry, 129, 132, 134

Chamberlain, Neville, xiii, 10, 20, 23–24, 26, 30, 34, 35–36, 51, 102
Chaney, Maj. Gen. James E., 80
Churchill, Winston, 36, 38, 51, 73, 79, 80, 81, 82–83, 92–95, 143, 147–148, 156, 166, 170
Clarkson, Stoker Kenneth, 118
Cockatoo Docks and Engineering, 50, 53, 125
Cole, Capt. John, 120
Compangnie Generale Transatlantic (French Line), 8, 9
Conte di Savoia, SS, 22,
Conte Rosso, SS, 62
Cornwall, HMS, 57
Courageous, HMS, 73
Cowdray, HMS, 109, 117, 120
Cunard Line (later Cunard-White Star Line), 1, 2, 3–4, 6–7, 8–10, 11, 13, 20, 23, 29, 43, 44, 46, 57, 84, 106, 121, 163, 164, 166–167, 171–172
Cunliffe-Owen, Sir Hugo, 166
Cunningham, Adm. Andrew, 93
Curacoa, HMS, 99, 100–103, 106–107, 108, 110, 111, 112, 113–120, 121, 122, 157, 167
Curtin, John, 59
Czechoslovakia, 24

Dennis, Seaman Fred, 119–120
Deutschland, DKM, 37, 70
Deutschland, SS, 2
Dobbs, Sgt. Sid, 120

Doenitz, Adm. Karl, 25–26, 72–73, 74, 76–77, 96, 148
Duke of York, HMS, 35, 39, 71

Eaton, Leading Signalman Donald, 118
Eisenhower, Gen. Dwight D., 81, 144, 158
Emergency Quota Act ("Three Per Cent Act"), 8
Empress of Britain, RMS, 50, 62
Empress of Canada, RMS, 50, 62
Empress of Japan, RMS, 50
Enigma (German encryption system), 75, 92, 146–147
Enterprise, USS, 13
Europa, SS, 9, 21

Focke-Wulf Fw-200 (bomber), 69–70
Fredendall, Maj. Gen. Lloyd, 144

Gigantic, RMS, 4
Glasgow, Scotland, 1, 134, 135, 167
Glass, Emily (Mrs. Robert), 161
Glass, Sgt. Robert. 161
Gloucester Castle, RMS, 62
Gneisenau, DKM, 37, 70
Goebbels, Joseph, 73, 91
Gourock, Scotland, 51, 52, 86, 91, 116, 117, 120, 138, 142, 145
Graf Spee, DKM, 37, 70, 71
Grattidge, Staff Capt. Harry, 83, 116
Graziani, Gen. Rudolfo, 54

Halifax, Nova Scotia, 166–167
Hamburg-Amerika Line, 2–3
Hartenstien, Capt.-Lt. Werner, 75–76
Hearn, Signalman Dennis, 120
Heighway, Junior Third Officer William, 110, 113
Heinkel He-111 (bomber), 68–69, 103
Hermes, HMS, 172
Hewitt, Third Officer Albert, 110
Hitler, Adolf, xiii, 19–20, 23–25, 26, 30, 34, 35, 34, 35, 57, 58, 73, 90
Holmes, Lt. Patrick, 117–118, 119, 122
Hood, HMS, 13, 71

Ile de France, SS, 21, 44, 91, 137
Illingworth, Capt. Gordon, 90, 91, 106, 110, 111, 112, 113, 114, 115–116, 120, 121–122, 162, 167
Imperator, SS, 4,
Inflexible, HMS, 104
Iron Duke, HMS, 105
Irving, Capt. William, 49, 53
Italian Line, 9

John Brown & Sons, 1, 7, 11–12, 20, 33, 37
Johnson, Lt. Tony, 112
Junkers Ju-87 (Stuka dive-bomber), 67–68

Kaiser Wilhelm II, SS
Kaiser Wilhelm der Grosse, SS, 2
Kessler, Capt.-Lt. Horst, 91–92
King, Adm. Ernest J., 79
King George V, 11, 12, 20
King George V, HMS, 71
King George VI, 20, 165
Kriegsmarine (German Navy), 25, 65, 70–72, 96, 148
Kronprinz Wilhelm, SS, 3

Laconia, SS, 75–76
"*Laconia* Order," 76–77, 96
Lady Drake, SS, 62
LaForce, Airman James, 134
Lemp, Lt. Fritz Julius, 73, 75
Leviathan, SS, 6
Levin, Sgt. Phillip, 115
Lewin, Capt. Terrence, 172
Leyden, Quartermaster John, 112, 114
Lockhart, Quartermaster John, 110, 112
Luftwaffe (German Air Force), 40, 41, 65, 66–70, 133, 142
Lusitania, RMS, 1, 3–4, 6, 27, 48, 73

MacKelden, Joan, 162
Majestic, RMS, 6, 46
Marien, Pvt. Daniel, 134
Marshall, Gen. George C., 79, 80, 81, 82–84, 142–143
Martin, Telegraphist Allin,113–114, 118, 119
Masson, Crewman A. W., 115
Mauretania, RMS, 3–4, 46

Mauretania (II) , RMS, 44, 49

Maxtone-Grham, John, 43

Maxwell, Lt. John, 119

McMeekin, Seaman Tom, 105

Molotov, Vyacheslev, 165

Mountbatten, Field-Marshall
　　Lord, 93

Munich, Germany, 20, 24

Murphy, U. S. Atty-Gen. Frank,
　　27

Murray, Stoker William, 119

Mussolini, Benito, 54, 57, 58

Neptunia, SS, 62

New York Times, 43

New York Sun, 49

Nieuw Amsterdam, SS, 91

Norddeutscher-Lloyd Line, 2–3,

Normandie, SS, 9, 10, 14–15, 16,
　　17, 21–22, 29, 33, 34, 44, 62

O'Connor, Gen. Richard, 55

Oceania, SS, 62

Oceanic, RMS, 7, 8

Olsen, Lt. David, 137–138

Olympic, RMS, 3, 15, 46

Operation Bolero, 81–82

Operation Overlord, 125, 141,
　　142–143, 146

PBY (bomber), 87

Pearl Harbor, Hawaii, 58, 59

Pembroke, HMS, 104

Phillips, Rear-Adm. Tom, 38

Poland, 20, 23–24, 26, 30

PQ-17 (convoy), 71–72

Prien, Lt. Gunther, 73

Prince of Wales, HMS, 38, 71

Prisoners of war, 56, 95–96

Queen Elizabeth, 20

Queen Elizabeth II (Princess Eliz-
　　abeth), 165

Queen Elizabeth, RMS, xiii, xiv,
　　16, 29, 30, 31, 35, 37, 46,
　　54, 59, 63, 65, 75, 79, 81,
　　89, 90, 93, 126, 127–134,
　　135–136, 138–139, 168,
　　169–170

　　appearance, 18–19, 22, 33–34

　　attacked by U-704, 91–92

　　converted for US trooping
　　　duties , 84–85, 123–125

　　deception measures utilized,
　　　85–87, 149

　　defensive armament, 84–85

　　design and construction, 18, 19

　　destroyed by fire, 172–173

　　dimensions, 19, 175

　　enters passenger service,
　　　163–166

　　escapes to United States, 42–44

　　first conversion to troopship,
　　　53–54

　　Indian Ocean service, 56–59

　　interiors, 22

　　last meeting with *Queen Mary*,
　　　173–174

　　launched, 20, 34–35

　　living conditions aboard,
　　　55–56, 57, 128–134

　　number of troops carried, 83,
　　　89, 144–145

　　Pacific Ocean service, 61

possible conversion to aircraft
carrier, 38
requisitioned for trooping
duties, 39
returns troops to United States,
153–155
riot aboard, 56–57
secret departure for the U. S.,
39–41
service as medical transport,
150–153
subject to German bounty, 90
transports POWs, 95–96
Queen Elizabeth 2, RMS, xiv, 171
Queen Mary, 11, 12
Queen Mary, RMS, xiii, xiv, 22,
26, 31, 46, 49, 50–52, 53,
55, 59–60, 61, 63, 65, 75,
79, 81, 83, 89, 90, 91, 93,
107–108, 110, 111, 112,
126, 127–134, 135–136,
138–139, 157, 167, 168,
169–170, 171–172,
appearance, 14–15, 33
captures Blue Riband, 17
carries families to U. S.,
159–163
collision with HMS *Curacoa*,
99, 113–115, 117–118, 120,
121, 122
construction, 10–11
converted for US trooping
duties, 84–85, 123–125
deception measures utilized,
85–87, 149
defensive armament, 84–85

design and construction,
10–11, 13
dimensions, 13, 175
escapes to New York, 27–28
first conversion to troopship,
46, 48, 50, 53
formally requisitioned, 29
freak wave strikes, 96–97
Indian Ocean service, 56–59
interiors, 15–16, 22–23
laid up in New York, 28–29, 30
last meeting with *Queen Elizabeth*, 173–174
launched, 11–12
living conditions aboard,
55–56, 57, 128–134
maiden voyage, 16
named, 11
numbers of troops carried, 50,
83, 89, 91, 121, 144–145,
153, 167
popularity, 17–18, 21–22, 23
powerplant, 13
retired to Long Beach, 172
returned to passenger service,
167–168
returns troops to United States,
153–155
sea trials, 14
security arrangements, 52–53
service as medical transport,
150–153
subject to German bounty, 90
transports POWs, 95–96
Queen of Bermuda, SS, 91

Raeder, Adm. Erich, 70, 72
Rashilee Light, 40, 41
Repulse, HMS, 38
Rex, SS, 22,
River Clyde, 1, 12, 20, 29, 37,
    39, 40, 91, 120, 125,
    133–134
Robertson, Cmdr. Douglas, 119
Robinson, Senior First Officer
    Noel, 109–110, 111,
    112–113
Rodney, HMS, 71
Rommel, Gen. Erwin, 54, 57, 58
Royal Air Force (RAF), 59, 66,
    134, 142
Royal Canadian Air Force
    (RCAF), 134, 138
Royal Canadian Navy (RCN),
    125, 126, 159
Royal Marines (RM), 120
Royal Naval Reserve (RNR), 28,
    37
Royal Navy (RN), 35, 36, 45, 59,
    70, 80, 88–89, 93, 104–105,
    106, 125, 126, 148, 171
Royal Oak, HMS, 73
Russell, Harold, 150

St. Claire Pilcher, Justice Sir
    Gonne, 121
Saladin, HMS, 109, 117, 120
Scapa Flow, Scotland, 100, 103
Schacht, Lt. Harro, 76
Scharnhorst, DKM, 37, 70, 71
Schuart, Cdr. Otto, 73
Short Sunderland (bomber), 87

Singapore, 53, 55
Skate, HMS, 109, 117, 120
Southampton, England, 15, 26,
    39–40, 133–134, 142, 145,
    160, 163
Sydney, Australia, 49, 50, 55, 56

Tirpitz, DKM, 70, 71–72
Titanic, RMS, 3–4, 15, 60
Townley, Capt. Jack, 41, 42
Tyrwhitt, Rear Adm. Sir Regi-
    nald, 100
"Tyrwhitt's Navy," 100

U-boats, 25–26, 27, 72–77,
    86–87, 96, 126, 149, 158
    U-29, 73
    U-30, 73
    U-47, 73
    U-129, 61
    U-161, 61
    U-407, 91
    U-704, 91–92
"Ultra" decryption system,
    146–147
United States, SS, 170–171
United States Army, 59, 82, 143,
    144
United States Army Air Force (Air
    Corps), 60, 66, 138, 142,
    157
United States Army Transporta-
    tion Corps, 125–126, 154,
    159
United States Navy, 79, 80, 125,
    126

Vaterland, SS, 4, 6
Vishinski, Andrei, 165
Wavell, Gen. Archibald, 55, 93
Wehrmacht (German Army), 20, 24, 35, 141–142, 146
White, Sgt. Edward, 120
White Star Line, 3–4, 6–7, 8–10

Whitley, HMS, 105
Wilhelm Gustloff, SS, 62
Woerdemann, Capt.-Lt. Erich, 76
Wright, Junior First Officer Stanley, 109, 111, 112, 114
Wyler, William, 150